OAKTON COMMUNITY COLLEGE

DES PLAINES, ILLINOIS 60016

HAROLD W. AURAND

from the Molly Maguires to the United Mine Workers

60886

THE SOCIAL
ECOLOGY OF AN
INDUSTRIAL
UNION
1869 - 1897

TEMPLE UNIVERSITY PRESS
Philadelphia

Temple University Press, Philadelphia 19122
© 1971 by Temple University
All rights reserved
Published 1971
Printed in the United States of America

International Standard Book Number: 0-87722-006-9
Library of Congress Catalog Card Number: 73-157737

Contents

PART V
The Collective Response:
The Physical Plant

Introduction

Scholars have long lamented the neglect of Pennsylvania's history during its "Gilded Age" (the latter part of the nineteenth century).[1] In no area of the Commonwealth's development is this oversight more marked than in that of the anthracite (hard coal) regions. A virtually unexplored desert lies between the well-documented "Molly Maguires" and the coal strike of 1902.[2]

The coal regions are too important to suffer historical indifference. Throughout the late nineteenth century the hard coal industry was a major employer in Pennsylvania. Anthracite provided important fuel to the iron industry.[3] The hard coal regions were among the first state areas to yield to corporate domination.

The anthracite regions of Pennsylvania also played an important role in the economic development of the nation. Anthracite was marketed more widely than any other coal. Its economic influence extended beyond the provision of fuel: hard coal stimulated many pioneering developments in American railroading. Socially the anthracite regions underwent rapid industrialization and assimilated every major ethnic group found in the nation, except Orientals and Puerto Ricans. Indeed, the area is a microcosm of American economic and social development.

Although the area can be placed within the mainstream of American history, the anthracite regions developed a unique identity. "A community of interests and the ties of labor unions," Francis H. Nichols reported in 1902, "have so bound the [anthracite] counties together that they constitute a sort of separate and distinct state, called by its inhabitants 'Anthracite.' "[4]

How did the anthracite regions develop their unique identity? The answer can be found by studying the largest group in the area, the mine workers, and their problems between 1869 and 1897. The two dates mark key institutional developments in the area. In 1869 the mine workers organized their first industry-wide union, the Workingmen's Benevolent Association, and in 1897 the United Mine Workers of America became firmly established in the region. During the same period the corporation rose to its dominant position within the industry.

What effects did these institutions have on social groups, values, and patterns of identification within the area? To answer that question I have adopted a functional approach to labor history. The functional approach begins with the assumption that work creates problems. By analyzing the work of mining coal it is possible to define the occupational problems of the miners and the alternative solutions to the problems. With a knowledge of the difficulties, one can measure the effectiveness of the miners' response.

But a solution cannot be arrived at within a social vacuum. Each attempted response will affect, and in turn be conditioned by, other social groups and institutions. The physical environment places restrictions on institutional development. The functional approach must therefore survey the total effect of these reciprocal influences.

By using the functional approach I found that the anthracite mine workers encountered two sets of problems—wages and the high accident rate in the mines. The organization of work precluded successful individual responses and compelled the mine workers to seek a collective response. Yet an environment disrupted by cultural, geo-economic, and ethnic forces made a collective response difficult. The obvious successes of their occasional unified efforts, however, forced the miners continually to strive to overcome the disruptive forces, and victory made the labor union the primary integrative force in the anthracite regions. In this way the labor union played a key role in the formation of a laboring class identity.

While the labor union reflected the needs of the mine workers, it also often sympathized with management. Concern over wages led labor to an analysis of the coal industry, from which they discovered that the industry suffered from a basic sickness. Incorrectly diagnosing the sickness as low prices resulting from overproduction, labor sought to maintain prices rather than attack management. The initial inclination of the mine workers to support capital permitted the middle class in the regions to receive the union in a more or less cordial fashion.

The middle class in the anthracite regions feared the vast economic, social, and political power of the mining industry. Local businessmen resented the company store and the exploitation of the mineral wealth of the region for the benefit of other areas. Shattered by the disruptive forces in their environment and prisoners of a parochialism which rarely extended beyond the political limits of a particular town, regional businessmen were unable to identify with a larger community. Rejecting the corporation as an integrative institution, the middle class accepted the labor union as a symbol of a larger community bound together by the problems of work.

In the end the large corporation often proved more ready to respond to the problems of the mine workers than did the small individual entrepreneur, perhaps because it could better afford to respond. The corporations, for example, voluntarily abolished their company stores. While big business fought legislation proposed by labor, it complied with safety and wage laws. Finally, most corporations sponsored paternalistic welfare plans for their employees which few entrepreneurs matched.

I am deeply indebted to Professor Ari Hoogenboom for his constructive criticism and constant inspiration. Professor Gerald Eggert read the entire manuscript and offered valuable advice, suggestions, and encouragement.

Mrs. Mary Ferry, librarian at the Hazleton Campus of The Pennsylvania State University, fulfilled an almost endless stream of requests. The late David W. Davis, curator of the Historical Society of Schuylkill County, Ralph L. Hazeltine, director of the Wyoming Historical Society, and Robert C. Mattes, curator of the Lackawanna Historical Society, placed the resources of their respective organizations at my disposal. I would like to express particular thanks to Nicholas B. Wainwright, director of the Historical Society of Pennsylvania, for making the as yet unopened Reading Company Papers available to me.

Milton Cantor, managing editor of *Labor History,* granted me permission to use parts of my article "The Workingmen's Benevolent Association" and William G. Shade, editor of *Pennsylvania History,* permitted the inclusion of portions of my article

"The Anthracite Strike of 1887-88." I am indebted to the Johns Hopkins Press, the McGraw-Hill Book Company, and the University of Pennsylvania Press for their permission to include copyrighted materials. I am particularly grateful to my wife, Frances D. Aurand, for her understanding and encouragement.

Harold W. Aurand

The Environmental Setting

Anthracite mine workers lived and worked within an environment that caused their problems and conditioned their response to the problems. Attempting to understand the hard coal miners' history by focusing on employer-employee relations and neglecting the surroundings would be like trying to understand a play by noting only the actions of the major actors and forgetting dialogue, scenery, and supporting cast. To be meaningful, a history of the mine workers must explain their actions within the context of their environment; in such a history one must attempt to re-create the milieu of the industry at the time.

The anthracite miners' environmental setting consisted of three major planes—the physical, the industrial, and the communal. The natural surroundings determined the location of jobs and imposed limits on institutional development. Management organized and rewarded work, but the industry's internal logic circumscribed the employers' freedom of action. The community provided the context within which the problems arising from work were solved. To reemploy the theatrical analogy, the physical environment provided the backdrop, the industrial environment the script, and the communal environment both stage and supporting cast.

The Physical Surroundings

Anthracite (hard coal) is a coal with a high percentage of fixed (nonvolatilized) carbon; true anthracite is 91 to 98 percent carbon. High carbon content gives the coal its peculiar characteristics. It is jet black with a high luster, hard, and does not burn readily. Once ignited, it emits a short blue flame and gives off an intense heat with little smoke.

Many laymen confuse semianthracite with hard coal. Semianthracite is 85 to 90 percent carbon, is softer and less lustrous than anthracite. When lit it burns with a yellow flame, but the flame quickly dies and the coal then assumes anthracite's heating characteristics.[1] Since the two coal types are often equated and both are found in the same region, the term anthracite as used in this book includes coal that is 85 to 98 percent carbon.

All of America's usable anthracite deposits lie in Pennsylvania within a 1,400-square-mile area, of which only 439 square miles contain coal. Three rivers—the Susquehanna, the Lehigh, and the Schuylkill—drain the region, while a double ring of mountains surrounds the coal measures.[2]

The story of anthracite antedates historical time; it begins in the Pennsylvania Period[3] of the Paleozoic Era. During the Pennsylvania Period much of eastern North America was a broad and level lowland and subject to periodic submergences. When above sea level, the terrain's lowness afforded poor drainage, thus creating swamps of continental size. Encouraged by a universally mild and wet climate, thick forests of lipodenderons, sigiliaria, and calamites thrived in the swampy areas. Foliage, twigs, and dead trunks fell into the murky water and underwent a biochemical process resulting in peat.

The weight of the peat depressed the flexible crust of the earth, causing the peat to be covered by sediment washed down from higher ground. Submergence continued until the subsidence either stopped or proceeded so slowly that sediments could again build up continental conditions. Cyclical conditions of uplift and submergence built a distinct geological structure—the cyclothem—which would give the coal measures a unique feature. Although not all need be present, the cyclothem usually contains ten layers. Layers one to three represent the preswamp era of uplift, and consist of sandstone, shale, and limestone. Underlay, believed by many to be the swamp's soil, composes the fourth layer, while coal (peat) is found in the fifth. Shale, representing continental sediments, overlies the coal, and marine deposits compose layers seven to ten.

While locked into position by the cyclothem, the peat underwent a dynamochemical change which completed its metamorphism. Pressure from the overlying strata drove off volatile matter and water, thus transforming peat into lignite, and, as the pressure increased, lignite into bituminous coal. The final conversion required more pressure than that provided by the weight of overlying sediment. Indeed, only a crustal movement (diastrophism) could supply the necessary pressure.

The diastrophism occurred during the Permian Period of the Paleozoic Era. At about the middle of the Permian Period, Appalachia (now the eastern United States) was thrust westward against the Appalachian geosyncline. Moving from the southeast, the compressive force was so great that it folded strata, causing the surface area to shorten; the distance between present-day Philadelphia and Altoona shrank 100 miles. Rock strata

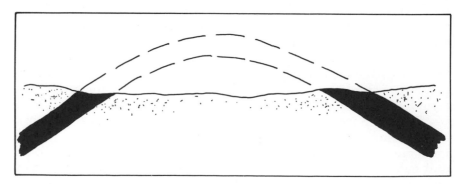

Fig. 1   The Division of Coal Beds by Erosion

underwent the greatest folding in the eastern United States, with the deformations gradually ceasing toward the west. The area experienced six subsequent uplifts.

As the folding receded, there was only a partial conversion to anthracite. Semianthracite is found in the Shamokin area, where distance combined with faults to reduce the pressure. Near Scranton the reduced force could not bend the coal beds' dense underlying strata and again we find semianthracite. One may trace the decreasing force waves by noting the degradation of the coal's rank (anthracite to semianthracite to semi-bituminous to bituminous) as he travels west through Pennsylvania.

The gradual transition from anthracite to bituminous, plus the approximate identity of seams, suggests that the two deposits originally belonged to the same field. Erosion divided the fields (see Fig. 1). Water washed away most of the mountains created by the Permian thrust and subsequent uplifts permitted increased denudation.

Erosion also divided the anthracite field into four basins.[4] The northern field, 176 square miles, is crescent-shaped and extends from Forest City on the Lackawanna to Hartville near the Susquehanna. The 38-square-mile eastern middle basin is a collection of small parallel troughs situated on a plateau bordered by Spring and Green Mountains, with Hazleton its principal city. Locust Mountain partitions the 95-square-mile western middle basin into southern and northern sections. The southern section extends from Locust Gap to Ashland, while the northern begins at Shamokin and ends at the headwaters of the Catawissa.

Fig. 2 Coal Seam Folded Back Over Its North Dip

(Source: Daddow and Bannan, 287-288)

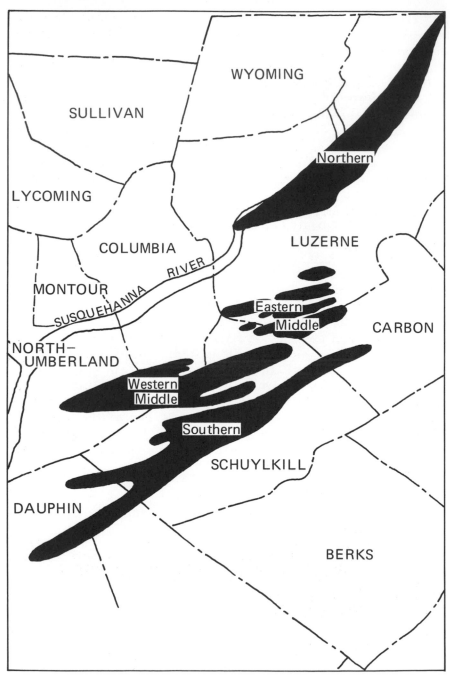

Fig. 3 The Anthracite Coal Basins

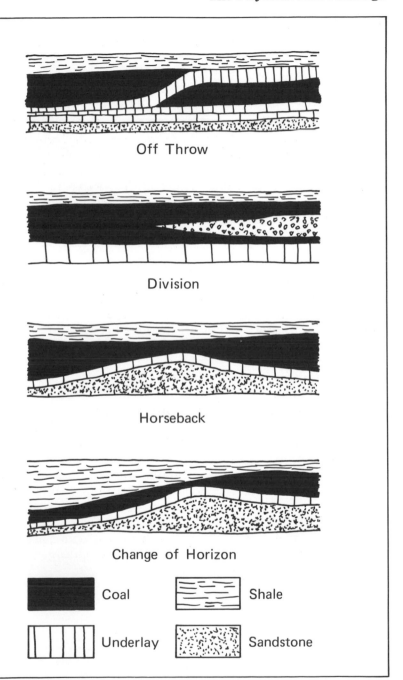

Off Throw

Division

Horseback

Change of Horizon

Coal

Shale

Underlay

Sandstone

Fig. 4 Types of Anthracite Faults

(Source: Daddow and Bannan, 291-294)

Shaped like a fish, the southern basin covers 149 square miles in Carbon, Schuylkill, and Dauphin Counties.

Geological differences between the northern and the remainder of the basins give the former a distinct identity. During the Pleistocene Epoch of the Cenozoic Era a glacier covered much of the northern basin. Drift buried the valley gouged out by glacial activity. The Susquehanna flows over the buried valley, and its water-clogged material, resembling quicksand, poses a threat to the workmen below.[5] As already noted, the northern basin experienced less folding; therefore its beds are in a more or less horizontal position, whereas the seams in the other basins incline over 90 degrees from the horizon (see Fig. 2). The dense underlying strata which retarded folding in the northern basin also proved less susceptible to faulting, but the remaining basins have numerous faults.

The basins' topography reflects their differences in structure. The northern basin lies in a broad river valley broken by gently rolling ridges. The eastern middle resides on a high plateau, and the ridges separating the troughs are more pronounced than those in the northern basin. Both the western middle and southern basins occupy narrow valleys with ridges approximating the surrounding mountains' height.

Soil fertility caused the regrouping of the three topographically distinct areas into two regions. The Wyoming Valley, under which lies the northern basin, contained a rich soil that attracted both Connecticut Yankees and Pennsylvanians during the colonial period. In fact, the valley once enjoyed a reputation for being the nation's "garden spot." A sterile soil, however, covers the remaining three basins. Barren soil and inaccessibility discouraged would-be settlers; even the Indians shunned the area, which they called *Towamensing*—the wilderness. White explorers agreed: while traveling through the region in 1742 Count von Zinzendorf dubbed it "Saint Anthony's Wilderness," a name it would carry until the discovery of coal changed it forever.[6]

The Industry

The geological forces that transformed primeval slime into anthracite coal created four basins with contrasting terrains. Steep mountains and narrow valleys covered the three southern basins, while the northern basin was hidden under the broad and fertile Wyoming Valley. It was inevitable that the more attractive area would yield first its secret cache of mineral wealth.

The conflict between Connecticut and Pennsylvania over the possession of the Wyoming Valley led to the discovery and use of anthracite. In 1762 John Jerkins, mapmaker for the Susquehanna Company, reported the existence of coal in the Wyoming Valley, and six years later the survey of Sunbury Manor revealed the presence of anthracite on Ross Hill in what is now Edwardsville.[1] Enterprising Yankees quickly found a use for the new fuel; in 1769 Obadiah Gore successfully burned the native coal in his forge.[2]

Table 1
Coal Shipped from Wyoming Valley, 1807-1820

1807	55 tons	1814	700
1808	150	1815	1,000
1809	200	1816	1,000
1810	350	1817	1,100
1811	450	1818	1,200
1812	500	1819	1,400
1813	500	1820	2,500

Source: George B. Culp, cited by Bradsby, *Luzerne County*, 272.

Wyoming's anthracite apparently remained a regional fuel until 1775, when patriots shipped "stone coal" from the valley to the Continental armory at Carlisle, Pennsylvania.[3] Although the Wyoming Valley's anthracite trade began during the Revolution, statistics are not available until 1807.[4]

As can be seen in Table 1, the Wyoming Valley possessed an expanding coal industry by 1820, the generally accepted date for the opening of the southern basins.

Discovery of the southern basins quickly followed the detection of the northern field. In 1770 William Scull placed the legend "coal" near present Pottsville and on the Mahanoy Creek on his famous map of Pennsylvania.[5] Another early map of the region, this one by Jacques Nolin, contained the inscription "Charbon de terre" at the confluence of Norwegian Creek and the Schuylkill River.[6] But "Saint Anthony's Wilderness" swallowed the cartographers' information until folk heroes rediscovered the coal. In 1790 Neco Allen, a local hunter, made camp near present Pottsville and awoke during the night to find the earth burning—his campfire had ignited an outcrop of the southern basin. One year later another hunter, Philip Ginter, stumbled over a fallen tree near Summit Hill and discovered another outcrop.[7]

Ginter gave a sample of his discovery to Colonel Jacob Weiss who, in turn, sent it to Philadelphia for analysis. Upon learning that Ginter's black stones were coal, Weiss, with Robert Morris, Jacob Cist, and others, formed the Lehigh Coal Mine Company and began buying land. By 1793 the company controlled 7,108¾ acres and was looking forward to a prosperous future. But the high hopes were unjustified.

Before an anthracite industry could develop, it had to be demonstrated that the product would burn with relative ease. Anthracite's high carbon content made it difficult to ignite, and many dismissed the new fuel as stone. In 1803 the city of Philadelphia graveled footwalks about the water works with hard coal after it failed to ignite.

The efforts to convince the public that anthracite would burn anticipated Madison Avenue. The Lehigh Coal Mine Company distributed handbills in both German and English which described the proper method for burning its coal, and accompanied the notices with affidavits attesting to anthracite's value.[8] The Delaware and Hudson Company installed stoves fired with hard coal in its New York banking house. In Boston a Mr. Badger hung iron cages which contained burning anthracite from the trees in Bowdoin Square.[9]

It was the War of 1812 which provided a large market for anthracite. The British blockade of the eastern coast diminished the supply of Richmond and Liverpool coals. The scarcity of bituminous coal, plus the increasing cost of wood, caused many to experiment successfully with anthracite. Although the public returned, temporarily, to the more familiar fuels at the end of the war, the growing knowledge that anthracite would indeed burn provided the industry with the opportunity to develop its markets.

Anthracite found its first use in the processing of iron, but it was not until the 1830s that it was used to smelt the ore. In 1820 the Lehigh Coal and Navigation Company, successor to the Lehigh Coal Mine Company, built an anthracite iron furnace at Mauch Chunk. The furnace was a failure, but enterprising iron masters were not dismayed. Experiments continued until 1830 when Frederick W. Geisenheimer received a patent for making pig iron using anthracite.[10] Geisenheimer's success prompted others to enter the field. The anthracite pig iron industry can be dated from 1839 when William Lyman of Pioneer Furnace near Pottsville received a $5,000 prize for making pig iron with anthracite continuously for 100 days.[11]

Anthracite quickly replaced charcoal as the most important iron-smelting fuel. Iron masters favored the new fuel because "Its [anthracite's] comparative freedom from waste by transportation, and its little liability to change by atmospheric influences, have marked it as singularly for use *in furnaces at a distance from the place of its origin.*"[12] More important than hard coal's transportability, however, was its relative cheapness. Some iron masters claimed that the cost of anthracite was half that of charcoal, a saving of from $10 to $14 a ton. After 1875 the major iron-producing fuel became bituminous coal and coke, but, as is evident in Table 2, iron furnaces remained a sizable market throughout the century.

Anthracite also found other industrial markets. Hard coal was used in the steam engine as early as 1825, but its intense heat burned out the grate. By 1830 this problem was solved by making the grate heavier in the center than at the ends. Superiority over wood made anthracite better suited for small markets. Great savings for lime burners were reported. Two cords of wood (at a cost of $3.50) were needed to produce 100 bushels of lime. The same amount of lime could be produced with a half-ton of anthracite, which cost only $1.50, a saving of 57 percent. Use of anthracite further reduced fuel costs by providing a more efficient kiln: " . . . by burning with coal, we can keep on hand a constant supply of lime, whereas by using wood, the lime must be all hauled off before we can renew, but by using coal we can continue burning and hauling at the same time."[13]

Table 2
Iron Production, by Fuel

Year	Anthracite (short tons)	Charcoal (short tons)	Bituminous (short tons)
1855	381,866	339,922	54,485
1860	519,211	278,331	62,390
1865	479,558	262,342	122,228
1870	930,000	365,000	570,000
1875	908,046	410,990	947,545
1880	1,108,651	537,558	1,950,205
1885	1,454,390	399,844	2,675,635
1890	2,448,781	703,522	7,154,073
1895	1,397,989	247,895	8,745,073
1898	1,323,600	326,452	11,301,302

Source: E. Levasseur, *The American Workingman.*
Translated by Thomas G. Adams, Baltimore: The Johns Hopkins Press, 1900, 15.

The brick industry found that coal offered it the same advantages; William Everhart reported that the increase in production achieved by burning coal instead of wood covered the cost of coal; he could burn 1,000 more bricks per load when using anthracite.[14]

Although anthracite's cheapness recommended its use to many industries, the greatest use of it was as a domestic heating and cooking fuel. Smokeless anthracite was a natural household fuel, but the obvious economy of using hard coal overrode every other consideration. By the 1840s anthracite was a necessity for rich and poor.

By 1860 anthracite was firmly established as an important industrial and domestic fuel. To a degree, the industry owed its growth to advertising, but the most important factor was efficiency. Anthracite's natural advantage, however, could be realized only when it was delivered to market at competitive prices.

Irregular terrain and distance from main markets, plus coal's bulkiness and low unit value, were the greatest hindrances to low prices.[15] Overland hauling was prohibitive; expenses for the trip ($25 a ton) could not be covered. The rivers draining the coal fields offered more risks than efficient transportation. In 1803 the Lehigh Coal Mine Company lost four of the six arks it sent to Philadelphia.[16] Even if river transportation had proved feasible, the cost of hauling coal from the mines to the river was high. In 1815 Jacob Cist paid Aaron Dean $4.50 a ton to haul 60 tons of anthracite from Summit Hill to the Lehigh River, a distance of six miles.[17] In the northern basin the cost of transporting coal from Carbondale to the Wallenpaupack ran $2.50 a ton. The need to cut the exorbitant hauling costs makes the history of anthracite "first and last a story of transportation."[18]

Canals provided the first high-capacity, low-cost transport system. Two private companies and the state improved the three rivers draining the coal region. The Lehigh Coal and Navigation Company and the Schuylkill Navigation Company tamed their respective waterways, while the Susquehanna became part of the Pennsylvania State Canal System. The Commonwealth also improved the Delaware, thereby making possible slack-water navigation from Mauch Chunk to Philadelphia. Because they had to follow the southern flow of water, the three canals did not provide direct access to the lucrative New York market. The Delaware and Hudson Canal opened the New York trade for the

TABLE 3
Heating Costs of Wood and Coal

Wood		Coal		
2 cords of hickory $6.75	$13.50	4 tons $6.50	$26.00	
hauling $.50	1.00	breaking and putting		
sawing $1.00	2.00	in 37½	1.50	
piling 18¾¢	.37½			
cordage $.06	.12	Total	$27.50	
6 cords of oak $5.25	31.50			
hauling $.50	3.00			
sawing $.80	4.80			
piling 18¾¢	1.12½			
cordage $.06	.36			
Total	$57.78			

Source: *Hazard's Register of Pennsylvania*, October 10, 1829, 237.

TABLE 4
Canal Transportation Costs

Year	Cents per ton mile
1826	1.5
1843	1.25
1845	1.00

Source: Roberts, *Industry*, 64.

northern basin, and two canals—the Morris and the Delaware and Raritan—crossed New Jersey to tap the Lehigh fields. By 1846 the anthracite canal system totaled 643 miles and brought about a substantial decrease in transportation costs.

Water transportation, however, suffered from serious defects. Travel, paced by a mule's gait, was necessarily slow. Freshets could wipe out improvements overnight; the 1827 flood destroyed the upper sections of the Lehigh Canal. Water transportation was doomed by the more efficient railroad.

High transportation costs from the mines to the canals compelled the building of feeder railroads. The Lehigh Coal and Navigation Company constructed a gravity road from its Summit Hill mines to its canal and realized a savings of 64¾ cents per ton in haulage. The economies of rail transportation, plus the imperious attitude of the canal owners, led capitalists to construct railroads as competitors, not as feeders for the canals. By the end of the nineteenth century 11 railroads served the anthracite regions.

Development of the transport system accentuated the regions' geological differences and created three geo-economic units. The western middle and most of the southern basins comprised the Schuylkill region, which found its market in Philadelphia via the Philadelphia and Reading Railroad. The extreme eastern section of the southern basin and the eastern middle basin formed the Lehigh region, which, served by the Lehigh Valley and the Central of New Jersey Railroads, shipped to New York and, to a lesser degree, Philadelphia. The northern basin, better known as the Wyoming region, shipped over the Delaware and Hudson Canal and the Delaware, Lackawanna, and Western Railroad and found its major market within the New England–New York–Buffalo area. Within each of the three regions the transport companies became dominant, not only as carriers but as miners.

The anthracite regions were one of the first areas in Pennsylvania to yield to corporate control.[19] The concentration of ownership into the hands of the few carrying companies proceeded with a logic that led one group of observers to conclude: "There is probably no other commodity entering into human consumption which possesses so much the character of a natural monopoly as the anthracite coal of Pennsylvania."[20] The compactness of the anthracite regions explains in part the ease with which concentration was accomplished; but the main explanation lies in the industry's economics.

Capital needs formed one of the jaws of the vise that squeezed the individual entrepreneur out of the industry. The cost of entry became increasingly prohibitive as the industry matured. The first consideration, thanks to speculation, was the rising cost of land. Indeed, some regarded speculation in coal land as the primary source of profit in the anthracite industry. Purchase of land formed only a part of the entry costs; there remained the expenditures for opening the mine. As the outcrops became exhausted, the mines became deeper, requiring increased outlays for pumping water and for coal-hoisting machinery.

Certain special features of the market also caused increases in the initial outlay. For example, the customer became more fastidious—he demanded a clean and uniform product. To meet the demand the mine operator installed coal-breaking, screening, and -cleaning machinery in a separate building called the "breaker." As the breaker became more sophisticated it appreciated in value; the Lehigh Coal and Navigation Company reported an expenditure of $16,998.56 for a new breaker in 1857, and by 1876 a moderate-sized breaker cost over $77,000.[21] Increasing land values, deeper mines, and more sophisticated preparation processes denied the individual entrepreneur access to the industry.

Mining also required a great deal of operating capital. Many individuals received no return until their coal was sold at retail, which often took months. Capital was needed to meet current expenses during the interim. And current expenses were burdensome. Below-water-level mines had to be pumped continuously; timbering had to continue. Indeed, the fixed operating costs were so great that operators found it more economical to sell at a loss than to suspend operations. By so doing, they at least covered part of their operating costs.

Falling prices due to overproduction was the other jaw of the vise closing on the individual operator. It is ironic that an industry requiring great capitalization suffered from overproduction resulting from overinvestment. But the very nature of the market made for overinvestment. Heavily dependent on the domestic fuel market, the anthracite industry had to have an overbuilt plant in order to meet sporadically heavy demands.[22]

Given the need for overinvestment, the industry's mechanics provided overproduction. We have already noted how heavy fixed operating costs, to say nothing of increasing capital charges, compelled the operator to continue mining at a loss. The land system also provided for overproduction. Many operators saved initial outlay by leasing their land, but most leases called for the raising of a minimum tonnage on which a royalty had to be paid. The minimum royalty forced operators to cut their losses by producing at least that amount of tonnage regardless of price. High fixed costs placed the operators on a vicious carrousel: low prices prompted greater production which resulted in still lower prices.

TABLE 5
Cost of Entry in 1837 and in 1897

1837		1897	
Coal land	$ 3,500	Boiler and engines	$ 75,536.62
Opening mine,		Tools and machinery	2,330.47
wagons, etc.	3,000	Breaker building	64,006.46
Boats	2,500	Breaker machinery	33,846.72
Working capital	1,000	Shops, etc.	35,603.87
		Rolling stock	16,529.83
Total cost	$10,000	Electrical plant	11,441.83
		Opening mines	431,191.18
		Total cost	$670,486.98

Sources: Packer Report, and D.L. & W. Papers.

Eckley B. Coxe, a wealthy mine operator, admitted that only a few entrepreneurs caught the carrousel's gold ring: "The actual fact is, that until a comparatively recent time, out of every ten men who went into the coal business, nine of them have become bankrupt."[23] Franklin B. Gowen, president of the Philadelphia and Reading Railroad, warned that success might be more painful than failure:

I practiced law for seven years in the County of Schuylkill, and in all that time, and up to it, there were but three men who ever retired from the business of mining coal with any money, and one of those died in an insane asylum and another had softening of the brain. The shock was too great to their systems.[24]

The tendency toward collapse of the entrepreneurial order can be seen in Schuylkill County, long considered the bastion of individual enterprise. In 1865 Schuylkill County boasted 109 shippers controlling 146 collieries and shipping 3,735,806 tons. But the top 25 shippers accounted for 60 percent of the production, while the top 10 operators shipped 35 percent.

Increasing demand for capital, coupled with falling prices, destroyed the individual mine operator and set the stage for domination by the carrying companies. Being corporations and enjoying intimate contacts with the money market, the transport companies were better prepared than the entrepreneur to meet the industry's insatiable appetite for capital. Furthermore, their strategic position at the industry's "bottleneck" enabled them easily to exert control.[25] But access to the money market and strategic position only explain the power to implement the decision to rule, not the decision-making process.

Fear, not imperial designs, governed that process. The transportation companies, with the exception of the Philadelphia and Reading Railroad, enjoyed mining privileges, but their primary interests were in carrying coal. The failure of the independent operators created a power vacuum which, each company feared, a competitor might rush to fill.[26] Once created, the atmosphere of fear and distrust led to a cycle of defensive buying of coal lands. In 1867 the Lehigh Coal and Navigation Company's managers reported to their stockholders that the Delaware and Hudson Company bought some coal land near Wilkes-Barre and explained:

This movement following others of like character, less threatening, perhaps, but all indicating the same disposition to monopolize, as far as possible, the coal land of Wyoming to one or other of the three great mining and transporting companies in that valley with their capital and principal offices located in the City of New York, excited the apprehensions of your managers, lest at some future day there might be a deficiency of trade from that quarter. . . . It was thought advisable, therefore, to endeavor to secure the control of coal lands in the Wyoming region with the view of making them tributary to our improvements.[27]

At first the transporting companies limited their defensive scramble for coal land to the Lehigh and Wyoming regions where they held mining privileges. But in the late 1860s the northern companies began to extend their lines into the Schuylkill region. Threatened by a loss of tonnage, the Philadelphia and Reading, which heretofore had opposed the union of the mining and carrying operations, decided in 1871 to go into the mining business. The Reading's decision to enter the mining sector of the anthracite industry sealed the independent operators' doom. The percentage contract, which consigned the independent operator's entire output to the transporting company for a percentage of the tidewater price, reduced the few remaining entrepreneurs to vassals of the railroads.[28]

Control of the mines forced the carrying companies to confront the problem of falling prices. Conceiving the problem as one of restoring the market to a profitable equilibrium, management sought to equalize production with demand. Under Franklin B. Gowen's leadership the carrying companies formed their first pool in 1872. The pool maintained prices despite the depression the following year, but its very success spelled its doom. In 1876 the Lehigh Valley, in anticipation of greater profits, broke the agreed-upon limitation on its production and the other companies followed its lead. Other pools followed the first; the pattern of the various pools were the same. The carrying-mining companies assigned each other quotas based on the company's productive capacity. Each company was honor bound to observe its quota, and in one pool, to pay a fine for exceeding its quota.

Restriction of output maintained prices, but it failed to solve the basic problem of overinvestment. Indeed, the pools accentuated the problem as each company strived for a larger share of the total allotment by increasing its productive ability. In so doing, management reacted to social pressures. Expansion, not stabilization, was the hallmark of economic success of an industry and, within that industry, of each company. Managers had an obligation to the owners and to their own reputations to promote growth. In addition, they did not realize that expansion for expansion's sake could result in overinvestment; an abiding faith in the economy as a self-adjusting mechanism precluded such an expectation. Trapped by an intellectual framework that was fast becoming obsolete, management found itself in a vicious spiral of increasing investment to offset overinvestment.

Overinvestment was new (and eventually destructive) to the anthracite industry; in the long run, it spelled bankruptcy to management as ever-increasing capital charges had to be earned by a decreasing percentage of capacity. The precarious fiscal position can be demonstrated by correlating the various pools' failures with the Reading's bankruptcies. The pool failed in 1883, and within the year the Reading went into receivership. During the competitive years 1893-96 the Reading failed twice—once in 1893 and again in 1896.

Labor also suffered from the industry's overinvestment. Faced with a precarious capital position, management had to keep large profit margins even if it meant the depression of wages. And surplus of labor had to be kept within the region to keep the unnecessary plant operative. Management met the requirement for excess labor by instituting three-quarter, one-half, or one-quarter time and, whenever necessary, laying off men altogether. The miners' twin plagues of low wages and less work were rooted not in the operators' parsimony, but in the impersonal logic of an industry staggering under the burden of overinvestment.

The anthracite industry grew from a precarious birth into a giant. But despite its impressive growth, it remained basically sick. Management diagnosed the symptom—overproduction—as the sickness and treated it in a manner that aggravated the real illness—overinvestment—with the resultant bankruptcy and labor discontent, both of which boded ill for the communities of the anthracite regions.

The
Community

Mining supported the anthracite communities. "It [coal] has raised up in our formerly barren and uninhabited district, an intelligent and permanent population, and converted the mountains into theaters of busy life, and hitherto waste and valueless lands into sites of flourishing and populous villages."[1]

But the coal industry was sick. Management, therefore, sought to use its economic power to structure a set of industry-community relations which would create sympathy for the industry's problems.

The simple fact that mines are geographically fixed by the mineral's location determined the anthracite industry's community relations. An environment so forbidding that one could travel 35 miles and see only three dwellings, "two of which were taverns recently errected [sic]," forced mine operators to become community developers.[2] The Lehigh Coal and Navigation Company built "Summit Hill" to house its miners, and the Delaware and Hudson constructed Carbondale for the same purpose. Even after industrial development attracted a population base, the isolation of a new mine often necessitated the building of towns by the mining company. "For the accommodation of this new working, twelve blocks of double miners' houses have been contracted for, and are now being built."[3]

Industry-community relations within the company town, or "mine patch," were unilateral. The mine provided the inhabitants with their only source of employment, and control over the job made the operator master of the individual's, and indeed the community's future. Ownership of the land enabled the operator to consolidate his control; he could evict "undesirables" and refuse entry to those who aroused his displeasure. The "mine patch," in fact, resembled a feudal fief: "Everything in the region belongs to the operators and must be subject to their autocratic domination. They are the lords of the domain and no man is allowed to encroach on their territory, even the Jew peddler is not allowed to expose his wares within their borders."[4]

The "free towns" sharply contrasted with the company towns; not owned by a company, they escaped the operator's domination. Although mining provided employment for most of the free towns' male population, these communities enjoyed subordinate economic pursuits. Three—Pottsville, Wilkes-Barre, and Scranton—were county seats; most boasted of at least one factory; and all served as entrepôts for a surrounding cluster of mine patches. Relative economic diversification gave the free town a more heterogeneous class structure and made industry-community relations more complex and less absolute than in the company town.

Economic diversification, however, did not mean that the free town completely escaped the influence of the anthracite industry with its preponderant financial power. The coal companies were the largest employers. Besides furnishing the community's economic base, they often provided such essential needs as water. Railroad subsidiaries could easily influence transportation policies.

Economic power gave the coal industry great social suasion. Attorneys found a lucrative practice in the leases and contracts inherent in a complex and confusing industry. Some operators maintained company doctors. Favored merchants, as well as the "company stores," issued credit without risk when the operator agreed to deduct debts from his miners' paychecks. Even priests and ministers received their salaries through the company, which the company also deducted from its employees' wages. Although operators charged from 2 to 5 percent for their collection service, the assurance of a steady income with little trouble was so eagerly sought after that those who availed themselves of the service practically became the operators' agents.

Land ownership provided another lever with which mining officials could persuade the community's opinion-makers. The group most affected by the coal companies' real estate holdings were the clergy. Charged with the responsibility for building churches, schools, and cemeteries at low cost, ministers and priests appealed to the operators for land donations. Concern for the future salvation of souls usually demanded that the request be granted, but hard reasoning dictated a return in the present. George Jones, secretary of the Lehigh–Wilkes-Barre Coal Company, wrote to Reuben Downing: "I enclose a letter from Rev. Felix McGulken asking for a lot at Wanamie for a church. I believe in good influences and would like *your views*, and if you think favorably, see the Rev. Father and find just what he wants and let me hear from you."[5]

Charity was another channel for the conversion of economic power into social power. Operators gave free coal to hospitals and churches. The companies' apparently bulging treasuries made them logical targets of requests for donations. Churches not only asked for land, but also solicited gifts to building funds and aid in maintaining the church. Reverend William Roberts, for example, asked the Delaware, Lackawanna, and Western Company for either another contribution (he had already received $600) or an interest-free loan of $4,000 for his church's upkeep, and indirectly requested private charity by remarking that his income for two months totaled only $53.[6] Libraries and volunteer fire companies also shared the anthracite industry's bounty.

The mining companies' relations with railroads provided another outlet for wielding influence—the free pass. Worthwhile undertakings such as benefit picnics received free transportation. Convention delegates traveled without cost. Although organized groups enjoyed most of the free transportation, individuals were not shy about applying for the gift. W.S. Jones, editor of the "only Welsh language paper in the state," solicited a pass, promising that if it were granted he would "repay double value" through the medium of his newspaper.[7]

The ability to employ professional people, collect debts and church "offerings" from their employees' wages, give land away, bestow charity, and grant railroad passes enabled the coal industry or more correctly, its representatives, to increase their social power. Mine managers were the most influential men in the anthracite communities. W.R. Storrs, General Coal Agent for the Delaware, Lackawanna and Western, could stop a movement to sever the community of Throp from Dickson City with a simple protest.[8]

Naturally the coal industry converted its vast economic and social power into political power. To gain political power, mine officials lobbied, influenced officials, and reduced offices to mere company agencies. Anthracite lobbying agents operated on both the local and state levels of government. On the local scene respected attorneys protected the companies' interests. M.E. Olmsted, Harrisburg lobbyist for the anthracite industry, had the governor's ear as well as the legislature's. Such distinguished members of the bench as George Woodward pleaded eloquently on "king coal's" behalf.[9]

Patronage gave management a measure of control of appointive offices. Operators were influential in national and state parties, using their power to gain patronage.[10] W.H. Tillinghast, president of the Lehigh–Wilkes-Barre Coal Company, was successful in having Miss Kate Koons appointed postmistress in Audenried. Politicians, in return, asked company officials to hire certain people. W. Ward, a congressman, requested that the Philadelphia and Reading place one of his supporters on its police force.[11]

Management and elected officials shared economic interests. Simon Cameron had a vested interest in anthracite through his connection with the Northern Central Railroad. Congressman Hendrick B. Wright derived part of his private income from mine royalties and owed at least one operator money.[12] Congressman William L. Scott owned and operated mines near Mt. Carmel.

Some local officials could be identified with the anthracite industry. In 1896 the mercantile firm of Dailey and Robert asked the Lehigh–Wilkes-Barre Coal Company to collect their store bills from its employees and pointed out that one of the firm's members was a justice of the peace and deputy coroner and "has been and can be of great assistance to the company." The company granted the request.[13]

If the industry's economic power could be used to guarantee "great assistance" from some politicians, it could also be exercised in a manner which would reduce offices to empty shells. The industry functioned as the tax collector by deducting the miners' per capita and other taxes from their paychecks. The elected tax collectors paid a 2 percent commission for the privilege of not working, but they also lost their power.

Township supervisors also lost their power. An act of 1883 permitted taxpayers to commute their taxes into actual services and mining companies escaped payment by maintaining roads. Performance of service in lieu of taxes might have assured the public better roads, but to the coal companies the practice had a more important implication:

> At a meeting of a few of the representatives of the Larger Tax-payers [the coal companies] in Old Forge Township it was thought advisable, in order to reduce taxation, that the larger Taxpayers should work the road according to the Act of 1883, as is done in other townships in Luzerne County, thus taking the matter out of the hands of the supervisors.[14]

Supervisors occasionally reduced their own independence by allowing mine operators to provide or pay for special services required by the public servants:

> The treasurer will send you a voucher for $50 to pay John Mc-Gahran for services as Attorney for the Supervisor for Hanover Township. Please take a loose receipt for same and forward to me, and oblige.[15]

The reduction of the offices of tax collector and supervisor was so complete that the Pottsville *Daily Republican* observed on April 29, 1890: "There would seem to be no necessity for the election of supervisors in townships where the Reading Coal and Iron Company own property. They insist upon paying their taxes in road work performed by their own men. They can collect the tax from the majority of the payers in cash at the pay-window."[16]

Stripping the tax collectors and supervisors of their power reflected the anthracite industry's concern over taxes, but the community's coercive potential also interested the operators. For industry concern for police control was as logical as care about taxes. The police protected property, and the mines were the largest form of property within the region. Furthermore, the presence of a sympathetic police force could be a valuable asset in times of labor strife.

Operators in Schuylkill County attempted to influence the police by bypassing local government. In 1867 they secured from the Pennsylvania legislature "An Act for the better protection of persons, property, and life in the mining regions of this Commonwealth." Limited to Schuylkill County, the act gave the governor authority to appoint a special marshal of police and not more than 100 officers upon an appeal from 20 local citizens that the regular police were unable to maintain order. The marshal, who along with his force was paid from the county treasury with funds raised by a special tax on coal, enjoyed the same authority as the sheriff. The most interesting features of the act were that the coal industry financed the special police through the guise of an extraordinary tax, while local politicians exercised no control over the new force. The creation of a special criminal court with the same jurisdiction as the county court increased the Police Marshal's independence of the local government. Removal from local political control, however, did not place the police under the operators' dominance.

In 1866 anthracite mine operators gained an effective instrument of police control when the Pennsylvania legislature extended to them the railroad companies' privilege of maintaining private police. Nominated by the coal company and appointed by the governor, the Coal and Iron Police had the same authority as the city police of Philadelphia and the right to call for assistance. "If the railroad mining company can pay a hundred men under that law," observed a congressional committee, "it can maintain and use a standing army."[17]

Maintenance of a livery force gave the operators the ability to reduce public law enforcement agencies to puppets. Coal region boroughs had a wholly inadequate police force. In 1891 Shenandoah, with a population of 15,944, boasted two policemen and three officers; Pottsville, with 14,117 persons, had a force of nine men. Understaffed local police forces had to expand rapidly to meet emergencies, and the most expedient method to do this was to use the Coal and Iron Police as auxiliaries. The sheriff also found the private police a welcome and necessary source of manpower for his posses. The dependence of borough police and the sheriff on the coal companies for extra men in times of emergency, the most common of which were strikes, made them essentially agents of the operators.

The degree of control exercised by the anthracite industry over the community's police power was clearly evident in the Molly Maguire incident (see Chapter 9). Historians have debated whether the Mollies were hardened criminals or innocent labor leaders; many, in the heat of argument, have completely neglected the episode's true significance.[18] The Molly Maguire investigation and trials were one of the most astounding surrenders of sovereignty in American history. A private corporation initiated the investigation through a private detective agency; a private police force arrested the alleged offenders; and coal company attorneys prosecuted them. The state provided only the courtroom and hangman. The fate of the Molly

Maguires taught the people of the anthracite regions that the Coal and Iron Police were supreme within the area.

Wielding their economic influence, mine officials achieved so much political power that for all practical purposes they provided the de facto government of the anthracite region. Given the extent of the coal industry's economic, social, and political power, it must be concluded that the term "free town" was only a euphemism for "large town," because in reality industry-community relations within such communities were as unilateral as in the "mine patch." But such a conclusion would be superficial; for within the free town there existed a class whose challenges to industrial dominance made the power of the operators less than absolute.

As a group the independent merchants revolted against industrial control. In part, social discontent nourished the revolt. It must be remembered that company bureaucrats wielded the coal industry's power. They were not the product of only the large companies; most independent operators were absentee owners and depended on managers. Social tensions existed between the avant garde of the "new middle class" and the classical bourgeoisie.[19] Owning property and not merely managing it, the merchants regarded themselves as the legitimate social leaders; but obviously they were not.

The social conflict between the merchants and the industrial élite can be seen in their differing definitions of industry's obligations to the community. The mine superintendents sought a profit, with little concern about what area benefited from their business acumen. Local businessmen, on the other hand, wanted to see their region's wealth reinvested at home. "It is not a fair thing," they argued, "to rob our coal lands without a return of some sort."[20] Economic motives were combined with motives of social status and civic pride in the merchants' challenge to the power of the operators. Businessmen regarded the company stores as "a drawback to legitimate business houses wherever they exist."[21] Many merchants felt the industry was doing them, and indirectly their towns, great harm by purchasing its supplies outside the community.

For reasons such as these, the businessmen of the anthracite region concluded that their best interests were not necessarily synonymous with those of the coal industry. Organized into boards of trade and merchant protective associations, they fought either to improve or maintain their position in their particular towns. Merchants were free to challenge the operators despite the industry's formidable power because the mines were fixed. Although businessmen needed the mines to survive, the mines could not exist without the community.

The struggle between industry and local business betrayed a social order which lacked cohesion. Because of the layout of transportation routes, the four coal basins were grouped into three geo-economic units which resented each other's prosperity. Geology and soil conditions subdivided the three units into two basic regions—the north and the south. Divergent cultures enhanced the geological differences. The northern region boasted a colonial history and gloried in its Yankee heritage, while the southern region had no pre-industrial history and traced its cultural roots to the Pennsylvania Dutch.[22]

Within each region society was fragmented along ethnic lines. Immigrants always formed the majority of the anthracite laboring force and each new wave of immigrants brought forth denunciations from the native and older inhabitants. Convinced that the foreigners were a threat to them, the "natives" organized anti-Catholic societies. The Junior Order of American Mechanics flourished in the anthracite regions, and Schuykill County boasted of being the stronghold for the Patriotic Order of the Sons of America in Pennsylvania.[23] Older immigrants feared for their jobs and held the new arrivals in contempt. Both demanded protection from the swarming hordes of undesirables: "Are miners protected from filthy, pauper Poles, laborers from water and flower earthly Italians, ignorant Swedes, English-murdering, rice and rat eating Chinese?"[24]

Fear and contempt preceded indifference and violence. "Natives" forgot the concept of neighborly help: "I happened to ask the employer ... whether the American families looked after the Hungarians at all times of sickness, and his answer photographed the whole situation: "We don't know they are sick till we see the funeral go by."[25] "Americans" applauded violence when directed against the immigrants: "Two Hungarians were walking down Lackawanna Avenue yesterday in front of the Delaware, Lackawanna and Western depot when one of them, without any cause, was set upon by a drunken brute and beaten and kicked in a shameful manner, and a crowd stood by and laughed."[26]

"Old immigrants" clashed with the "new," but ethnic identification within each major group prevented a united front of

the old against the new immigrants. Foreign-language news-
papers abounded in the region. Hazleton was the home of the
Volksblatt (German), the *Onallas* (Hungarian), and the *Jednota*
(Czech). Fraternal organizations kept ethnocentrism alive. The
English joined the Sons of Saint George and the Welsh united in
Urdd y Gwir Iforiaid Americanaidd (American Order of True
Ivorites) and maintained their own philosophical societies and
young peoples' clubs. Germans mingled in *Liederkranzes* and
Vereins. Newer immigrants organized paramilitary groups such
as the *Gwardia Pulaskiego Rycerzy Polskich* (Guards of Pulaski,
The Polish Knights).

Each group maintained its own beneficial society. The Polish
had a Pulaski Beneficial Society and the Irish could choose between the Hibernian and Emerald Societies. Social events adver-
tised one's ethnic origins. The Polish celebrated Pulaski Day and
held Kosciusko picnics, while the Irish marched on Saint Patrick's Day and the Scotch celebrated Robert Burns' birthday.
Not to be outdone, the Welsh sang at *eisteddfods* and Germans
enjoyed *Sängerbunds*. Even charity could be organized on ethnic
foundations; the Scranton Germans held an excursion to Jones'
Lake for the benefit of the Lackawanna Hospital.

Normally integrative institutions such as churches and political parties failed to cross ethnic lines. Denominationalism splin-
tered Protestantism; ethnic churches existed within each denom-
ination. There were Welsh and English Methodists, German and
Dutch Reformed, English and German Lutherans. Although de-
void of denominationalism, the Catholic Church failed to
achieve unity among its adherents. Each national group demanded and received its own parish. In 1902 the anthracite regions supported 142 Catholic churches, of which 62 were Irish,
19 Polish, 18 Greek, 15 Slovak, 12 Lithuanian, 10 German, and 6
Italian.

Organized into national parishes presided over by priests
from the homeland, many immigrants chafed under the rule of
an Irish-dominated hierarchy. "People," a layman urged, "let
us pray that God might have pity on us, and might deliver us
from the domination of foreign bishops, restore our churches to
us, and give us bishops after our own heart."[27]

Ethnocentrism, coupled with a dispute over control of the
parish finances, caused a separatist movement within the Catholic Church. In 1897 the Polish in Scranton demanded lay control of parish property but the priest refused to relinquish his

authority. The congregation forced the issue by denying the priest entrance into the church and appealed to the bishop for his removal. When the bishop refused to grant their petition, the parishioners asked the Reverend Father Francis Hodur to administer the sacraments to them and to take up their cause. Hodur agreed; when rebuffed by the hierarchy, he formed the Polish National Catholic Church. Using the Polish language in its rites and ceremonies, the Polish National Catholic Church displayed its ethnocentrism in the preamble of its constitution; "Shall only we Poles form an exception and allow ourselves to be forced to follow a line laid down for us by others?"[28]

Political parties also experienced the centrifugal force of ethnocentrism. Party leaders attempted to balance their ticket with representatives from each immigrant group. Welsh and German Republican central committees conducted their own campaigns. Immigrant groups maintained their own political organizations outside the major parties. Italians in Scranton formed the Italian Political Association which auctioned their votes. In 1887, for example, they went Republican. Schuylkill County Poles also sold their votes. In Scranton the Negro community named representation on the police force as the price of their support.

Strong enough to withstand integrative forces, ethnic groups themselves broke into factions. Deep lines of division cut through the Irish community. The differences became noticeable in Clarks Summit "Irish War of 1850," a fight between Corkonians and Fardowns which resulted in three deaths.[29] Antagonism between the Russian and the German and Austrian Poles was so great that the two subgroups founded separate churches and societies. The existence of the Polish National Catholic Church alongside the Roman Catholic Church further fragmented the Polish community. So great were these inter- and intra-ethnic conflicts that they weakened normal class lines.

Apparently chaos ruled in the anthracite community. Operating in an area divided and subdivided by economics, geology, and culture, management used its vast economic resources to stabilize the region with a unilaterally set system of industry-community relations. Independent merchants took advantage of the immobility of the industry to frustrate management. And ethnic divisions atomized an already fragmented society.

Work

Defined as earning a living, "work" is an economic pursuit. But viewed in a sociological context, work becomes a system of social interrelations governed by rules and directed toward a given goal.

Anthracite mining was a collective productive system involving "a technological process carried on by a production organization, with a reward system, in a social setting."[1] Every industry must have a function; it must fulfill a socially determined need. To fulfill its function an industry employs technology and organizes its labor force around the technology. A reward system insures the smooth operation of the resulting system. Functioning within such a productive system, the anthracite mine workers confronted problems derived from both the technological process and the reward system while they simultaneously discovered that the social relations inherent in the organization of work conditioned their response to the problems.

Chapter
4

The Productive System

Operators viewed the anthracite industry as a source of profit, but profit was simply the reward for fulfilling a socially defined function. Sociologically providing a clean and uniformly sized fuel was the industry's raison d'être. Social demand dictated the industry's two major operations, mining and preparation, and thus outlined the structure of work.

Dominated by the culm pile, a huge black mound of coal, slate, and dirt spewed out by the breaker, the surface plant housed the preparation operation. The breaker was the heart of the operation; inside the tall unsightly building freshly mined coal underwent cracking, screening, and cleaning processes. A cluster of drab smaller buildings housing boilers, pumps, and hoisting machinery surrounded the breaker and completed the surface plant.[1]

Mine workers penetrated the earth through four distinct types of opening: "drifts," "slopes," tunnels, and shafts. The "drift" was an inclined plane driven into the coal at an upward angle from the outcrop. "Slopes" followed the coal seam's dip from the outcrop. Divided into "lifts" of approximately 100 yards each, the "slope" was an inclined plane driven through both coal and strata. The tunnel provided entry to coal beds lying above water level which failed to outcrop. The shaft reached coal seams lying 200 or more feet below the surface.

Once inside the mine, the miner was confronted by a bewildering maze of gangways and airways. Heavily timbered and laid with railroad track, the gangways were the mine's haulage routes. Airways ran parallel to the gangways and were connected to them at regular intervals by cross-headings. Furnaces located at the bottom of an upcast shaft rarefied the air to insure circulation. During the late 1870s, however, fans began to replace the furnaces. The gangway and the airway met at the miners' working place, the mine face.

Most anthracite mines followed the pillar and breast method of mining. Rectangular working compartments (breasts), usually five to twelve yards wide and from four to six hundred yards long, opened from the gangway. A thick block of coal (the pillar) stood between each breast and supported the mine's overhead burden ("overburden").

Miners worked one of three types of breasts, depending on the coal seam's dip. "Wagon breasts" opened at full width at the gangway in seams dipping less than six degrees. "Buggy breasts" were used to work coal beds dipping from six to twelve degrees. Since the grade was too steep for the heavy mine wagon, smaller cars—"buggies"—brought the coal to the gangway where it was reloaded into the regular wagon. "Shute breasts" were needed for coal seams inclining from 12 to 90 degrees. Freed coal slid down the grade of the breast into a shute which extended into the gangway. Wooden barriers, the "battery," held the coal back until an empty wagon was to be filled.[2]

The mine contained two separate plants. The surface plant, built around the breaker, was for processing freshly mined coal. The subsurface plant, a confusing complex of gangways, airways, and breasts, was used to retrieve coal from underground. Mine owners had to integrate work in such a manner that the two plants would operate smoothly and thereby realize the industry's social function.

Operators naturally divided their employees according to plant, and organized each unit functionally. Comprising roughly 36 percent of the total personnel, the outside force, those working above ground, contained three major classes. Skilled artisans such as blacksmiths, carpenters, machinists, and stationary engineers formed the first class. Mule drivers, common laborers, and other unskilled employees who did not work in the breaker made up the second group. The third and largest class may be labeled the breaker division, and contained everyone who spent most of his working day in the breaker.

Management organized the inside, or underground, force into four functional divisions. Miners and miners' laborers were the

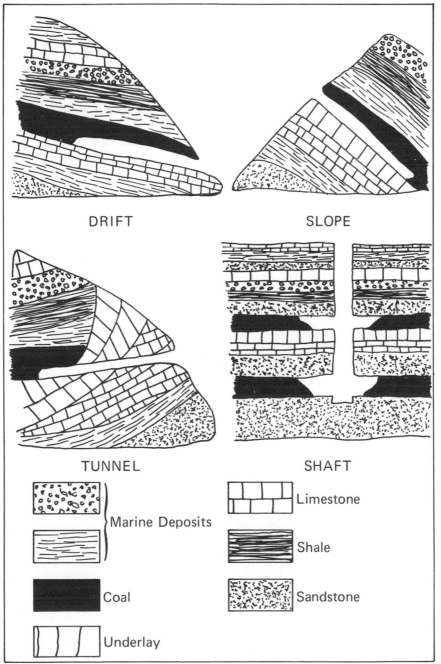

DRIFT   SLOPE

TUNNEL   SHAFT

Marine Deposits

Coal

Underlay

Limestone

Shale

Sandstone

Fig. 5 Types of Mine Openings

only employees engaged in the actual digging of coal. Mule drivers, runners, stable men, and stable bosses constituted the transportation group. Door and fan boys concerned themselves with ventilation. Both skilled and unskilled workers functioned as the maintenance group.

Technological innovation only slightly altered the structure of the various functional groups. Slate pickers felt some pressure from technological advancement. During the late 1870s many collieries began adopting mechanical slate pickers such as the jig which separated coal from dirt and slate by specific gravity. Mechanization of the cleaning process, however, did not completely destroy the slate-picking occupation, for in 1886 the anthracite mines still employed 19,995 slate pickers.[3] Outside mule drivers suffered a small displacement with the introduction of conveyor belts, but the job itself was never jeopardized.

The inside transportation group also experienced some changes. Locomotives, first steam and after 1887, electric, replaced mules in the larger gangways. Subsidiary haulage routes, however, continued to use the mule's power well into the twentieth century.

Neither was machinery a threat to the miners. Some miners did trade their hand drills for crank-turned boring machines, but the use of machinery that would displace miners was almost nil. Operators knew of coal-cutting machines as early as 1866, but both management and miners agreed that the hardness of anthracite and the distorted horizons of the coal seams made the use of such machines impractical.

Unlike most other industries, anthracite mining remained immune to sweeping technological changes. The inability to apply machinery to the mines not only gave the mine workers a sense of security but allowed the social relations derived from organization of work to remain untouched.

Organization of work into functional operations created a status hierarchy for the anthracite mine workers. The contract miner, who was paid by the piece, was at the top. Working for definite wages, the "day miner" ranked directly below. Highly skilled employees were next, with the miners' laborers next below. The remaining employees were assigned to their jobs on the basis of skill and/or the importance of jobs. Job location ascribed status differentiation within each position; inside mule drivers, for example, enjoyed higher status and wages than their colleagues above ground.

The mine workers' hierarchy was not rigid; men passed freely from one level to another. Age was the chief determinant of mobility. The mine worker usually began his career as a slate picker between the ages of four and ten. Between 12 and 14 he graduated into the "nipper" class, a kind of puberty rite which provided the errand boys in and around the mines.[4] At 14 he was old enough to enter the mine, usually as a door boy. From door boy the budding mine employee progressed to mule driver, laborer, and finally, miner.

In many respects the functional hierarchy resembled the age-skill hierarchy found in the New England shoe factories. But the miner's hierarchy was not a vertical ladder; one did not remain a miner after he grew old. Instead he found that age closed the circle; when too old or infirm to perform the miner's arduous tasks he returned to picking slate. It was just as the saying went, "twice a boy and once a man is a poor miner's life."[5]

Not all mine workers entered the mines through the breaker. Immigrants usually began their careers as mule drivers or laborers and worked their way up to the rank of miner. As can be surmised from Table 6, many immigrants experienced opposition as they moved up in the ranks; but the continuous increase in production, combined with the lack of mechanization in the mines, tended to cause the breaking down of ethnic barriers.

Operators were adept at organizing work according to function, but they were surprisingly inept at defining the relationship of the diverse groups. Some companies wrote detailed job descriptions (see Appendix II). Other operators, however, delegated the authority to compose work rules to individual mine superintendents, and at least one major employer published rules which defined only the working day and the mine boss's function.[6]

The apparent disregard for work rules reflected the impossibility of enforcement rather than professional ineptitute. Mine inspectors repeatedly called for greater discipline in the mines. Working in the labyrinth of a mine, many employees escaped continuous supervision, and the use of the piece rate reinforced the freedom gained by being far from the source of supervision; many miners refused to assume a subordinate position to the foreman. One miner explained how he instructed his immigrant laborer (who loaded the coal) in the "etiquette" of the mines: "Here's the boss. Don't work. Always sit down when the boss is around."[7]

TABLE 6
Nationality of Certified Miners in the Western Part
of the 7th Inspection District

Nationality	Number
American	847
German	64
Irish	62
English	43
Welsh	44
Scotch	14
Austrian	13
Hungarian	7
Polish	4
French	2
Turkish	1
Canadian	1

Source: *Daily Republican,* October 30, 1889.

Although anthracite mine workers enjoyed freedom from supervision to a degree rarely experienced in other industries, they were not completely without discipline. Custom dictated certain procedures. It was customary for the contract miner to quit work whenever he felt he had freed enough coal for the day. In the northern basin by tradition four men worked a breast, while in the two southern basins there were only two.

Because of the interdependence of the groups, each group had to fulfill its obligation to the others. The anthracite mine was operated in much the same way as an assembly line; a break at any point caused the entire operation to stop. If the slate pickers quit working, for example, the mine had to shut down. Interdependence, combined with shared working conditions, overrode normal intergroup conflicts and made for a common identity.

By modern standards working conditions above and below ground were abominable. Inside the breaker, young boys found it difficult to sit through the day, and "picker bosses" used whips and switches on mischief-makers. Corporal punishment formed only part of the deleterious working conditions. The slate pickers' compartment was choked with dust, which necessitated open windows. Open windows and poor heating made it impossible to keep warm during the winter months, and some boys sabotaged machinery in order to go home and get warm.

Weather was not a problem for the workers inside. The temperature remained fairly constant throughout the year. Water, however, did cause trouble. The mines became giant cisterns which collected huge amounts of subsurface water. In some mines men worked knee-deep in water. Also, the water soaked the workers' clothing, making coal dust adhere to it.

The mine's atmosphere teemed with dirt. Anthracite could be broken loose only by blasting; the combination of powder smoke and coal dust made air even in the best-ventilated mines filthy. Coal-burning locomotives contributed their share of soot to an already dirt-laden air. Sometimes the dust and smoke inside the mine became so thick that the laborer had to feel his way through the tunnels.

Light was a problem even in the cleanest mines. Inside workers got their light from oil lamps measuring less than three inches in height. Required to furnish their own oil, many employees contributed to their gloomy circumstances by using as little oil as possible and thereby cutting costs. Rather than use more expensive fuels which burned with a clean bright light, many mine workers bought poorer grades of oil such as "Wild Fire Jack." Cheaper fuels had a tendency to cake on the wick, which reduced the light so much that it "would require another light to see it."[8] Some mine workers mixed kerosene with cheap oil to avoid crusting, but the mixture usually gave off more smoke than flame.

For safety as well as tolerable working conditions, adequate light was mandatory. Danger was always present in the mines (see Table 7). Blasting was a common cause of accidents. Gas was equally dangerous—and invisible. Anthracite coal seams contained pockets of carbonated hydrogen—"fire damp"—which was explosive. After an explosion the burning gas rolled down the mine's gangways singeing everything and everybody in its path. Suffocating "black damp" (carbonic acid) usually followed the fire damp. Penetration of abandoned mines often released water that had collected; in 1891, for example, 17 men drowned when miners at J. C. Hayden Company's Slope Number 1 at Jeansville broke into an old mine. Miners worked under the constant threat of the overburden caving in on them. In 1896 there was such a cave-in at the Twin Shaft Colliery near Pittston,

TABLE 7
**Causes of Fatal Accidents in Schuylkill County,
1869 to 1874**

Cause	1874	1873	1872	1871	1870	1869	Total
Falls of coal	24	37	21	26	37	18	163
Falls in slopes and shafts	4	7	8	6	4	5	34
Falls of rock and slate	2	3	4	5	5	2	21
Explosion of fire damp	16	10	15	26	8	2	77
Explosion of powder	1	1	9	2	1	6	20
Explosion of blasts	1	2		5	4	2	14
Explosion of boilers	2			1	5		8
Crushing by wagons	7	7		8	15	4	41
Crushing by timbers	2	1	3	1	1	1	9
Cage accidents	2		2	2	6	5	17
Rope and chain accidents	4	6	1	3	12		26
Animal accidents	2	1			3		6
Machinery accidents	2	6	1	5		5	19
Roller accidents		4	2	3	4	1	14
Misc. accidents	9	6	3	9	7	5	39
Total	78	91	69	102	112	56	508

Source: Mine Inspectors, *Report, 1874*, 17.

which killed 58 men. Above ground, unguarded machinery and inquisitive boys who worked around the mines often proved a fatal combination.

The accumulated dangers in the mines took a frightful toll in fatalities and injuries. Between 1876 and 1897, 7,346 men were killed in the anthracite mines of Pennsylvania (see Table 8). indeed, the hard coal mines were among the world's most dangerous. Although there were approximately 1.9 anthracite mine workers for every bituminous coal miner in Pennsylvania during the decade 1887 to 1897, roughly 2.7 hard coal miners died for every soft coal miner killed, while 2.6 men received injuries in anthracite mines for every injury in the bituminous mines (see Table 9). A comparison of fatal accidents per 1,000 employees in the world's coal mines during the period (Table 10) reveals that the anthracite mines deserved their unenviable reputation.

To some degree the operators were responsible for the high accident rate in the anthracite mines. Not willing to bear the added costs of extra openings, they provided only one opening

TABLE 8
Fatal and Nonfatal Accidents in
the Anthracite Mines

Year	Fatal	Nonfatal
1876	228	453
1877	194	567
1878	187	504
1879	262	791
1880	202	670
1881	273	835
1882	294	850
1883	323	1,093
1884	252	751
1885	356	868
1886	279	848
1887	316	1,048
1888	364	1,032
1889	385	998
1890	378	1,007
1891	427	997
1892	396	1,023
1893	455	1,069
1894	439	919
1895	420	1,075
1896	502	1,115
1897	424	1,106
Total	7,346	17,709

Source: Mine Inspectors' Reports.

to the mine—which made every mine a potential deathtrap. One of the most terrible accidents occurred on September 6, 1869 at Avondale, when a breaker above a shaft caught fire, suffocating 110 men and boys. "Robbing the pillars" and mining the pillars after the breasts had been worked increased the likelihood of a cave-in. Failure to keep adequate maps of abandoned mines and their positions vis-à-vis mines in operation contributed to accidents such as that at J.C. Hayden's Slope Number 1.

The anthracite industry's basic weakness also contributed to a high accident rate in the mines. Frequent suspensions caused by overproduction (mentioned above) made the mines "so often idle that, from standing gas, decay of timber, the absence of

TABLE 9
Comparison of Accidents in Pennsylvania's
Anthracite and Bituminous Mines

	Anthracite		Bituminous	
Year	killed	injured	killed	injured
1887	316	1,048	84	271
1888	364	1,032	89	290
1889	385	998	105	297
1890	378	1,007	146	381
1891	427	997	226	333
1892	396	1,023	133	393
1893	455	1,069	131	346
1894	439	919	124	357
1895	420	1,075	155	419
1896	502	1,115	179	398
1897	424	1,106	149	426

Source: Mine Inspectors' Reports.

proper ventilation, and standing water [they became not only] unsafe but virtually dangerous."[9]

But mine workers also must share the blame. Many of them were guilty of "rushing into danger without using the proper precautions."[10] Eager to blast coal free in the shortest time possible, and thereby leave the mine early, some miners would not take the precious minutes needed to timber their breasts. During the winter months they would not go out into the cold to secure the necessary props. Some mine workers were guilty of gross carelessness. One miner blew himself up when he mistook a keg of powder for oil, and poured the powder into his burning lamp. Lack of discipline contributed to the high accident rate. Also, mine inspectors blamed most of the mine accidents on employees' refusal to obey normal safety rules.

Both management and labor were thus responsible for the excessive accident rate in the anthracite mines. The operators' eagerness to cut costs, failure to keep maps, and desire to recoup the coal in the pillars, plus the frequent suspensions induced by overinvestment, contributed to the hazardous working conditions. But many, if not most, accidents were attributable to the mine workers' "inexcusable negligence, or the most stupid disobedience of orders."[11]

TABLE 10
Comparison of Fatal Accidents Per 1,000 Employees
in the World's Coal Mines

Location of Mines	1891	1892	1893	1894	1895	1896	1897
Austria	2.54	1.18	1.11	5.13	1.96	1.20	0.95
Belgium	1.40	2.84	1.12	1.62	1.49	1.14	1.03
Germany	2.80	2.30	2.60	2.12	2.44	2.57	2.27
England	1.50	1.49	1.55	1.60	1.48	1.48	1.32
France	1.67	0.95	0.93	0.85	1.19	1.30	1.07
Colorado	4.40	4.49	6.31	3.06	3.05	10.75	4.99
Pa. Anthracite	3.08	3.05	3.25	3.15	3.64	3.35	2.84
Pa. Bituminous	3.18	1.69	1.64	1.44	1.83	2.14	1.72

Source: *Report of the Coal Strike Commission,* 28.

The
Reward
System

Mining anthracite was a dismal and risky occupation. Climate, subsurface water, poor light, and air choked with coal dust and blasting powder were combined in terrible working conditions. Managerial and employee irresponsibility accentuated an already hazardous occupation until Pennsylvania's anthracite mines were among the world's most dangerous. The men, nevertheless, were induced by its reward system to overlook discomfort and risk injury in order to enter this collective productive industry.

The anthracite industry's reward system was chaotic. Operators took advantage of both piece and daily rates to fix wages for employees. Skill and age were the determinants of the daily wage rate which remained fairly uniform throughout a company. But management paid by the piece in one of three ways. Some operators paid their miners according to each ton of coal produced. Others paid by the wagon of coal sent to the surface. Operators working mines with greatly folded seams paid by the yard, or "run." A miner working by "the run" received an agreed-upon sum for opening his breast, and thereafter for each linear yard of breast driven. In each case the wage per yard varied according to the amount of propping and other necessary nonproductive work.

The actual rate within each piece-rate system varied between mines and within each mine. To a large extent the varying geological features serve to explain the difference in rates, but since the rates were the result of individual negotiations between the foreman and miner, they also reflected the foreman's tenacity and the miner's skill in bargaining.

44

Although it was the result of individual negotiations, the piece-rate system was the source of many grievances. Miners working by the ton complained that the "miner's ton," which ranged from 2,464 to 3,360 pounds, was an unfair weight. Those paid by the wagon insisted that the tendency of the operators to increase the amount a wagon could hold lowered their earnings. All contract miners found the practice of "docking"—deducting a certain amount from each payable unit for dirt and slate—a constant irritation.

All mine employees agreed that their wages were too low. The mine workers' charges seem to have been substantiated (see Table 11). But "low" is relative, and it is only by comparing wages in the anthracite industry with other industries that we can arrive at any conclusion. During the period 1875 to 1888 bituminous coal miners in Pennsylvania received slightly higher wages than did the anthracite miners.

Comparison with the wages paid in Pennsylvania's rolling mills (Tables 13 and 14) reveals that the steel mills also paid higher wages than the hard coal mines during the same period. Blast furnaces (Table 15) paid lower wages than did the anthracite industry, but the furnaces were one of the few industries that did. In 1884 the anthracite industry ranked 34th among the 58 industries in Pennsylvania reporting average weekly wages.

Irregularity of employment caused even lower wages. Employment levels reflected seasonal fluctuations in demand.

TABLE 11
Average Daily Wages in 1884, by Class and County

Class	Carbon	Columbia	Schuylkill	Luzerne
Contract miner	$3.00	$3.05	$2.53	$2.72
Miner on wages	2.02	1.90	1.86	1.92½
Loaders	1.72	1.77	1.75	1.46
Inside laborer	1.58	1.70	1.56	1.55
Outside laborer	1.16	1.37	1.27	1.23
Platform man	1.20	1.33	1.33	1.26
Slate picker boss	1.27	1.54	1.37	1.49
Slate picker boy	0.51	0.65	0.67	0.62
Door boy	0.80	0.90	0.76	0.70
Driver	1.32	1.38	1.25	1.27
Engineer	1.80	1.86	1.81	1.85
Fireman	1.38	1.36	1.51	1.45

Source: Pennsylvania *Industrial Statistics, 1884,* 4.

TABLE 12
Average Daily Wages in the Anthracite Mines

Class	1875	1876	1877	1878	1879	1880	1881	1882	1883
Contract miner	$3.00	$2.97	$1.91	$1.97	$2.09	$2.71	$2.52	$2.52	$2.70
Miner on wages	2.40	2.33	1.78	1.66	1.63	1.88	2.05	2.05	2.00
Inside laborer	2.00	1.82	1.69	1.38	1.37	1.62	1.72	1.72	1.78
Outside laborer	1.65	1.56	1.47	1.21	1.19	1.30	1.27	1.27	1.40
Platform man	1.66	1.66	1.51	1.21	—	1.31	1.39	1.29	1.40
Slate picker, boss	1.40	1.29	1.06	—	1.05	1.44	1.37	1.37	1.55
Slate picker, boy	0.60	0.61	0.53	0.51	0.56	0.57	0.65	0.65	0.64
Door boy	1.05	1.03	0.63	0.61	0.61	0.77	0.75	0.75	0.45
Engineer	2.50	2.28	2.15	1.68	1.65	1.80	1.78	1.78	1.88
Mule driver	1.64	1.63	1.62	1.30	1.19	1.26	1.29	1.29	1.43
Fireman	—	—	—	1.26	—	1.44	1.40	1.40	1.58
Blacksmith	2.50	2.28	2.87	—	1.65	1.80	1.81	1.81	1.91
Carpenter	2.50	2.28	2.50	—	1.65	1.80	1.83	1.83	1.88

Source: Pennsylvania *Industrial Statistics.*

TABLE 13
Average Daily Wages in the Bituminous Mines

Class	1875	1876	1877	1878	1879	1880	1881	1882	1883
Miner	$2.47	$2.59	$1.65	$1.88	$1.74	$2.25	$2.16	$2.16	$2.05
Inside laborer	1.90	1.71	1.64	1.47	1.42	1.69	1.81	1.81	1.82
Outside laborer	1.76	1.52	1.34	1.47	1.42	1.46	1.63	1.63	1.62
Mule driver	1.81	1.61	1.57	1.46	1.41	1.63	1.80	1.80	1.80
Blacksmith	2.29	2.15	1.80	1.91	1.75	1.96	2.16	2.16	2.09
Carpenter	2.29	2.15	1.80	1.90	1.75	1.84	2.06	2.06	1.93

Source: Pennsylvania *Industrial Statistics.*

TABLE 14
Average Daily Wages in the Rolling Mills: Eastern Division

Class	1875	1876	1877	1878	1879	1880	1881	1882	1883
Puddler	$3.11	$2.78	$2.40	$2.40	$2.53	$2.80	$3.03	$3.03	$2.72
Puddler's helper	1.57	1.51	1.35	1.27	1.32	1.40	1.60	1.60	1.45
Heater	4.60	3.26	3.10	3.03	3.03	4.20	3.81	3.81	3.60
Heater's helper	2.25	1.71	1.50	1.55	1.55	1.60	1.50	1.50	1.79
Roller	4.00	3.68	3.05	3.12	2.95	4.70	4.69	4.69	4.21
Rougher	2.45	1.88	1.75	1.60	1.57	1.89	2.56	2.66	2.36
Catcher	2.33	1.88	2.40	1.51	1.57	1.76	2.06	2.06	1.74
Hooker	1.75	1.23	1.80	1.15	1.22	1.20	1.25	1.25	1.15
Shearman	1.43	1.67	1.58	1.40	1.41	1.55	1.50	1.50	1.33
Straightener	2.54	1.67	—	1.56	1.58	1.48	1.50	1.50	1.58
Engineer	2.24	1.87	2.25	1.72	1.90	1.90	2.00	2.00	1.75
Blacksmith	2.56	2.06	1.82	1.73	1.71	1.75	1.96	1.96	2.06
Machinist	2.37	2.02	2.52	2.00	2.08	2.17	2.17	2.17	2.35
Carpenter	2.37	1.97	1.80	1.59	1.43	1.58	1.67	1.67	1.83

Source: Pennsylvania *Industrial Statistics.*

"When things begin to improve," one operator explained, "we must have enough employees on hand to satisfy the demand, and that means, when business slacks up, that many have to be idle."[1]

Regulation of production to offset overinvestment increased the unemployment caused by seasonal demand. As mentioned earlier, the coal pool instituted three-quarter, half, and one-quarter time to keep production in line with demand. Occasionally some companies worked less time than that suggested by the coal pool; during January 1890 the Delaware, Lackawanna, and Western mines worked only one day a week.

As can be seen in Table 17, the long periods of compulsory unemployment bit deeply into the workers' pay. In addition mine workers had to furnish their own tools, oil, and powder, which they bought from their employers.

The mine operators discovered that the sale of supplies was a good source of extra profit. Operators purchased oil at 25 to 35 cents a gallon and sold it for 75 cents a gallon. But the sale of blasting powder was the most lucrative. Paying 90 cents per 25-pound keg of powder, management retailed it at $3.00 a keg. Prudent operators realized an even greater return: powder companies paid 5 cents for each reusable keg returned, and they

TABLE 15
Average Daily Wages in the Blast Furnaces

Class	1878	1879	1880	1881	1882	1883
Foundryman	$2.11	$2.48	$2.70	$2.92	$2.92	$3.09
Keeper	1.40	1.50	1.56	1.75	1.75	1.81
Keeper's helper	1.15	1.40	1.35	1.55	1.55	1.46
Filler	1.15	1.61	1.33	1.63	1.63	1.39
Cinderman	1.16	1.32	1.26	1.43	1.43	1.34
Barrowman	—	—	1.18	1.31	1.31	1.38
Hot blast man	1.26	—	1.45	1.62	1.62	1.63
Weighman	1.40	—	1.39	1.55	1.55	1.43
Metal carrier	1.25	1.41	1.41	1.68	1.68	1.67
Engineer	1.24	1.60	1.67	1.69	1.69	1.75
Fireman	1.06	1.38	1.30	1.52	1.52	1.38
Blacksmith	1.34	1.37	1.63	1.80	1.80	1.79
Blacksmith's helper	1.08	—	1.16	1.25	1.25	1.23
Carpenter	1.49	1.52	1.60	1.69	1.69	1.68
Laborer	0.96	1.19	1.05	1.15	1.15	1.18

Source: Pennsylvania *Industrial Statistics.*

TABLE 16
Number of Working Days in the Anthracite Industry

Year	Days worked	Year	Days worked
1875	132	1886	194
1876	155	1887	210
1877	161	1888	221
1878	134	1889	195
1879	209	1890	191
1880	172	1891	182
1881	218	1892	205
1882	217	1893	207
1883	214	1894	179
1884	190	1895	182
1885	200	1896	171

Source: Roberts, *Industry*, 121.

usually gave a discount for early payment. As would be expected, the companies maintained a monopoly of the sale of powder. If a thrifty miner bought powder elsewhere, he was not allowed to blast with it in the company's mines.

Deductions for mining supplies fell most heavily on the inside workers, but all mine employees paid the high cost of paternalism. Because of geographic isolation many mine owners were forced to become community developers. Despite the warning of the Pennsylvania Bureau of Industrial Statistics, that "the demand for rents out of proportion to cost of construction is not only wrong itself, as taking advantage of men's necessities, but it engenders and nourishes the feeling of discontent among wage earners," company houses were rented at exorbitant rates. Some mine operators found another source of profit in the company house system—they charged each renter for a ton of coal per month regardless of whether he used it or not.

The truck system was still another drain on the mine laborers' wages. Under the system workers received their pay in scrip, or store orders, rather than cash. Employees often complained that the scrip was discounted or that the store on which the order was drawn furnished shoddy goods at high prices.

Closely related to the truck system was the company store. Many operators maintained their own stores and compelled their men to trade at them. Other employers entered into an agreement with independent merchants whereby they would

collect their employees' store bills for a commission and encourage their workers to trade at the favored merchant's store. In
the latter case, a contract between the miner and the business-
man preserved legality.[2] In both types of store, a man's wages
determined the extent of his credit. The bookkeeping department furnished the merchant with a daily report of the earnings of each employee, and no person's bill could exceed his
earnings.

Payroll deductions for store bills meant a reduction in real
wages (because of higher prices) as well as less pay. The company store usually took advantage of its captive clientele; one
independent merchant testified that company store prices
ranged as high as 160 percent above his.[3] Merchants who had
their bills collected by the operator increased their mark-up to
recover the operator's commission.

Some operators developed a system of paternalism that included virtually all of the community's life. Married workers had
75 and single employees 50 cents per month deducted from their
pay for the services of the company doctor, a deduction, however, which did not cover all medical expenses. Delivery of a
baby required an extra payment ranging from $5.00 to $8.00.

The end result of low wages and numerous payroll deductions was little or no pay. Contract miners, the highest-paid
level, received only a fraction of their earnings in cash. Other
workmen often received the infamous "bob-tail check," a statement that the total deductions equaled wages. Some unfortunate
employees learned at payday that their hard work had only

TABLE 17
Theoretical and Actual Wages in 1884

Class	Theoretical wages (at full time)			Actual wages		
	Day	Week	Year	Day	Week	Year
Contract miner	$2.70	$16.20	$842.00	$2.70	$8.84	$459.68
Miner on wages	2.00	12.00	624.00	2.00	7.00	364.00
Inside laborer	1.78	10.68	553.36	1.78	6.14	319.28
Outside laborer	1.40	8.40	436.16	1.40	4.91	255.32
Driver	1.43	8.58	446.16	1.43	5.32	276.64
Blacksmith	1.91	11.46	595.92	1.91	7.16	372.32

Source: Pennsylvania *Industrial Statistics, 1884*, 4.

placed them in debt to the company. Some went for long periods before their labor produced cash. One miner reminisced: "There was a man that worked very hard continuously for a little over five years, and he never drew a dollar. It is only that he drew $5 at the end of the five years and he came to me and told me of it, and the old gentleman was almost crying with joy that he had received $5 on that occasion."[4]

Operators were usually slow in informing their employees whether the reward for their labor would be cash, nothing, or a debt. Most mines paid on a monthly basis, but the time lapse between the end of the pay period and the date of actual payment was such that mine workers received their pay five or six weeks after they did the work. In some instances management did not make payment until forced to; in June 1884 the men around Ashley had to threaten to strike before they finally received their wages for April.

To a large extent mine owners structured wages so as to enrich themselves rather than recompense their employees. But the basic weakness of the industry also partly explains the operators' tendency to view their employees' reward system as an extension of their own. Squeezed between high capitalization charges and falling prices due to overinvestment, management often found labor to be the only source of profit. To a surprising

TABLE 18
Prices in Company and Other Stores

Article	Company store	Other store
Flour per barrel	$8.00	$7.75
Chop	1.50	1.25
Corn meal	1.50	1.25
Butter per pound	.35	.30
Bacon per pound	.10	.08
Lard per pound	.13	.12
G. sugar per pound	.13	.11
A. sugar per pound	.12	.10
C. sugar per pound	.11	.09
Ham per pound	.13	.11-.12
Cheese per pound	.20	.16-.18
Teas per pound	.60-1.00	.25-.75
Coffees per pound	.28-.37	.25-.30

Source: Pennsylvania *Industrial Statistics,* 1878-79, 377-378.

TABLE 19
Pay Check for Contract Miner

By balance	
By 85 ½ wagons, 88	$75.46
By 10 yards, 1.58	15.80
By . . . . hours	
To balance	$91.26

To powder	$8.10	
To smith	.50	
To labor	41.33	
To labor		
To labor		
To team, 75, 75	1.50	
To rent	3.65	
To coal	1.50	56.58
Balance		34.68
By board		
Amount		
To merchandise	23.34	
To board		
To doctor	.75	
(extra adult in family)	.50	24.59
		$10.09

Source: *Labor Troubles,* 488.

degree, labor appreciated management's predicament, and instead complained about the perversions of a system that needlessly lowered their wages and callously struck at their pride.

The anthracite industry's reward system tended to deprive the mine workers of their self-esteem. Compulsory unemployment caused the mine employee to feel impotent. "My wife needs medicine. She needs nourishing food, but I have not the common necessaries of life to give her. My God what am I to do? I am idle through no fault of my own; I shrink from making it public."[5]

There was no sense of security even in company housing, expensive as it was. Often forced to sign a lease waiving his legal protections, the tenant-miner continually faced the threat of sudden eviction. The operator's ability legally to do anything he pleased with company houses sometimes stung the miners to the quick. One day in 1890 a miner named Edward Monaghan returned home from work to find his invalid wife on the pavement. The company had evicted her and their seven children after deciding to tear down the house to make room for a growing culm pile.[6]

Deductions for mining supplies and for the company store, along with other features of the operators' system of paternalism, deprived the mine workers of nearly all freedom. Mine laborers tended to view people who were able to buy wherever they pleased as "a superior class of freeman." Denial of the right to choose one's physician and pay one's taxes continually ate away at the pride of the miners.

In addition, the industry's payroll deductions reduced already low wages while the system of company paternalism, which the payroll deductions financed, further undercut the mine workers' pride. Indeed, the industry's reward system for anthracite mine workers appears on the whole to have been more of a studied insult than a reward.

The
Individual
Response

Improving his working conditions and bringing about a more equitable reward system were the anthracite mine worker's two major problems. Since mine operators would resist attempts to do anything about either problem, the solution depended on power.

The individual mine worker, of course, had little power, partly because the anthracite miners functioned in task groups. Stripped of power and even individual identity by the collective productive system, the mine worker could solve his major problems on an individual basis only by escaping from the mine. Effective action within the industry could be undertaken only by the group.

Chapter
6

Mobility

Working within a collective productive
system, the individual mine employee had little opportunity
even to ameliorate his occupational problems. Since quitting his
job was the only alternative open to him, his ability to rid himself of occupational problems was directly proportional to his
mobility.

Contemporary observers disagreed over the mine worker's
ability to change his position. George Virtue reported a "re-
markable lack of mobility" among the anthracite miners.[1] Peter
Roberts, however, described the anthracite communities' social
structure as being "in a condition of flux," through which "the
thrifty members of our society rise to more congenial employ-
ments."[2] The disagreement reflects different standards of
measurement and, possibly, different interpretations of mobility.
I use the term "mobility" in this book to mean movement from
one occupation to another regardless of change in status or in
geographical position.

Certain structural elements in the anthracite industry encouraged geographic mobility. Because they were mining a mineral found exclusively in a relatively isolated area of northeast-
ern Pennsylvania, the mine operators depended on imported
labor. The very presence of the anthracite workers demonstrated
their tendency to be geographically mobile, and there is no
reason to assume that those who had already moved would
suddenly become stationary. Also, in the company houses and
towns, built in locations necessitated by the isolation of the
mines, the mine employees were denied the right to own property; otherwise they might have been more inclined to remain in

one region. Frequent suspensions to regulate production and quiet labor disturbances prompted many to seek work elsewhere. Finally, the well-developed transportation system became an excellent way out.

When mine workers left the anthracite regions they went one of two ways. Those who had come recently from Europe often returned to the "old country"; in 1891, for example, a group of about 200 Welsh miners in Scranton returned en masse to their homeland. Those who could not—or would not—recross the Atlantic went west.

Operators of the bituminous coal mine frequently encouraged the anthracite miners to move west by advertising for labor in regional newspapers. In 1877 the Waverly Coal and Coke Company of Pittsburgh ran an advertisement for workmen in the *Scranton Republican;* two years later mine operators in the state of Wyoming experienced a great response to their "Men Wanted" ads. Some miners who responded to such advertisements found the western mines inhospitable. Wilkes-Barre miners who journeyed to Krebs, Indiana in 1890 reported that they lived in small huts and were forced to live and work with strike-breakers. The disillusioned miners would gladly have returned to the anthracite fields if they had had sufficient money. Although the miners at Krebs were not the only ones sending back unfavorable reports of working conditions farther west, the migration to the soft coal mines continued unabated.

While some anthracite mine workers sought work in western bituminous coal mines, others pursued new careers in the west. In 1872, 200 men left Beaver Meadows for Texas, and another group went to the Black Hills of Dakota. Western cities were also magnets that drew ambitious and adventurous men; in 1893 a group left Pottsville to find work in Chicago.

Although difficult to document, there is ample evidence, both circumstantial and direct, that the individual mine worker could solve his occupational problems by "moving on." The freedom with which he could reach a managerial position within the collective productive system or change his occupation while remaining in the anthracite regions also influenced his ability to reach an individual solution to his occupational problems.

A model of upward movement within the anthracite industry can be constructed from the empirical evidence furnished by the biographical sections of county histories.[3] A random sample of 165 men in managerial positions indicates that mine workers

TABLE 20
Miners in Managerial Positions

	Number	Percentage
Miner	117	71
Nonminer	48	29
Total	165	100

Source: Compiled by author.

could advance into managerial positions, although the greatest concentration of mine workers was at the inside foreman level.

The inside foreman was responsible for the mine's day-to-day operation. He instructed "the workmen in their several duties and vocations," had charge of safety, and negotiated contracts with the miners. The performance of such duties demanded a practical knowledge of mining which could be gained only by working in the mines. In 1885 the state recognized the need for work experience for inside foremen by requiring a certificate which was granted to those who had passed an examination and had "given satisfactory evidence of at least five years practical experience as a miner."[4]

Superintendents found practical training useful; more than half of them began their careers in the mines. Exemplary performance as an inside foreman often resulted in promotion to superintendent. But the growing demand that superintendents have technical as well as practical skill soon pushed the managerial position beyond the reach of the average mine worker.

The skills required for the position of outside foreman made it less accessible to the mine worker than the position of either inside foreman or superintendent. Responsible for the maintenance of the surface plant as well as the preparation of coal, the outside foreman required for his job little experience in practical mining. Ten of 18 nonminers who were outside foremen were carpenters before their appointment.

An unexpectedly high percentage of mine operators began their careers in the mines. Four of the ten mine operators who had been miners were over 64 years of age, which implies that they were able to enter the industry before the entrance costs became prohibitive. Another mine worker who became an operator had a father who was an operator. Although scanty, the information on the occupations of the remaining five members of

TABLE 21
Miners at Various Management Levels

Position	Miner		Nonminer	
	Number	Percentage	Number	Percentage
Inside foreman	70	96.4	2	3.6
Superintendent	20	55.6	16	44.4
Outside foreman	17	49.6	18	51.4
Operator	10	45.4	12	54.6

Source: Compiled by author.

the sample indicates that they were highly mobile before becoming mine operators.

The number of mine workers who were in managerial levels of the anthracite industry clearly demonstrates that opportunities for advancement were present within the collective productive system. But when considered in the light of the total labor force (over 100,000 men and boys), the opportunities for advancement were limited. At the lowest and most accessible level of management, inside foreman, there was one position for every 200 employees.

The mine worker who was unable to take advantage of the limited opportunities for promotion within the industry could still seek a solution to his occupational problems by changing occupation. The pattern of movement away from the anthracite industry is based on information in the biographical sections of the county histories mentioned above. A random survey of 498 persons engaged in the professions, industry, business, and politics, indicates that the mine worker found it more difficult to move away from the industry than to move upward within it. In Table 23 we see that there was a continuum of accessibility to the various occupational categories.

The professions were least accessible to the mine worker. Access to specific professions, however, varied greatly. Education was the main determinant of the mine worker's ability to enter professions. Two of the four pharmacists who worked in the mines, for example, worked less than three years in the mines, and the third left the mines while young enough to learn another trade. Only one mobile miner became a pharmacist directly, and he entered college after thirty-three years in the mines. The single dentist who started in the mines left them

TABLE 22
Miners in Other Occupations

	Number	Percentage
Miner	150	30.1
Nonminer	348	69.9
Total	498	100

Source: Compiled by author.

TABLE 23
Miners in Occupational Sectors

Sector	Miner		Nonminer	
	Number	Percentage	Number	Percentage
Professions	15	10.2	132	89.8
Industry	12	27.9	31	72.1
Business	103	37.4	172	62.6
Politics	20	60.6	13	39.4

Source: Compiled by author.

after two years. Both lawyers studied law in local law offices at night. Teaching apparently required little formal education; one ex-miner who had become a teacher described himself as "self-educated."

The parent's ability to give his child a chance for a better life was instrumental in helping the mine worker to escape into the professions. One of the two journalists listed in Table 24 got his break when his father was appointed postmaster, and the other mine worker-turned-journalist listed his father's occupation as "merchant." Both physicians' fathers were also merchants.

The professions remained nearly closed to the mine worker trying to solve his own occupational problem. Only those who were able to leave the mines at an early age or who had fathers who were already mobile could hope to enter the professions. Since the ability to leave the mines at an early age implies that the parent had become mobile, it seems likely, judging from the sample, that entry into the professions was restricted to a second or later generation of mobile mine workers.

Mine workers found it slightly easier to move into managerial or entrepreneurial roles in other industries than into the professions. Possession of the prerequisite skills at the managerial level, however, was a formidable barrier even to the mobile

TABLE 24
Miners in Specific Professions

Profession	Miner		Nonminer	
	Number	Percentage	Number	Percentage
Medicine	2	3.0	61	97.0
Law	2	4.9	39	94.1
Dentistry	1	11.1	8	88.9
Journalism	2	17.3	9	82.7
Funeral directing	1	25.0	3	75.0
Education	3	30.0	7	70.0
Pharmacy	4	40.0	6	60.0

Source: Compiled by author.

mine worker. William Charles, the only mine worker who became a manager, left the mines after two years to become a machinist; working as a machinist gave him the experience and training needed to become manager of the Hazleton Machine Shops.

Occupational histories of the mine workers who became entrepreneurs vary, but we can determine two patterns of mobility. Five of the mine workers in the entrepreneurial sample (Table 25) left the mines before they were 20. Their comparative youth suggests that, as in the case of the managers, skills were a major stumbling block to the mine worker aspiring to become an industrialist. Yet four of the remaining six miners in the sample first worked in the mines for 18 years or more. The long years in the mines enabled them to accumulate the necessary money to enter another industry.

The need for less money initially made business more attractive to the mine worker than did industry. Mine workers were concentrated in the liquor and hotel businesses (Table 26)—enterprises which promised a rapid turnover of money and whose greatest asset was good will. The overwhelming majority (seven of the eight) of mine workers who were agents were in insurance, a field with fewer capital demands than real estate. The relatively high investment commitment, combined with the need for special skills, made lumber and building almost prohibitive to the mine worker. Occupational histories of mine workers in the mercantile and livery stable categories were too varied to be interpretable.

TABLE 25
Miners in Industry

Position	Miner		Nonminer	
	Number	Percentage	Number	Percentage
Manager	1	8.3	11	91.7
Entrepreneur	11	35.5	20	64.5

Source: Compiled by author.

TABLE 26
Miners in Various Businesses

	Miner		Nonminer	
Business	Number	Percentage	Number	Percentage
Lumber	1	11.1	8	88.9
Building	4	17.4	19	82.6
Banking	3	27.3	8	72.7
Mercantile	41	30.6	93	69.4
Agents	8	42.1	11	57.9
Livery stable	5	50.0	5	50.0
Hotel	33	56.9	25	43.1
Liquor	8	72.7	3	27.3

Source: Compiled by author.

The occupational histories of the three ex-miners in the banking sample show that they were highly mobile. An example is John P. McGinty, president of the First National Bank of Tamaqua. McGinty left the mines to open a grocery store; later he became a brewery agent, and this led to the establishment of a wholesale liquor business. Next he built his own brewery, and finally combined his position as president of a brewery with the presidency of a bank.

The political sample—those persons whose livelihood depended primarily on office-holding—contains the highest percentage of former miners. The concentration of mine workers among the politicians can be explained by the occupational requirements of a personal following and an acceptable reputation, both of which could be acquired with a minimal economic outlay.

Education and capital resources were the major obstacles to the mine workers' occupational mobility. Yet we can see that an impressive number of mine workers surmounted the obstacles. When compared to the total labor force in the anthracite industry, however, the number who were mobile becomes insignificant.

The nature of the individual solution must be questioned. The departure of a relatively small number of mine workers was not a constructive alternative to the problems inherent in mining anthracite. In fact, their leaving hardly made a dent in the collective productive system; the miners' problems would remain regardless of the action of any one individual. Nor did the flight of a few—or even many—mine workers force the operators to change the conditions of the system. Opportunities for escape were so limited that the influx of immigrants more than offset the exodus of some mine workers. Seen from the point of view of those in the collective productive system, the individualistic solution simply meant a change in personnel. The failure of the solution to remedy basic faults in the system made collective action the only possible method for solving the system's problems.

The Collective Response:
The Reward System

Since the individual mine worker's response to his occupational problems was limited to escape, his action had little influence on the collective productive system; it became increasingly clear that within the system effective action could be taken only by the group.

The most visible, and perhaps most pressing, problems of the mine workers arose because of the reward system. The workers organized themselves into labor unions in an attempt to demand a restructuring of the reward system by increased wages, lowered supply costs, and restrictions on the abusive practice of payroll deductions.

This collective response of the miners, however, could not transcend the system itself. Met by employer resistance, the mine workers' united effort to improve their condition often took the form of strikes. The strike affected the community as well as the industry, and raised serious questions about industry-labor-community relations, as well as about the anthracite industry itself. Regionalism, ethnocentrism, and the tensions inherent in the functional organization of work were barriers to united action. In a very real sense, the need for collective action produced a crisis of identity for the mine worker, who tended to view himself as a member of an ethnic or regional group rather than as a member of an occupational class.

The
First
Union

Group reaction by the anthracite miners to the reward system of the mining industry took the form of labor unions; and the success or failure of the unions depended primarily on their ability to come to terms with the mine workers' environment.

Economic geography, ethnocentrism, and the industry's form of work organization were serious obstacles to united action by the miners. The four anthracite fields were divided by lines of transportation into three geo-economic regions. The mine workers, who thought of the region's welfare in the same terms as their own, were not inclined to cooperate with other regions. Ethnic tensions were so great that "[even] the less adroit of employers could play upon these race prejudices so effectively as to weaken the strongest union."[1] Finally, the organization of work contributed to tensions between work groups. Laborers, for example, were often at odds with miners; one disenchanted laborer asked: "When have the operators ever treated the miners so bad as the miners have treated their laborers at Ashley?"[2]

There were several integrative factors inherent in the industry, however, which tended somewhat to offset the disruptive forces—the piece-rate system, function mobility, low wages, and interdependence. Because of the piece-rate system, miners became adept at bargaining with management. Occupational animosities were softened by mobility up through the graded functional task groups. In the uniformly low wages all ethnic groups had something in common. Finally, the interdependence inherent in the functional organization of work made it imperative that any efforts to organize or to react collectively to management be on an industrywide basis rather than a trade basis.

The first united action by anthracite mine workers was taken in July 1842 when mine workers at Minersville spontaneously protested against the truck system, demanding higher wages. Arming themselves with clubs and other weapons, the disgruntled men marched to Pottsville in an attempt to close the mines around the town. When they reached Pottsville the strikers were confronted by the Orwigsburgh Blues, a militia company, and promptly disbanded without gaining any of their objectives.[3] The ease with which the militia broke up the Minersville men's protest demonstrated the need for organization.

In 1848 John Bates, an English Chartist, organized a union among the mine workers in Schuylkill County. Within a year the Bates Union had enrolled 5,000 members and felt strong enough to press its demands on the operators. During the summer of 1849 union members aimed for higher wages—$8 to $9 a week for miners, $6 for inside laborers, and $5.50 for outside laborers.

The members of the Bates Union devised a unique strategy for securing their objective. Blaming their low wages on an unstable market rather than their employers' greed, they decided to raise coal prices. A strike could be used, they argued, to raise the price of coal by decreasing its supply. Meeting at Deer Park Farm on July 4, 1849, union members passed a strike resolution in the belief that "such a suspension is required for our own good, for the good of our employers and for the interests of the coal region generally."[4]

The strike lasted three weeks and caused a decrease in the supply of coal on the Philadelphia market. But when the strikers returned to work, they found themselves locked out by the mine operators. The lock-out continued a few weeks until the growing number of orders forced the operators to compromise. Although somewhat successful, the union collapsed amid rumors that Bates had absconded with the union funds. The fate of the Bates Union proved so discouraging that mine workers in the Schuylkill region waited 11 years before attempting to reorganize.

Mine workers in the northern basin became active in 1853. That year the Delaware and Hudson Canal Company's miners struck for a 2½ cents per-ton increase in the piece rate. The short strike ended with the company promising to meet the men's demand, but its success did not encourage imitation, and collective activity in the Wyoming-Lackawanna region ceased until the Civil War.

Inflation during the Civil War and the example of the American Miners' Association, a union of soft coal miners, prompted anthracite mine workers to organize locally. An increased demand for coal and a dwindling labor supply made it possible for the new unions to be successful. A series of strikes pushed wages up to the point where some contract miners were earning $500 a month. In 1863 the miners in the Pittston area achieved a significant victory when they received formal recognition from the operators in the form of a written contract.[5] Success apparently ensured the continued united action of the anthracite mine workers.

A series of disastrous strikes in 1865, however, temporarily impeded growth of unionism in the anthracite fields. On January 1, 1865 miners of the Lehigh Coal and Navigation Company began a strike which lasted until March 10, when they returned to work on the company's terms. In the Wyoming region the Pennsylvania Coal Company announced a 20 percent wage cut, to which its employees responded by striking. The strike spread throughout the region as other operators lowered wages. As the strike grew in intensity, the Wyoming men appealed for support from the Schuylkill region miners, but local unions in the southern field rejected the request. With no outside help, the Wyoming strike collapsed.

The defeat of the unions, along with a growing manpower pool as soldiers returned home, encouraged the operators to adjust to the postwar recession by forcing down wages. The operators were successful; by 1867 wages had fallen below the 1857 level.

As wages rapidly declined mine workers reorganized in an attempt to protect the status quo. The most important new union was the Workingmen's Benevolent Association of Saint Clair. Led by John Siney, an Irish immigrant who had formed the Brickmakers' Association of Wigam, England, and encouraged by such well-known leaders as Jonathan Fincher, the W.B.A. enrolled 500 members within a month.

Initially limited to local interests, the various new unions' only chance of succeeding depended on the operators not uniting. But in 1867 operators in the western middle basin formed the Mahanoy Valley and Locust Mountain Coal Association, and in the southern basin mine owners contemplated a firm combination. At the same time that the mine operators were organizing themselves into subregional associations, the local unions were unable to overcome petty jealousies and adopt a parallel movement. An outside stimulus was needed.

In 1868 the Pennsylvania legislature provided the stimulus by defining the legal workday as eight hours unless a contract for a longer day existed. Wage miners and laborers demanded the shorter day without a comparable reduction in wages. When operators in the Mahanoy Valley refused, a spontaneous strike broke out. Armed strikers carrying signs reading "Eight Hours" marched through the coal fields shutting down mines.

Mine workers in the Schuylkill and Lehigh regions responded to the call, but the strikers were unsuccessful in the Wyoming region. There the press argued that a strike would only benefit the Schuylkill region and urged mine workers to remain loyal to the area. But the men needed no prodding. Still smarting over the rejection of their request for aid by the Schuylkill miners in 1865, the Wyoming men informed the southern strikers that they would support them only if the Lehigh and Schuylkill regions organized larger unions.

Despite the Wyoming region's lack of participation, the "Eight Hour" strike ended in August with a compromise. The operators granted a 10 percent increase in wages, and the men agreed to work the normal ten-hour day. Limited victory, however, did not diminish the force of the Wyoming men's insistence on an organization with a wider base.

Meeting in Mahanoy City a week before the strike ended, the Eight Hour strikers decided to form countywide unions in Schuylkill, Carbon, Northumberland, and Luzerne Counties. Local unions in Schuylkill County met in Saint Clair on September 3rd and implemented the resolution by merging with the Workingmen's Benevolent Association. On September 23rd the Northumberland County unions organized the W.B.A. of Northumberland County.[6] In Carbon County the local unions had already moved toward a countywide organization before the strike; the new society, The Workingmen's Beneficial and Benevolent Association, received its charter in October.[7]

Once the unions were organized on a county basis it was obvious that what was needed next was an association encompassing the entire industry. County delegates attended a convention in Providence, Pa. on November 7 and agreed to "organize the six counties in one organization."[8] But the Wyoming-Lackawanna men were hesitant to join the new unions. In December John Siney, president of the Schuylkill County W.B.A., tried to hasten a favorable decision by offering them control of the proposed union, but was unsuccessful.

Despite the rebuff, the new unions sent representatives to Hazleton on March 17, 1869, where the convention established the General Council of the Workingmen's Associations of the Anthracite Coal Fields of Pennsylvania.[9] The General Council defined W.B.A. policies and set the date for general strikes. No county organization, however, was bound by the General Council's decisions. The County Executive Board governed the county unions, and the Executive Board could expel branches, set initiation fees, levy assessments, and bargain with mine operators at the county level. The county union consisted of districts which had their own officers and representation on the Executive Board; they were supreme in purely local matters. Individual mines within each district were formed into branches which could send delegates to the district convention; the branches were to take care of grievances within the mines. Since each superior body's actions required a referendum from the subordinate organization, the General Council was a loose confederation in which power flowed only upward.[10] The W.B.A., composed largely of and led by men with experience in English trade unions, followed its prototypes' outlines. The W.B.A. sought to exclude nonunion workmen and to maintain a higher, standard wage.

In its efforts to secure higher wages, the W.B.A. sought to cure what it considered the basic sickness of the anthracite industry—low prices resulting from overproduction. Analysis of the miners' predicament by the Bates Union, plus their own experience in British coal mines, led W.B.A. leaders to conclude that the best way to get higher, standard wages was through the maintenance of coal prices. Labor sought an alliance with capital to increase coal prices and wages; the constitution of the Carbon County union proclaimed that one of the association's objectives was "to make such arrangements as will enable the miner and laborer and operator to protect and promote their mutual interests."[11] The Summit Hill district of the union was more explicit: "the object of this society is to make such arrangements as will enable the operator and the miner to rule the coal market."[12]

Business elements and small mine operators agreed with

labor's diagnosis of the problem, and encouraged such a policy. "If a strike must take place," the *Miners' Journal* editorialized on the eve of the Eight Hour strike, "this is the most desirable time when the trade is extremely dull." The editor predicted that the strike, if it became industrywide, "must result in the raising of the price of coal."[13] Operators in Schuylkill County agreed with the editor and informed the union that it could accomplish its mission if it would dictate coal prices at the tidewater markets.

Such advice was heady stuff to the mine workers. At the March 17 meeting they resolved that since overproduction had glutted the market, the president of the General Council should order an industrywide strike. The strike would take place when four counties had confirmed the order and both operators and consumers had received a week's notice.

In April 1869 the General Council tested its power by calling a strike for May 10. Unions in the Schuylkill and Lehigh region issued the strike call, and it appeared that, although they were not members of the General Council, the Wyoming men would join in the effort. The Delaware, Lackawanna and Western miners served notice of a strike on April 30, but for some unknown reason immediately postponed the strike. The action of the D.L.&W. miners caused the other unions in the northern region to vote against the strike at the last minute.

Not discouraged by the Wyoming men's adverse decision, the General Council met in Hazleton on May 11 to plan strike strategy. The Council gave the county unions permission to resume work when the price of coal reached $5 a ton at Elizabethport, the distribution center for the Lehigh region, and $3 a ton at Port Carbon, the shipping point for the Schuylkill region. Each county union was free to set other conditions for a resumption of work in its area. To limit production after the strike, the General Council requested each contract miner to decrease his production by one car a day, or if he worked by the yard, to restrict his work accordingly.

The W.B.A., which wanted to cure the industry's sickness by equalizing production with demand, adopted the "basis system" to achieve this important goal. The basis system was a sliding wage scale based on coal prices. By establishing a base coal price and wage schedule, it was intended that wages would increase as prices rose. Base wages would not be reduced if the price of coal fell below the base price; rather, the operator had the alternative of working at a large marginal loss or suspending work until the market readjusted. Any attempt to reduce wages would provoke a strike.

To be successful the basis system had to be implemented in all regions; therefore the W.B.A. vigorously tried to enlist the Wyoming men in the movement. By late May the northern miners had begun to reconsider their earlier position and in early June the Delaware, Lackawanna and Western miners voted to join the General Council and its strike, thereby making the Council an industrywide union.

It was more difficult to establish the basis system in the Wyoming region than in the Schuylkill or Lehigh regions. The small operators in the latter two acknowledged their inability to cope with the vicissitudes of the market, and urged labor to save them. The large corporations in Wyoming-Lackawanna, however, could regulate their market without the intervention of labor. Thomas Dickson, president of the Delaware and Hudson Canal Company, summarized the attitude of the corporations when he remarked, "We are not prepared to take in new partners."[14]

While the entrepreneurs in the Schuylkill and Lehigh regions gladly extended their hands to labor when labor proposed a partnership to regulate production, they found the conditions distasteful. The W.B.A., true to its English heritage, demanded a closed shop. The second and more important area of conflict was the union's insistence on local committees. Under the local committee system, members presented grievances to a committee which investigated the claim. If the committee found the complaint valid, it would demand redress and, if refused, would order a strike.

The operators viewed the closed shop and the local committee system as unwarranted interference with their managerial prerogatives. The Shamokin Coal Exchange, a local organization of mine operators, agreed not to resume work until the union agreed to "abandon or cease to claim that such [local] committees shall act, or be allowed to act, or be allowed to exert any influence whatever in the working management of our collieries."[15]

The increase in coal prices averted a complete estrangement. In June 1869 the General Council announced that the strike had depleted the market, and gave the county unions permission to return to work. Eager to take advantage of high prices, management and labor tried to settle the major points of disagreement. They compromised on the closed shop issue; management agreed not to fire any union member without just cause, and labor promised not to insist on the discharging of "blacklegs" (strikebreakers). Both sides ignored the local committee issue. To implement the basis system, the union and operators selected a committee which would meet once a month to determine the average coal price from which wages would be determined. By June 16 the Schuylkill and Lehigh miners had returned to work.

While the Schuylkill and Lehigh mines reopened, the Wyoming strike continued. The General Council supported the strikers by levying a $1.25-per-month assessment on miners and $1 on laborers in the two southern regions. In July the large corporations tried to entice their men back to work with the promise of a contract rate of $1 per car. The Pittston men met on July 23 and voted to accept the Pittston operator's offer. The united front in Wyoming would have been broken sooner had it not been for the miners' wives, who stopped the back-to-work movement by throwing stones at the men as they walked to the mines.

Despite the support of the wives and the General Council, the strike collapsed under a demonstration of overwhelming power. Rumors of the hiring of Chinese strikebreakers spread. At least one company ordered strike leaders to vacate its houses. In Scranton a special police force and 350 volunteers, ostensibly there to keep the peace, overawed the strikers. Astonished at the display of power by the corporations, the miners returned to work on August 31 with higher wages but without the basis system.

The W.B.A. failed to achieve its main objective in the 1869 strike. The partnership labor sought with management in which to rule the coal market broke up in the face of opposition from the large corporations in the Wyoming region. Although individual operators in the two southern regions eagerly accepted labor's proposal, the closed shop and local committee issues made the espousal precarious. Operators and unions accused each other of violating the closed shop compromise. Local committees embarrassed the union with incessant striking. Indeed, the Carbon County Executive Board found it necessary to levy a $100 fine on each member who struck without its permission. In Schuylkill County the local committee issue resulted in the arrest of one committee for conspiracy to restrain trade.

Some operators felt the base wage schedule was too high. Within weeks after the settlement of the strike the operators around Hazleton notified their men that they could not pay the new wages. The men responded with a second strike that lasted two months. By the end of 1869 the small operators were ready to wash their hands of labor.

In Schuylkill County the operators gained new strength in November 1869 when they combined their local trade associations into the Anthracite Board of Trade; they quickly reopened the wage question. The Board of Trade proposed a new wage schedule of $10.50 a week for miners, $8.50 for inside laborers, and $7.50 for outside laborers. The operators also demanded a 5 percent reduction in wages for every 25-cent decrease in coal prices below the $3-a-ton base until a maximum wage reduction of 20 percent was reached. The Schuylkill County Executive Board of the W.B.A. regarded the new proposals as a declaration of war, and in January 1870 called a strike.

The Schuylkill County strike was local; the other county unions remained working. Within Schuylkill County labor maintained a united front, but the operators did not; some members of the Anthracite Board of Trade agreed to maintain the 1869 schedule and the W.B.A. gave its men permission to return to work at those places.

Prodded by its more restive members, who were not disposed to see their competitors work while they remained idle, the Board of Trade offered a compromise solution on February 10 by proposing a $2.50 base price with a wage schedule of $12 a week for miners, $10 for inside laborers, $9 for outside laborers, and a 30 percent reduction in contract rates. Viewing the Board's action as an omen of weakness, the union rejected the compromise proposal.

Rumors of a pending general strike encouraged the Schuylkill miners to believe they could bring the Board of Trade to its knees. The general strike was not to be a sympathy strike—its objective was to raise the price of coal. The coal region's newspapers bluntly described the issue involved in the strike: "As the understood object of this strike, if it shall really take place, is to advance the price of coal, and is to keep up wages at the mines, there is no knowing how widely it may extend or how long it will continue."[16] With the exception of the Wyoming corporations and Schuylkill County operators, the area would have welcomed a strike if it had become general. But as each county union ordered its men on strike at its leisure, the community became alarmed. *The Shamokin Herald* mournfully asked, "What remedy have we then in case the strike is not general?" But there was no need to fear that the strike would not be industry-wide, for, "if the thirty thousand miners in Pennsylvania are true to themselves and each other, they will regulate the price of coal without the aid of operators and railroad companies."[17]

But the miners were not "true to themselves and each other"; the Wyoming men refused to support the strike. Angered over the betrayal, the General Council met in Tamaqua and severed all connections with the "men of the three large companies."[18] The delegates from lower Luzerne County voted against their northern brethren because regional and not county loyalties counted. Its solidarity shattered, the General Council authorized a resumption of work whenever the county unions attained the 1869 base wage schedule.

The operators, however, would not have a resumption. Seventy-six Lehigh and Schuylkill region operators meeting in Pottsville agreed to support the Anthracite Board of Trade, vowing to close down their mines on April 2 if the unions did not accept the $2.50 basis.

During April the Schuylkill County men gained allies, which made the strike more effective. Workmen on the Philadelphia and Reading Railroad's lateral lines struck when the company reduced their wages. The railroaders became so violent that the Reading refused to haul coal unless the coal owners provided their own protection. The small operators could not afford to hire guards and were therefore unable to ship coal. Experiencing a combined coal strike, lock-out, and railroad strike, Schuylkill County had to import coal over the main line of the Reading for its own use.

As the strike became more intense business elements in the region sought a resumption of work by becoming alternately patronizing and vituperative toward the miners. The *Miners' Journal* appealed to the regional loyalty of the miners, asking them to return to work so "our operators can go into the market and make sales before the other regions secure their customers."[19] When the strikers failed to respond, the *Journal* tried to sow discord by raising the issue of nationality. It reported that the union was "composed almost exclusively of adopted citizens."[20] Undaunted by pleas or sneers, the Executive Board remained firmly committed to the strike.

By late May it appeared as if the Wyoming men were about to rejoin the flock. Still refusing to join the strike, the Archbald district assessed each miner $3 and each laborer $2 a month to support the Lehigh and Schuylkill strikers. The Hyde Park men gave the southern miners a brief glimmer of hope when they walked out in June to protest the firing of two men. The Hyde Park miners quickly settled the issue, but the Wyoming men reassessed their position relative to the southern strike. In late June they agreed to divide their work with "the brothers now out on strike in Schuylkill and elsewhere" by taking an extra man in each breast.[21]

The share-the-work plan came at an opportune moment; the strike was beginning to exhaust the miners' resources. Hard pressed, the miners first turned to the independent merchants for credit. The merchants, hoping to strike a blow against the company store, responded generously. But some strikers still found it difficult to make both ends meet.

The operators sought to take advantage of the fact that their workers were ill prepared to weather a prolonged strike by trying to starve them out. As the operators probed the ability of union to support a strike, they discovered what they thought was the miners' Achilles heel. *How clever of the miners and laborers to pretend they allowed dead work (work which produced no coal) because they had the operators' welfare at heart.* This ruse had worked in 1869, but now the operators refused to be fooled. On May 16 the Board of Trade advised its members that:

> Complaints are made about the large number of men employed about the collieries doing dead work, amounting, it is admitted, to twenty percent of those usually employed, thus enabling the men to prolong this contest. In order, therefore, that it may be short, sharp, and decisive, it is earnestly recommended that all dead work cease after Wednesday the eighteenth instant.[22]

Pursuing its starvation campaign, the Board of Trade tried to close all working mines. Two days before it forbade dead work, the Board of Trade expelled the Philadelphia Coal Company for resuming on the 1869 basis. The Reading aided the Board by increasing its freight rates for coal by 20 percent and discontinued all drawbacks.[23] The railroad promised that it would rescind the increase and restore the drawbacks after a general resumption of work "upon any satisfactory basis of wages."[24]

Not dismayed by the power arrayed against it, the W.B.A. introduced new issues into the strike. It announced that it would concede a 20 percent reduction in wages if the operators granted the eight-hour day. The union also called for a more equitable difference between the contract rates and the wages of other mine employees. In taking the position that a new balance in wages should be secured, the W.B.A. never lost sight of its major goal—limitation of production. It would allow the contract miner an average daily wage of $3 with a 25-cent-per-day bonus if he worked in an especially wet or dangerous place. To police its ruling the union would instruct each miner to give his pay docket to his branch or district officers and pay everything over the allowed average into the district treasury. To further limit production, the contract miner could not make up a lost day. The union also ruled that the contract miner could no longer pay his laborer directly; hereafter the company would pay the laborer and deduct the amount from the contract miner's wages. The introduction of the eight-hour day was an effort to gain a bargaining point and was soon dropped.

Neither the operators nor the union enjoyed the prospects of a drawn-out strike as long as the Wyoming region worked. Both, therefore, were eager to find a face-saving device that would end the strike. Benjamin B. Thomas, a mine operator, came from Philadelphia and talked to John Siney. Shortly after his return he visited Franklin B. Gowen, president of the Philadelphia and Reading Railroad, and asked him to act as mediator. Gowen accepted the commission and both parties accepted his good offices. Gowen's efforts resulted in a compromise: the basis remained at $3 but wages would be reduced when the price of coal fell under $3 a ton until it reached a floor of $2 a ton. The Board of Trade rejected the "Gowen Compromise" on the grounds that it was "an unfair adjustment of the wages in question in favor of the men giving them more than they are entitled to."[25]

Benjamin Thomas, however, forced the Board of Trade to reconsider its action by resuming work on the terms of the "Gowen Compromise." The Board of Trade rescinded its earlier decision and met with union officials on July 28 to write the compromise into a contract. An important clause in the contract bound the operators to uphold the W.B.A.'s "equality resolution." The clause provided graduated reductions in the contract miner's pay, ranging from 10 percent if he should earn more than $100 but less than $125 a month, to 40 percent if he should earn more than $200 in a month.

The contract did not bring peace to the Schuylkill and Lehigh regions. The Northumberland County organization rejected the "Gowen Compromise" and remained on strike until October 1, when it agreed to the "Shamokin Compromise." The "Shamokin Compromise" retained the 1869 basis, with a sliding scale of 25 percent which could go below the basis as well as above. In the Hazleton area the employees of A. Pardee Brothers began a month-long strike in September because the firm employed non-union men. Schuylkill County workers changed their opinion of the "Gowen Compromise" when they received their first pay and found 8½ percent deducted because the price of coal had fallen below $3 a ton. Talk of a strike aroused John Siney to write an open letter advising the men to refrain from such thinking. The men followed Siney's advice and did not strike, although wages fell by 24¾ percent by December.

The 1870 strike seriously weakened the W.B.A. Both the leaders and the rank-and-file realized that the goal of a regulated market was beyond their reach if one region remained working. The Wyoming region's failure to strike and the subsequent bitter feelings made a general strike improbable. Indeed, it was questionable if the General Council could enforce its will on the Schuylkill region. In Dauphin County the union disbanded during the strike. The Shamokin area men bolted from the Northumberland County W.B.A. and created an independent organization which represented the employees of 21 collieries. Inside the regular union, adherence to the "equality resolution" left many contract miners restive.

The actions of the Reading during the strike were an external threat to the union. The coal carriers appeared quite capable, and willing, to regulate production by increasing freight rates. If it proved possible for the railroads and the small operators to agree on a suitable policy of market regulation, the W.B.A. would be of no value to the operators, who would move to crush the union. As the union leaders surveyed the lessons derived from the strike, a change in policy seemed forthcoming.

The Collapse
of the
W. B. A.

The 1870 strike disillusioned the an-
thracite mine workers. Weakened by regionalism, their union
appeared incapable of achieving its goal at the very time that
the railroad companies were demonstrating their ability to regulate coal production and hence coal prices. Certainly the Workingmen's Benevolent Association would have to adopt new
methods of obtaining higher wages.

The Schuylkill County Executive Board reflected the change
in thinking in November 1870 when it negotiated a contract for
the following year. Except for a 16½ percent reduction in contract rates, the agreement was essentially the same as that of
July. Both parties were careful to make the contract provisional
pending the Reading Railroad's sanction. The prospect of industrial peace was bright now that the strongest union in the two
regions had reached an agreement with the operators.

The Wyoming corporations destroyed this prospect. Expulsion from the General Council had not destroyed unionism in
the northern region; it merely freed the unions from involve-
ment with the other regions.[1] The Wyoming unions became active when the companies announced a 30 percent reduction in
wages. The unions met in early December to discuss their response. Prodded by the Irish members in the unions, the Wyoming men decided to strike. Seeking wider support for their
strike, the Wyoming unions petitioned for readmittance to the
General Council and promised to pay their back dues and obey
all orders if the Council would grant their petition. The General
Council, anxious to form an industrywide union, reinstated the
strikers.

At the first meeting of the General Council that they attended, the Wyoming delegates moved that an industrywide strike
be called for January 10, 1871. The Schuylkill County delegates,
knowing that they could not defeat the strike motion, sought to
postpone it until February 1. Joined by the representatives of
the Lehigh region, whose unions went out on strike in early January, the Wyoming delegates easily defeated the delaying action
and rammed the motion through.[2]

The miners and laborers in Schuylkill County protested the
vote. Almost to a man, they were against both the readmittance
of the Wyoming men and the strike vote. "A Miner," writing to
the editor of the *Daily Miners' Journal,* drew a novel conclusion
from his reading of the Bible, and declared that it was wrong to
welcome back a "rich Prodigal Son." The grievance was that the
same men who had become rich by refusing to join the Schuylkill strike now wanted the southern men to join their strike.
They expected too much in asking men who had "worked
only five months in the past thirteen" to join them.[3] The writer
threatened disobedience; "but if [the Wyoming men] voted down
those five delegates, from Schuylkill, they have not voted down
the men who sent those delegates."[4] John Siney confirmed this
opinion when he said later, "The Schuylkill Association was
outvoted in the General Council but it did not pledge the action
of Schuylkill."[5]

As the date for the strike drew closer, speculation on the
Schuylkill men's reaction increased. Contrary to the expectations of some, the Schuylkill region, with the exception of the
Shamokin and Lykens Valley areas, joined the strike. It was natural for the region to strike; since the resumption of work in July
1870, production had out-distanced demand and prices were
falling again. The operators favored a strike; they offered to
pay base wages for January if the union could make the strike
general. Since base wages would amount to a 16½ percent increase in pay, the men could not afford to reject the offer. There
was no decision to suspend work, for there were no alternatives;
the lack of orders meant a strike regardless of the desire to
work. The only two areas where demand existed—Shamokin
with its southern and western markets via the Northern Central
Railroad, and Lykens Valley, for whose "red ash coal" there was
never a lack of orders—remained working.

The Schuylkill region thought of the strike as a cooperative
effort between labor and capital to raise coal prices. As such,

both sides agreed to maintain the strike in a friendly manner.[6] The *Shenandoah Herald* outlined its opinion of the strike: "The strike is to end when production is reduced and prices raised. The other regions will then go to work, whether the difficulty in Wyoming is settled or not. After that each county will fix its own difficulties and wages, all [county unions] going out when the price falls too low."[7] The strike had revived the alliance between capital and labor, but it was an alliance that quickly broke. The miners and laborers longed for the return of the golden year, 1869, when they enjoyed higher wages and did not suffer a cut in wages when coal prices fell below the base. Stirred by hopes that the union could now maintain both high prices and high wages, they agitated for the $3 base, provided the Wyoming men would cooperate.

The operators in Schuylkill County and the Lehigh region proposed their own terms.[8] Under Gowen's tutelage they formed the Committee of Fifteen, which also included railroad presidents and the larger jobbers. The Committee offered the men a guaranteed wage of $10 a week for outside laborers, $11 for inside laborers, and $13 for wage miners. They reduced the 1869 contract rates by 10 percent.

The General Council considered the direct appeal to its members an insult, but it did not speak for all its units. The Columbia County W.B.A. and four districts of the Schuylkill County organization accepted the terms of the Committee of Fifteen. The rebellious districts, however, soon found that to agree to work was one thing, to work was another.

Though the majority of strikers were nonviolent, violence and fear enforced the strike resolution. In Mount Carmel a mob attacked a boarding house containing 29 strikebreakers. They shot into the bedrooms and exploded a keg of blasting powder on the first floor. The W.B.A. district met quickly, disavowed the act, and offered a $500 reward for the apprehension and conviction of the culprits. The union was undoubtedly sincere, but it was doubtful it could control its more violence-prone members. An attack on strikebreakers did not require authorization from the union to be effective. In Scranton, attacks on "black legs" by mobs became so violent that Governor John W. Geary ordered a company of militia to the city. The mob disarmed the militia, and, brandishing the militia's weapons, overawed the strikebreakers. Geary ordered another company of militia to Scranton, but this time someone fired a shot and the militia fired a volley into the strikers, killing two miners and wounding several others.

While violent strikers maintained a solid front, those operators who would have agreed to the union's demands experienced a more subtle, but effective, form of coercion. Both the Philadelphia and Reading and the Lehigh Valley Railroads supported the Committee of Fifteen. To discourage independent operators from resuming work on the union's terms, they raised their freight rates on anthracite in the middle of February by $2 a ton; ten days later the rates were raised another $2 a ton.[9] With shipping costs running $6.08 a ton, the operators knew they could not make a profit on their coal, and thus kept their mines closed. Miners, operators, and consumers complained about the railroads' arbitrary action.

Ever mindful of grassroots sentiment, the Pennsylvania Senate instructed its Committee on the Judiciary General to investigate the action of the railroads for a possible violation of their charters. On the first day of the investigation Franklin B. Gowen took the stand to defend his railroad. The Reading's charter gave it the power to set its own rates, and since operating expenses remained practically the same if it hauled 1,000 or 100,000 tons of coal a week it had to raise its rates whenever tonnage declined to meet those operating costs. If there had been no suspension of operation, Gowen maintained, there would have been no need to raise the rates. The union, and not the Reading, was clearly at fault. Asa Packer, President of the Lehigh Valley, seconded Gowen. Suddenly the investigation focused on the union. Gowen was so sure of the outcome that he gave union leaders free passes to attend the committee's sessions. The only satisfaction the W.B.A. got was an acknowledgment of the workmen's right to form a union and refuse to work, provided the union used only lawful means to arrive at lawful ends.

Assured of the legality of its existence, the W.B.A. experienced such internal difficulties that its existence was problematic. Desertions during the strike made the union's weakness plain. Ethnic animosities threatened to disrupt the union. English miners in the eighth district of the Schuylkill County union tried to stop rumors that they were disloyal to the union by publicly denouncing "those men who have circulated false reports concerning our actions."[10] The "three Scranton companies" played on ethnic hatred by firing their Welsh miners and hiring

Germans and Irish to replace them. Threats followed insults, and the Germans organized a committee to protect themselves. Two days later the Irish did the same. Animosities became so bitter that Irish, English, and Scots agreed never to associate with the Welsh because "in their late murderous outrages they have shown to us they are a class of beings who should never be allowed to associate with peaceable and law abiding citizens."[11]

After the conflict over national origin had run its course, a dispute between functional groups split the union in the Wyoming region. Because of their lower wages the laborers had less savings to see them through a long strike, and were anxious to return to work. They met at Hyde Park to discuss the possibilities of resuming work, but the miners violently broke up the meeting.[12] The angry laborers withdrew from the union and organized their own. The new union, aiming directly at the contract miner, demanded:

> That the miner pay to the laborer one third of the whole amount received by him each month, together with the price of any cars lost during the month through the neglect of the miner, and through bad or broken roads, that in case the miner is not capable of cutting his coal, the laborer will not be bound to assist him and also that any and every laborer in the mines shall be entitled to a chamber in his turn [to become a miner] if he is capable of working said chamber. That the work shall be equally divided among all nationalities for [sic] the future as has not been in the past.[13]

To gain wider support for their union the laborers resolved that they had no animosity for the Welsh. The Irish, German, Scotch, and English miners confirmed the resolution.

Confronting powerful antagonists and racked by internal conflicts and the knowledge that many members could not afford to remain on strike, the W.B.A.'s leadership searched for an honorable way to end the suspension. Arbitration appeared the best method. The idea to arbitrate differences came from a variety of sources. In March Franklin B. Gowen testified that he was trying to get operators and labor to agree to a hearing by an impartial judge.[14] In the same month the Carbon County W.B.A. offered to arbitrate, but the operators refused. Eckley B. Coxe, a large operator in the Lehigh region, however, renewed the idea. Coxe demonstrated his interest in arbitration by writing a paper on the subject for the American Social Science Association, and he outlined his specific plan of arbitration in a series of letters to the *Anthracite Monitor*. Coxe called for the establishment of three regional boards consisting of 13 men—six union representatives, six operators, and one umpire. Each regional board would select four delegates to a general board. A majority of two-thirds would be needed to decide any question, and the umpire would have to be chosen unanimously.

The General Council met at Mauch Chunk on April 12 and agreed with John Siney that the workingmen could not expect justice through arbitration, but that arbitration was the only way to end the strike. The Luzerne County delegates moved to adopt Coxe's arbitration plan. An amendment, however, provided for a general arbitration board whose membership would be determined by the General Council and whose life would be limited to the "present emergency."[15] The amendment carried by a vote of 17 to 8, and the General Council set the board's membership as: five members from Luzerne County, four from Schuylkill, two from Northumberland, and one from Columbia County. The board invited the operators to meet with it at Mauch Chunk on April 17.

Selecting the umpire was the first business taken up at the joint meeting. Each side proposed various men, only to have them rejected by the other. After two hours of haggling both groups agreed on Judge Elwell of Columbia County; they named Judge Harlin of Luzerne County as the alternate. Prospects for a successful conclusion to the suspension of operation faded when the Lehigh region announced it would not be bound by Judge Elwell's decision and when the "three Scranton companies" and their employees refused to attend the meeting. Arbitration continued, nevertheless.

On the morning of April 18 the operators submitted their grievances. They complained that they were subject to threats of strikes if they refused to maintain a closed shop. And they accused the W.B.A. of breaking its contracts.

The W.B.A. answered in the afternoon. The union denied that it wished to control the management of the mines by insisting on a closed shop. It promised not to sustain a man fired for incompetence or bad conduct. The W.B.A. asked, in turn, that the operators not fire men who were union officials for engaging in their official duties, and refused to surrender its right to strike in a body.

Judge Elwell held: (1) that the operators had the "entire and exclusive" right to control their mines; (2) that men could strike, but could not prevent others from working[16]; and (3) that operators could not fire a union officer for performing his official duties. As both sides fought over wages the General Council turned its back on its arbitration board and permitted each county union to set its own terms for resuming work.

Schuylkill and Columbia Counties waited for Judge Elwell's decision, which came on May 14th. The umpire split the differences by granting a $2.75 basis and setting wages at $10, $11, and $13 a week for outside laborers, inside laborers, and day miners, respectively. Contract rates were 10 percent less than those for 1869, and the sliding scale was 33 percent.[17] The Schuylkill region men returned to work the following day. One week later the Wyoming strike ended as the miners accepted the companies' terms. Strikers in the Lehigh region held out for the 1869 base wage, continuing their strike until June 21, when they returned to work with the base wage set at $4.50 a ton at Elizabethport, with the same wages for the Schuylkill men.

No sooner had the strike ended than there was further discord between the miners and operators. The men believed that the operators had blacklisted members of the union, a belief that was so widespread that David Lewis, a miner in Shamokin, published in his hometown newspaper sworn testimony that he had no connection with the W.B.A. In early October the Mahanoy Valley men won higher wages in a brief strike, thus starting a chain reaction of wildcat strikes which ended when the W.B.A. and the Anthracite Board of Trade agreed to pay base wages until the end of the year, regardless of coal prices.

The 1871 strike dashed the W.B.A.'s hope of achieving its goal. Quarrels between nationalities and splits between functional groups nearly destroyed the union in the Wyoming Valley. The weakness of the region precluded success in any attempted general strike, which was the W.B.A.'s only effective tool for controlling production. In the Schuylkill and Lehigh regions the hauling companies put into practice their decision to become miners. The appearance of large hauling and mining companies completely changed the economic situation in the regions. The W.B.A. could no longer dangle before the operators the promise of a regulated market; like the "three Scranton companies," the railroads were not considering new partners. At first the railroads suggested that, as a plan of mild production control, each colliery be allotted a certain number of railroad cars. In 1872 Gowen rationalized the allotment system by bringing the operators and carriers into the first anthracite pool.

The internal weakness of the W.B.A. and the creation of the coal pool forced the W.B.A. to submit its policy to an "agonizing reappraisal." The changed attitude of the union leadership became evident in August 1871 when the Northumberland County W.B.A., rather than strike, negotiated a reduction in the price of powder to $3.75 a keg and a decrease in the price of oil to $1 a gallon. By the end of the year other county organizations had demonstrated a desire for peace. The Wyoming-Lackawanna men traded a 10 percent reduction in wages for a promised decrease in powder and oil prices. The union in the Lehigh region extended the 1871 base wages for another year. The Schuylkill County Executive Board also maintained the 1871 base wages, but agreed to lower the base price of coal to $2.50 a ton and the contract rate 8½ percent in return for a promise by the operators to pay at least base wages for ten months out of the year. To forestall wildcat strikes the Executive Board and the Anthracite Board of Trade agreed that their presidents would investigate all grievances.

But everyone in the anthracite regions was not happy about the union's passiveness. Businessmen in the Schuylkill region were apprehensive about the entry of the Reading into mining; the Reading might use its immense power to undermine their already precarious economic and social position.[18] The region's middle class, mindful of their own weakness, called on labor to help combat the "monopoly." When the Reading increased its rates in May 1872 the *Shenandoah Herald* ranted against the railroad and exhorted the independent operators and labor to deal the Reading a blow. But labor was content simply to condemn the Reading at its July convention. When the railroad finally rescinded its increase in August, the *Herald* gloated unconvincingly that the Reading acted "just in time to save a general suspension." Other newspapers doubted that the railroad companies could regulate the market. In April the editor of the *Shamokin Herald* noted the coal trade's stock and advised labor that a short suspension of mining "now would improve the business."[19] A suspension was not forthcoming, however.

The W.B.A. was so wary of a strike that when the General Council authorized each county unit to negotiate its own contract for 1873, each union agreed to continue the 1872 wages, or took a reduction without protest. The eagerness with which the unions accepted the operators' terms showed that they had not surmounted the schisms of 1871. In the Wyoming region the

Scranton district could muster only 200 men for its annual parade, and the Wilkes-Barre district was unable to hold one. In the Schuylkill region contract miners protested a change in the Philadelphia and Reading Coal and Iron Company's work rules, but decided not to support the protest with a strike because they were afraid the laborers would not back them in a strike.[20]

The depression of 1873 began in the fall. Franklin B. Gowen tried to take advantage of the sluggish economy by forcing down wages during negotiations for the 1874 contract, and in December proposed that the base coal price should be $2.50 a ton. On January 11, 1874 the Schuylkill County organization rejected his proposal and went out on strike. The Wyoming men also struck over a wage reduction. The two strikes lasted most of the month, ending only when the operators restored the reductions.

The victory was not a sign that the union had recovered; the W.B.A. was still weak. There was renewed ethnic animosity in the Hazleton area when the German-Americans withdrew from the district union and established their own German-language union. P.M. Cummings, a Pinkerton detective infiltrating the Schuylkill County W.B.A., reported that the Saint Clair district did not have enough money in its treasury to send a representative to the National Labor Union's meeting in New York.[21] Insubordination inside the Northumberland County union became so pronounced that the Executive Board expelled six of its eight districts.

In addition to these troubles, the W.B.A. faced the threat of dual unionism.[22] Ironically, the General Council had been the driving force that created its rival. After a bitter dispute among the leaders the General Council sent John Parker, a member of the Council and editor of the union's newspaper, the *Anthracite Monitor,* to western Pennsylvania in 1870 to organize the bituminous fields. Enjoying some success, the union sent emissaries across the state line to rebuild the defunct American Miners' Association in Ohio, West Virginia, and Indiana. During 1872 horizontal expansion resulted in the formation of autonomous branches in Maryland, Kentucky, and Michigan. Such success caused many miners to envision a national union which would speak for all mine workers. A year later plans were made for just such a union at the Industrial Congress of Workingmen in Cleveland. After the congress adjourned, the miner delegates met and issued an invitation to all unions of miners to meet in

Youngstown, Ohio during October to form a national organization.

At the Youngstown convention the miners formed the
Miners' National Association of the United States. The founders
borrowed heavily from their English counterpart, Alexander
MacDonald's Miners' National Association. They stressed arbitration and conciliation and made legal strikes difficult to de-
clare; only after a district could show the national president that
it had exhausted all other methods of solving its problems and
had obtained his consent could it call a strike. The Miners' National Association would have nothing to do with the regulation
of the market through the judicious use of the strike. The convention, however, did pay tribute to the W.B.A. by electing its
chief spokesman and president of the Schuylkill Executive
Board, John Siney, as its national president.

Although delighted over the compliment of having its spokesman so honored, the W.B.A. began to feel that the M.N.A. was
encroaching on its territory. The Wilkes-Barre district adopted
the constitution of the M.N.A. on January 23, 1874; on February
4 the men at Plymouth did the same. Other districts and
branches followed. In the view of the W.B.A., with the strength
of the M.N.A. increasing so rapidly, some understanding between the two unions had to be reached.

In October 1874, the Schuylkill County W.B.A. sent delegates to the M.N.A.'s second annual convention with instructions to reach an agreement. The W.B.A. representatives presented a resolution which asked that the W.B.A. be allowed to
remain a separate union with the right to compel any national
union member to join it and pay its initiation fee. After some
debate, the M.N.A. offered a substitute resolution granting the
W.B.A. autonomy on the condition that it pay all requisitions
made by the national union. The W.B.A. hesitated. Thomas
Laire of Mercer County, Pennsylvania, broke the ice with an
amendment to exclude those M.N.A. members of locals requiring equal or higher initiation fees from paying the initiation
charges of the anthracite union. The amended resolution went
into committee and the committee reported it favorably. A free
exchange of traveling cards between the two unions was ar-
ranged; the person presenting an M.N.A. card to the W.B.A. had
to pay the difference, if one existed, between initiation fees
before he could become a member in good standing with the
anthracite union. The national organization agreed to recognize

the W.B.A. as a separate body and to settle all disputes between the W.B.A. and M.N.A. by arbitration. Both unions agreed that "whenever a reasonable possibility exists, the one should receive the moral countenance and practical support of the other."[23] It would not be long before the W.B.A. tested the M.N.A's willingness to lend this countenance and support.

Victory in the 1874 strikes did not reflect the strength of the union, but rather the eagerness of the operators to continue production. The operators felt that the coal pool would be able to maintain prices during 1874, but the strike caught them without a stockpile. The ability of the W.B.A., even when on the verge of collapse, to disrupt the coal pool's plans caused Franklin B. Gowen to conclude that the union must be destroyed.

During the year the Philadelphia and Reading collieries worked steadily; in the week ending November 29, 1874, for example, the Schuylkill region shipped out 159,532 tons of coal, whereas production in the same week in 1873 was 82,820 tons.[24] Trains of loaded coal cars highballed down the Reading's main line until the wharves at Port Richmond overflowed with anthracite. Philadelphia coal yards were filled to capacity. The railroad shunted onto sidings the cars that could not be unloaded.

While the Reading stored coal in anticipation of a great battle, Gowen wooed the remaining independent mine operators from the W.B.A. He talked them into forming a new association which followed the coal pool's example of restricting tonnage shipped to the line and city (Philadelphia) trade.[25] The resulting Schuylkill Coal Exchange cancelled any thoughts the independent operators may have had about an employer-employee alliance.

The groundwork laid, Gowen began to place his cards on the table. In late November he announced that the Reading had enough coal to last until spring, and ordered its collieries to close. To keep the operators who were not members of the Coal Exchange from working, Gowen announced that the coal pool could not receive or sell their coal after December 1, 1874, and suggested that if they could not find their own markets they should be shut down. Thirty-one independent operators suspended work. The Lehigh Valley followed the Reading's lead and the Wyoming companies cut their production in half. By December 1 most mine workers were either idle or working only part time.

The work stoppage did not alarm the men; the midwinter slump usually caused a brief suspension of work, and the depression had slightly reduced the market anyway. They suspected that the operators might use the shutdown as a ruse to get them to accept a wage cut, a suspicion that was partly correct. The Lehigh region operators met at Mauch Chunk and agreed on a 15 percent reduction in contract rates and a 10 percent reduction in wages. They also announced that the reductions were final, that there was no need for negotiation. Not to be outdone by its Lehigh counterpart, the Schuylkill Coal Exchange reduced contract rates by 20 percent and wages by 10. Both groups refused to establish a minimum coal price below which wages would not go, and denied the outside laborers the opportunity of having their wages determined by the price of coal. Furthermore, only the less expensive "white ash coal" would be used in calculating the average price of coal for the base wages, instead of a combination of "red ash" and "white ash" coals.

The Lehigh region and Schuylkill County unions promptly called a strike, but it was ineffective—the mines in the two areas had ceased production in late November. Even if the mines in Schuylkill County and the Lehigh region had been working, the strike would not have been effective, because the independent operators in Dauphin, Columbia, and Northumberland Counties remained working and their men ignored the strike call. Realizing that the operators had declared war on the W.B.A., John Siney abandoned his erstwhile comrades in arms and wrote an open letter dated January 6, 1875 to the *Daily Miners' Journal,* claiming that the M.N.A. and the W.B.A. were not related. Now isolated, the W.B.A. decided to fight. The Schuylkill County Executive Board agreed to serve without pay during the emergency, trying to break the operators' united front by promising to work for any operator who signed an agreement extending the 1874 contract. No operator took them up on the offer and the men remained idle.

Schuylkill County and Lehigh men hoped the strike would become general before the spring. Their hope seemed justified, for there was evidence that the strike was spreading. In February the Wilkes-Barre miners went out on strike. In Columbia County the Centralia district joined the strike and merged with the Schuylkill County union. The expectation that the small operators would back off from their earlier position also seemed to be bearing fruit when some indicated a desire to resume production. But the Reading vetoed any such move, and the operators remained shut down. The Schuylkill County W.B.A. was in a fight to the finish with a great corporation.

The union petitioned the Pennsylvania legislature to investigate the Reading's anthracite mining activities. The W.B.A. acquired strange allies when the coal merchants in Philadelphia, seeking to prevent the Reading from entering their domain, supported the union. The legislature yielded to the pressure and appointed a committee consisting of five members from each house to investigate the railroad.

Gowen eloquently defended his companies before the joint committee which met in Philadelphia. He appealed to the committee members' sense of fair play by pointing out that every other anthracite carrying company had the right to own coal land. The Reading had to own coal land for self-protection. Gowen invoked the committee's loyalty to Pennsylvania by pointing out that only the Reading did not go beyond the boundaries of the state. Would the Pennsylvania legislature vote against the only native anthracite railroad and in favor of those which served New York and New Jersey interests? While the hearings were in progress a heat wave hit Philadelphia. To spare the legislators discomfort, Gowen invited them to continue the hearing in Atlantic City, which they did. The conclusion of the committee was that the courts and not the legislature should determine the legality of the Reading's coal mining operations.

The hearings were only a skirmish, however; the main battle was fought in the anthracite fields. The men expected the operators to retreat by March 1875. The union tried to dislodge the independent operators by announcing that if the lock-out strike continued after March 1, the men would not return to work unless they received at least an 8 percent pay increase.

Much to the union's surprise, the operators refused to acknowledge the March 1 ultimatum. As the month wore on the mine workers realized that their union was involved in a death struggle, yet they continued to hope that the union could outlast the operators. The Lehigh region men read the refusal of the coal pool to publish coal prices in April as a good omen; the operators must be running short of coal, and hence would soon have to retreat. But then the mine operators brought the mules out of the mines.[26] Strikers were encouraged, nevertheless, by indications that a threat of the union's destruction would help to bring the autonomous W.B.A. units together again. The Northumberland County Executive Board published a warning that nonunion miners and laborers who were still outside the fold after April 1 would not be admitted to membership at any time. To some the announcement signaled the Northumberland County union's decision to enter the fray. In the Wyoming region the engineers and pump men at the Delaware and Hudson collieries went on strike for a return to January's wage. But the hopes inspired by these events did not last long; the Northumberland County W.B.A. never struck, and the Delaware and Hudson quickly settled its problem.

More encouraging to the striking miners and laborers in Schuylkill County was an alliance with a railroad union. The Reading lowered the wages of its railroad workers in the fall of 1874; the workers' union, the Mechanics and Workingmen's Benevolent Association, planned to strike when the coal dispute ended. Gowen, whose intelligence service warned him of the union's plan, decided to force the issue during the coal strike. He ordered that the leaders of the M.&W.B.A. be fired. This forced the hand of the union. It struck, and on March 13 held a joint meeting with the Schuylkill County W.B.A., at which the two unions formed an alliance. The M.&W.B.A. and W.B.A. exchanged traveling cards; the M.&W.B.A. agreed to increase its initiation fee to $50 for any prospective member who had mined coal without belonging to the W.B.A. But the alliance had no practical effect; the M.&W.B.A. represented shop employees, and it was doubtful that it alone could seriously injure the railroad's already diminished business. Nevertheless, the alliance did boost morale; it was comforting to know that other men were fighting the dreaded "monopoly."

Gowen was not idle while the W.B.A. sought allies. Since 1866 coal mine owners could hire their own police, so the Reading increased its police force until it approached the size of a small army. The police force served as a guard for strikebreakers and was, in Gowen's words, "armed to the teeth."[27]

As the strike progressed, the Coal and Iron Police paraded throughout Schuylkill County where the mutterings of the mine workers turned to violence. They focused all their hatred on Gowen. Not being able to get at Gowen physically, the strikers attacked the source of his power, the Philadelphia and Reading. They sidetracked its engines, upset or set on fire cars loaded with coal, and burned breakers and other buildings. John Welsh, president of the Schuylkill County W.B.A., begged his men to obey the law because Gowen *wanted* the mine workers to become lawbreakers. But the men ignored Welsh, and violence spread through Schuylkill County.

There was also violence in the Lehigh region. As riots near Hazleton began to spread, the Luzerne County sheriff panicked and called on the governor for help. When the governor ordered 500 militiamen to Hazleton the disgusted Luzerne County W.B.A. unsuccessfully petitioned the governor to withdraw the troops.

With the militia in Hazleton and violence spreading in Schuylkill County, Welsh offered to withdraw the basis system of wages and to agree to any reasonable offer by the operators. He also stated that the union would be willing to start work even if the operators refused to recognize the union by signing a contract, so long as they accepted the 1874 wage rates. Two small collieries at Mahanoy City agreed to Welsh's offer, but the Reading and the Schuylkill Coal Exchange ignored him. The end of the union was clearly in sight.

Neither the W.B.A. nor its members individually were financially prepared to maintain a long strike. The miners and laborers depended on the independent merchants to extend credit to keep themselves going. The middle class in Schuylkill County was inclined to cooperate with labor in a fight with a large company such as the Philadelphia and Reading, while the union overcame the merchants' fear of unpaid debts. Early in the strike, districts of the union one by one publicly promised to expel any member who refused to pay his store bill after work resumed and to publish both his name and the reason for his expulsion. The merchants extended credit, but with this vague collateral there existed limits to the amount that could be reasonably extended. The union tried to take up some of the slack, but its treasury was low. It appealed for aid to the Wyoming region, which responded with contributions. Delegates solicited funds in Philadelphia and New York, but returned home almost empty-handed. This failure to get financial help from outside doomed the union. The treasury of district six in Shenandoah, was empty and so were the treasuries of other districts.

Union leaders now conceded defeat in their effort to preserve wages, but they still sought recognition as the bargaining agent for the mine workers. They asked the operators for a token concession to preserve the principle of arbitration and, as a sop for this concession, offered to remove any committee member the operators objected to. They invited the Coal Exchange to meet with them in Shenandoah on June 12 to negotiate. The union committee assembled that day, but no operator appeared. The union decided to go over the Coal Exchange's head, and appointed a committee to travel to Philadelphia to ask Gowen for his terms. Gowen heard of the plan. Before the committee could board a train, newspapers carried an open letter from him in which he refused to meet with them. Reduced to near starvation the mine workers resumed work on June 14 on the operators' conditions. An unknown minstrel caught the mood of the men.

> Well, we've been beaten, beaten all to smash
> An now, sir, we've begun to feel the lash,
> As wielded by a gigantic corporation,
> Which runs the commonwealth and ruins the nation.[28]

For all practical purposes the Workingmen's Benevolent Association ceased to exist in Schuylkill County and the Lehigh region after the 1875 "long strike." The W.B.A. had been nothing more than a shadow in the Wyoming region since 1871. The more active locals there seceded from the W.B.A. in 1874 to affiliate themselves with the Miners' National Association, which lingered until 1876 when it began to give way to the Knights of Labor. Only the Northumberland County Union, which experienced neither strike nor lock-out in 1875, remained. In early July the Northumberland County Executive Board, in what proved to be its last public statement, declared itself "in favor of maintaining and strengthening the organization."[29]

The long strike of 1875 destroyed the W.B.A., but in many ways the union had committed suicide. Seeking to improve the mine workers' wage scale, it had pursued a policy based on a mistaken analysis of the anthracite industry's weakness. Diagnosing the industry's illness as overproduction rather than overinvestment, the W.B.A. attempted to regulate production without realizing that even if such a policy were successful it could not increase labor's wages. The unsatisfactory earnings of the mine workers resulted from low wages and irregular employment. Regulation of production through strikes might increase wages, but it also compounded the problem of enforced unemployment.

The union, however, used other methods to improve the

reward system. For one, it attacked the company store. The men, drawing on the experience of labor leaders in Britain and aware of Rochdale's success, fought the "pluck-me" store by forming cooperatives. But the cooperatives foundered on the very thing they were formed to destroy. The smaller operators made dealing at their store a sine qua non for employment. Ironically relief from the company store in the Schuylkill region appeared with the Philadelphia and Reading Coal and Iron Company: Franklin B. Gowen refused to become a shopkeeper.

The W.B.A. also tried to use politics to secure a more equitable return for labor. During the 1873 session of the Pennsylvania legislature, the union persuaded Schuylkill County's senator to introduce a bill entitled "for the better protection of wages," but it died in committee. The next year the W.B.A. successfully lobbied for the passage of a bill to increase the amount of the mechanic's lien. In 1875 the W.B.A., with the Miners' National Association, secured a law calling for "standard and lawful scales" and the enabling of mine workers to hire their own weighmaster to keep tabs on the company. The effects of the 1875 law were disappointing; the operators compelled the miners to sign away their right to hire a checkweighman after they lost the "long strike."

The failure of the W.B.A. to achieve any of its major goals betrayed its inability to cope with the structural realities of the anthracite regions and the production system of mining. Constructed as a loose confederation in which power flowed upward, the General Council lacked the force necessary to destroy the parochial barriers of regionalism. Within the separate regions its message of unity fell on deaf ears as ethnocentrism divided the union. Claiming to speak for all mine workers, the W.B.A. was unable to bridge the gap between contract miners and laborers; indeed, its "equality resolution" widened the breach.

Even in failure, however, the Workingmen's Benevolent Association left a legacy to the anthracite regions. At its zenith in 1869, the union did gain higher wages. For brief periods the W.B.A. sparked a comradeship among the mine workers; the fraternal identification can easily be seen in the Wyoming men's resolution to share their work with "the brothers now out on strike in Schuylkill and elsewhere." Moreover, the W.B.A. left a tradition of an underdog union fighting for the rights of the mine workers against great odds. The anthracite mine workers would remember the "old W.B.A." nostalgically; this memory would prompt other attempts collectively to attack their occupational problems.

A
Violent
Interlude

The anthracite mine workers' first union, the Workingmen's Benevolent Association, failed; its leaders' superficial diagnosis of the industry's sickness made any resuscitation unlikely. More important, the union had failed to take into account the parochialism of the mine workers, their ethnic and occupational prejudices, even though during its brief life the W.B.A. provided some means whereby the mine workers could attack their problems. With the collapse of the union, however, came a vacuum marked by violence.

Violence was not new in the anthracite regions. The high accident rate in the mines was the best example of the cheapness of life. The constant influx of foreigners produced tensions which broke normal institutional restraints. Shorn of restraints, the mine workers vented their frustrations through the use of terror. Many immigrants, it must be remembered, brought with them a heritage of violence. In South Wales a terrorist group known as the "Scotch Cattle" had functioned during the depression years of 1832 and 1842-45.[1] But the Irish Catholics were the most experienced in terrorism.

The Irish Catholic peasant led a miserable life in Ireland. Poor and harassed by an absentee landlord's agent, he often faced eviction. The threat became more pressing after the Napoleonic Wars as English landlords, themselves pursued by creditors, turned from grain cultivation to the more lucrative raising of livestock. If the evicted Irishman sought redress in the courts he found that the law favored the landowner. Denied legal relief he thus resorted to direct action through a secret society.

Secret societies and direct action had had a long history in Ireland. One group, the "White Boys," gained notoriety during the 1760s by fighting enclosures. In Ulster the "Hearts of Oak" imitated the White Boys. In the early nineteenth century a new secret society, the "Threshers," fought the tithe collector. Trials and hangings drove most of the Threshers underground, but they soon reappeared as the "Ribbonmen," in a conspiracy that flourished between 1810 and 1820.

In Ireland in the 1840s a new name—Molly Maguire—became well known between County Clare in the south and Counties Donegal and Tyrone in the north. Judging from the long history and wide range of secret terrorist societies in Ireland, it is reasonable to assume that Irish immigrants to the anthracite fields of Pennsylvania had knowledge of, and perhaps had even participated in such groups. And the terrorist group best known to the immigrants was the Molly Maguires.

In the anthracite fields the Irish immigrant was faced with a situation similar to that in the old country. An often absentee landlord, in this case the mine operator, enjoyed the privilege of arbitrary eviction. He exploited his employees with the ruthlessness of the old landlord's agent. Protestant Welsh, Scotch, and English miners maintained a monopoly over the more lucrative positions inside the productive system. The Irish immigrant responded in the old-fashioned way by invoking the familiar name of Molly Maguire.

A flurry of violence had been released in the anthracite regions during the Civil War. At a public meeting at Audenried in July 1862, John Kehoe, an Irishman and anti-war Democrat, allowed his political passions to overrule his reason and spat upon the American flag. F.W. Langdon, a mine foreman denounced Kehoe and his friends. Kehoe responded by threatening to kill Langdon. Later that day an unidentified person or group of persons attacked Langdon while he was alone and stoned him. Langdon died the next day.

Opposition to conscription also produced violence. In August 1862 some miners stopped a Harrisburg-bound train loaded with recruits and sent the (unwilling) draftees home. To avoid a confrontation (for political reasons) the federal government accepted bogus affidavits attesting that Cass Township, Schuylkill County, where draft opposition was greatest, had filled its draft quota with enlistments.[2] The second murder in Audenried occurred on November 6, 1863, when a mob broke into the home of George K. Smith, a mine operator, and killed him. Apparently Smith had incurred the wrath of the miners by giving a draft officer a list of his employees.

Violence engendered by war passions became a crime wave in the two southern regions. In 1867 the *Miners' Journal* reported that between 1863 and March 16, 1867, there were 52 murders in Schuylkill County. Moreover, in the period between January 1, 1867 and March 16, 1867 there were six murderous assaults and 27 robberies. The crime rate in the other counties did not increase so dramatically, but there is evidence that a terrorist gang or gangs operated in Schuylkill and Lehigh regions.

Law enforcement agencies were unable to cope with the terrorism. Whenever the police arrested a suspect, alibis were produced to free the alleged criminal. The ease with which the alibis appeared convinced many that a single and secret society perpetrated all violent acts.

Everyone "knew" the secret society's identity. Knowledge of the Molly Maguire's existence in Ireland and a popular belief that the Irish were behind the crime wave led many to conclude that the Irish terrorist organization was active in the anthracite fields.[3] Benjamin Bannan, editor of the *Miners' Journal,* circulated such a story in the 1850s. According to Bannan the Democratic party controlled the secret society for its own political purposes.[4] By 1864 the name Molly Maguire had gained such wide circulation that James F. Wood, Archbishop of the Philadelphia Diocese of the Roman Catholic Church, condemned the terrorist group by name in a pastoral letter.

Widespread violence and the equally widespread notion of a secret society called the Molly Maguires forced the popular equation of the two. In the resulting milieu there was an excellent outlet for pent-up frustration. It is easy to conceive of a person who, denied institutional outlets, found an outlet for his anger by evoking the Mollies. It was simple: one sent an anonymous note emblazoned with a pistol or coffin and promising vengeance on the recipient. Superintendents and foremen were the most likely targets in the anthracite regions. Men in managerial positions throughout the nation received similar warnings, but only in the Schuylkill and Lehigh anthracite regions did popular opinion make the receipt of a "coffin notice" a fearful experience. The number of "coffin notices" sent to managerial personnel was sufficient to complete a relationship in which violence equaled Molly Maguires and Molly Maguires equaled labor unions.

Calmer minds, however, could not grant the equation of the Molly Maguires and organized labor. The amount of violence actually declined during the period of the Workingmen's Benevolent Association's greatest strength. John Eltringman, state mine inspector in Schuylkill County, noted the correspondence of this decline with the union's advent, and reported that under the W.B.A. the region became "remarkably settled."[5] Mine operators agreed; testifying before the State Senate Committee on the Judiciary General, William Kendrick, the president of the Anthracite Board of Trade, remarked that the W.B.A. prevented crime by controlling "a very bad element."[6] The local newspapers praised the union for destroying "the reign of terror and outlawry that existed here a few years since."[7] A contemporary attorney and writer, F.P. Dewees, sought a connection between the union and the terrorist groups, but admitted that such a charge "is believed to be without foundation."[8]

But one important man—Franklin B. Gowen—disagreed. Serving as Schuylkill County's district attorney during the peak of the Civil War terrorism, Gowen failed to secure a single conviction.[9] Gowen had blamed his failure on a secret society. When the W.B.A. brought his actions as a railroad president under legislative scrutiny (see Chapter 8), Gowen identified the secret society which tarnished his legal record with the union. Appearing before the Committee on the Judiciary General, he drew attention to the union's goal of maintaining wages and prices, and explained its methods of reaching that goal: "In order to accomplish this object in 1869 they [the union] issued an order, from which there is no appeal. *The man who appeals from that order must go down into the tomb.*"[10] A secret society fulfilled the alternative to obedience:

> I do not charge this Workingmen's Benevolent Association with it, but I say there is an association which votes in the secret, at night, that men's lives shall be taken, and that they shall be shot before their wives, murdered in cold blood, for daring to work against the order . . . *I do not blame this association*, but I blame another association for doing it; and it happens that the only men who are shot are the men who dare to disobey the mandates of the Workingmen's Benevolent Association."[11]

Gowen, as befitting his position, mingled bellicosity with caution. In his mind the Molly Maguires were the labor union, but he had no supporting evidence. Renewed turbulence, however, would give Gowen an opportunity to corroborate his theory with facts.

Violence erupted again in the coal regions after the W.B.A. began to disintegrate. Concerned about the mounting crime wave, Benjamin Franklin, Philadelphia superintendent of Alan Pinkerton's national detective agency, sent agents already hired by the Philadelphia and Reading into the coal fields. The detectives reported the existence of a group of rowdies known as the Molly Maguires in the vicinity of Glen Carbon. When Franklin sent this information to Gowen, and the outbreaks of violence continued, Gowen and Pinkerton met and decided on an investigation of the Molly Maguires.

Pinkerton took care in selecting his agent, James McParlan, for the case. McParlan, born in Ireland, had emigrated to the United States in 1867, where he first worked as a store clerk and then became a "preventive policeman" of a small Chicago detective agency. In 1871 he joined the Pinkerton force.

Before assigning McParlan to the actual case Pinkerton asked that he produce a research paper on secret societies in Ireland. McParlan's paper demonstrated a fair knowledge of the "Ribbonmen," whom he identified as the Molly Maguires. He further noted that the Molly Maguires later "adopted a new name which was called the Ancient Order of Hibernians."[12] Obviously McParlan entered the investigation with preconceived notions as to the villains' identity.

In October 1873 McParlan left Philadelphia for the anthracite regions. Disguised as a tramp and calling himself James McKenna, McParlan disembarked at Port Clinton and proceeded to the western end of the southern basin. A brief tour of the mining towns of Swatara, Tremont, and Donaldson yielded nothing but rumors that Mollies flourished in the Mahanoy Valley. Emptyhanded, McParlan returned to Philadelphia for further instructions.

The new modus operandi called for McParlan to return to the coal fields and establish a base at Pottsville. In Pottsville he became acquainted with Patrick Dormer, proprietor of the Sheridan House and, rumor held, a leader of the Molly Maguires. Ingratiating himself with Dormer by demonstrating his dancing, drinking, and fighting abilities, McParlan carefully built his cover story. He was, the detective informed the gullible Dormer, a fugitive from justice, an active counterfeiter, and once a member of the Ancient Order of Hibernians. When challenged on the latter claim, he escaped exposure by feigning a drunken stupor. While at the Sheridan House, McParlan met reputed Mollies from Mahanoy Valley, the most important of whom was Michael Lawler.

"Muff" Lawler kept a tavern in Shenandoah and was a Bodymaster in the A.O.H. When Lawler invited McParlan to visit him in Shenandoah, McParlan gladly accepted. He remained there for more than a year.

McParlan's travels through the coal regions were enlightening. On March 25, 1874 he reported his first case of violence— the fatal shooting of a man named Lanahan in Centralia. But Lanahan, a Molly Maguire, had been killed by another terrorist group called the "Chain Gang."[13] Also known as the "Sheet Irons," the Chain Gang consisted of renegade Mollies, "Young Irish Americans," and "Kilkenny men."[14] Thus not one but at least two secret societies existed in the coal region. Moreover, the violence appeared to be the result of intra-ethnic feuding rather than a labor union's attempt to insure total obedience to its dictums.

But a connection between the dreaded Molly Maguires and organized labor might still be drawn. The detective reported that "Muff" Lawler was on strike. When McParlan expressed a desire to rejoin the A.O.H., Lawler told him that if he could get a job he would have no difficulty attaining membership. Following Lawler's advice, McParlan found work in a mine. On his first day of work a man named Mullany demanded that McParlan show his W.B.A. traveling card. McParlan explained that he had just begun mining, and Mullany told him he would have to join the union if he wished to keep his job.

While McParlan was learning that the W.B.A. maintained a closed shop, other Pinkerton detectives—P.M. Cummings, William McCowan, "W.R.H.," and H.B. Hanmore—infiltrated the union. Whether the detectives functioned as labor spies or sought a connection between the W.B.A. and the Mollies is unknown, but P.M. Cummings, a member of the Saint Clair District Board and soon to be elected vice president of the local, reported that Thomas R. Nash, once secretary of the local, was serving a prison term for killing his stepfather, who allegedly was a Molly Maguire, and Nash's brother kept a house of illrepute in Philadelphia.

There was little evidence that the labor union and the terrorist group were connected. If Gowen persisted in his belief that they were, McParlan punctured the belief by telling Gowen that the W.B.A. expelled known criminals. A case simply could not be made against the union as a fomenter of crime. Nevertheless, violence, which continued to occur in the coal region, *could* be the work of a secret society.

McParlan had begun his investigation firmly convinced of the existence of the Molly Maguires and of their connection with the Ancient Order of Hibernians. Through Lawler's efforts the Shenandoah lodge initiated the detective into the A.O.H. McParlan found the Order to be anything but a center for terrorism; at his first meeting only seven members attended, the treasury was empty, and the members grudgingly paid their dues. Traveling now as an insider, McParlan learned the names of the various Body-masters throughout Schuylkill County, reporting them to Philadelphia.

McParlan soon uncovered the relationship between the A.O.H. and violence in the coal region. Members presented grievances to the Body-master, who appointed the necessary men to redress the injury, all without the knowledge of the lodge as a whole. The actual terrorist group was an inner circle of A.O.H. Body-masters, and McParlan went after them.

But the next Molly Maguire murder did not follow the previous pattern. In Mahanoy City a group of Welsh and Protestant Germans known as the "Modocs," organized a fire company. The Irish had their own fire company too. Both companies answered calls from the town's central district, usually engaging in a fight in the course of duty. On October 31, 1874 a fire broke out in the center of town, whereupon the two companies indulged in the usual brawl. During the fight George Major, the chief burgess, tried to restore order, with disastrous consequences; he shot a dog and someone shot him. As Major fell he fired twice at his assailant. An Irishman named Daniel Dougherty was found shot in the head (it was apparently a glancing blow, which left a bullet in Dougherty's head but did not kill him). Dougherty was arrested and identified by the dying Major as the man who had shot him.

Feelings ran high both for and against the accused man. Dougherty was a member of the A.O.H., which came to his aid. Firmly believing in Dougherty's innocence, the Order raised a defense fund, while the *Miners' Journal,* thinking of the Molly Maguires, urged a hanging. Dougherty's defense received a

change of venue to Lebanon. At the trial the defense dramatically removed the bullet from Dougherty's head in the courtroom and showed that it had not been fired from Major's gun.[15]
Dougherty was found not guilty.

The killing of Major touched off an explosion of violence.
During November there were beatings and more fires. In
December Franklin B. Gowen forced the "long strike" on the
W.B.A. (it is noteworthy that the union's destruction came
about after the period of violence in Schuylkill County).

As the institutionalized methods of response failed, the frustrated men turned to direct action. Vandalism against the Philadelphia and Reading increased, and "coffin notices" gained
wide circulation. Gowen next ordered P.&R. field officers to forward reports of all incidents to him. Gowen presented the reports as "A List of Outrages" to a joint committee of the Pennsylvania legislature which investigated the Reading during the
summer.[16] The wily railroad president succeeded where his detectives had failed: by implication he again linked the W.B.A.
with the Molly Maguires.

While Gowen attacked the union McParlan uncovered plans
for another Molly murder. Although acquitted, Daniel Dougherty
remained guilty in the eyes of Major's friends. One evening two
men shot at Dougherty and two bullets pierced his clothing.
Dougherty identified the men as Jess Major, George Major's
brother, and William M. ("Bully Bill") Thomas. The Molly
Maguires agreed that their "brother," Dougherty, would not en-
joy peace while Major and Thomas lived. Jack Kehoe, Schuylkill
County Delegate of the A.O.H., appointed McParlan, who was
now a de facto leader of the Shenandoah lodge, to engineer the
murder of Thomas.

Obediently, McParlan, a member in good standing in the
A.O.H., notified members of a meeting. At the meeting, Thomas
Hurley, Michael Doyle, and John Gibbons volunteered to go to
Mahanoy City to eliminate Thomas. The three men invited
McParlan to join them, and he agreed. In Mahanoy City
McParlan convinced the others that they should postpone their
task because of the troops sent there to maintain peace during
the strike.

After his return to Shenandoah McParlan became ill, using
his illness as an excuse for not participating in the job. But the
project was postponed and on the night of June 27 McParlan
met Hurley, Gibbons, Doyle, John Morris, and Frank McAndrew

and learned that an attempt on Thomas's life would take place the following day. McParlan, however, did not tell anyone. On the morning of the 28th Doyle met McParlan and took him to Ringtown Mountain where they joined Morris, Hurley, and Gibbons. There the excited men told the undercover agent that they had killed "Bully Bill" Thomas.[17]

One week later Benjamin Yost, a policeman at Tamaqua, was murdered. Extinguishing the street lights was part of Yost's duties. He was shot as he mounted the ladder to put out the last light. Due to Yost's adverse relations with James Kerrigan, Body-master of A.O.H.'s Tamaqua lodge, popular consensus attributed the murder to the Molly Maguires. Kerrigan had been arrested several times by Yost and at least once the policeman used his club on Kerrigan. On the night of his death Yost and his fellow officer, Barney McCarran, stopped for a drink at James Carroll's tavern, reputedly a Molly Maguire rendezvous, and joined Kerrigan at the bar. While there the officers noticed two strangers whom Yost before he died identified as his assailants. But both Yost and McCarran cleared Kerrigan of the shooting.

Yost's murder created a popular outcry. An enraged populace organized a citizens' committee which went to Philadelphia and talked to Benjamin Franklin. The committee left with assurances that the Pinkerton Agency would assign an unannounced operative to the case—McParlan naturally. His reputation as the toughest of the Mollies preceding him, McParlan went to Tamaqua where he learned the facts from fellow Mollies. Kerrigan had sought revenge for a beating Yost gave him during the summer of 1874, and he enlisted James Roarity, Body-master at Coaldale. Roarity agreed to help Kerrigan kill Yost, but soon dragged his feet. When Kerrigan pressed him, Roarity finally offered two men, Hugh McGehan and James Boyle, if the Tamaqua lodge would return the favor with the murder of John P. Jones, a Lansford mine boss.

Kerrigan agreed. Hugh McGehan and James Boyle appeared in Tamaqua on the evening of Yost's murder. The host Body-master showed the two assassins an escape route and planted them where they could get a clear shot at Yost. Kerrigan then returned to Carroll's bar, where he joined Yost in his last drink.[18]

Later Kerrigan approached McParlan for help in fulfilling the obligation to Roarity. Nothing came of it. The A.O.H.'s

County Convention discussed the issue, but came to no decision. The proposed murder of Jones, however, became inter-
twined with the projected murder of a mine boss named Reese.
Some members of the Shenandoah lodge wanted Reese elimi-
nated. Frank McAndrews, the Body-master, decided the job
could be done safely only with an exchange of personnel. At a
lodge meeting he proposed that the Shenandoah group fulfill
Kerrigan's deal; in return the Tamaqua lodge would supply
Reese's murderers. The Body-master appointed John McGrail,
Mike Darcy, and Thomas Munley as Jones's assassins, and instructed McParlan to go to Tamaqua and seal the bargain with
Kerrigan.

McParlan and two of the others (McGrail was unable to go)
went to Tamaqua but could not find Kerrigan. Munley and
Darcy returned home, and McParlan sought his Pinkerton con-
tact, Robert J. Linden, whose cover was captain in the Philadelphia and Reading Coal and Iron Police. Unable to find
Linden, McParlan wrote a long report to Benjamin Franklin, the
most interesting aspect of which was McParlan's interpretation
of the relation between the W.B.A.'s destruction and the renewed outbreak of violence. At one point he congratulated himself:
"Now you can see yourself how this is, and what I predicted—at
the time of the suspension—that if the Union would fail there
would be rough times." McParlan later became more explicit:
"there was very little killing a doing whilst [the] Union stood,
but now it is quite the reverse."[19]

McParlan discovered later why he did not find Kerrigan. At
Carroll's tavern he was told that Kerrigan had made his own
plans to kill Jones. The next day Kerrigan put his plan into operation. Two strangers approached Jones as he mounted the
steps of the Lansford train station and shot him. Unfortunately
for the gunmen, a student named Samuel Beard returned to
Tamaqua with the news, and someone remembered seeing
Kerrigan with two strangers west of town. Taking a telescope to
the Odd Fellows' Cemetery which overlooked the valley, Beard
and the other man spied Kerrigan and his friends enjoying a picnic lunch. Gathering a posse in Tamaqua they proceeded to the
spot and arrested them.

The trial went badly for Kerrigan and his accomplices. The
prosecution, strengthened by the services of General Charles
Albright, attorney for the Lehigh-Wilkes-Barre Coal Company,
F.W. Hughes of the Philadelphia and Reading, and Allen Craig

of the Lehigh Valley, decided to try Doyle first. The prosecution built its case on circumstantial evidence supplied by 200 witnesses. Anticipating every move by the adversary, the prosecution successfully stymied the defense. Such anticipation did not stem from an astute knowledge of courtroom strategy, nor was it the result of clairvoyance. McParlan, as a high-ranking Molly, was privy to the defense's plans, which he relayed to the prosecution. Finding themselves hopelessly outmatched, the defense did not call witnesses. On February 1, 1876, the jury returned a verdict of "guilty of murder in the first degree."[20]

During Doyle's trial Kerrigan broke. Locked in solitary confinement, the Tamaqua Body-master became apprehensive and decided to save himself by turning informer. He called his Coal and Iron Police guard and confessed. The guard quickly notified Albright and Hughes, apparently overlooking the district attorney in his excitement. The prisoner repeated his confession before Albright and Hughes. The confession contained the principal outlines of McParlan's reports of the plans to kill Jones and their relation to the Yost murder. Now the authorities could bring that case to trial.

A telegram to Philadelphia brought Benjamin Franklin to the coal regions. Franklin and Linden formed a posse and arrested Carroll, Duffy, Roarity, McGehan, and Boyle. The arrests created a flurry of rumors. Fearing that others involved would leave the area, Coal and Iron Police rounded up additional Mollies. Since Kerrigan did not know the men arrested by the second posse, the Molly Maguires suspected the existence of a second informer.

About a week after the arrests, McParlan learned that some Mollies considered him a traitor. Frank McAndrew later told McParlan that some Mollies were placing bets on his being a detective and that Jack Kehoe warned the group to beware of McParlan. McParlan demanded and got a trial before the County Convention to confront the county delegate at his home in Girardville. While there McParlan talked to Father Daniel O'Conner, who, according to Kehoe, had informed Kehoe of the detective's true identity. Leaving O'Conner, McParlan went by train to Pottsville; from there he left the coal regions only to return as the prosecution's star witness at the "Great Molly Maguire Trials."

The trial of Edward Kelly for the murder of John P. Jones proceeded admirably for the Commonwealth. The prosecution felt that their case against Kelly was so strong they did not need

Kerrigan's confession. They were right; the jury found Kelly guilty of first-degree murder, and the judge sentenced him to be hanged. Attention then focused on Schuylkill County.

As in Carbon County, the district attorney, George Kaercher, had ample assistance. Guy E. Farquhar, a prominent local lawyer, joined the prosecution, and completing the team was no less a light than Franklin B. Gowen. Thus armed, the Commonwealth tried the Yost murder case.

On the first day of the trial District Attorney Kaercher announced that the prosecution would present as its key witness James McParlan, a Pinkerton detective, alias James McKenna. On May 6, 1876 McParlan took the stand and repeated his earlier reports. On the second day of McParlan's testimony the prosecution shifted the court's attention to the A.O.H., or Molly Maguires, instead of the defendants. Despite the defense's objections, the prosecution was successful. In the afternoon, Gowen had McParlan recite the A.O.H.'s ritual and organization. Finally McParlan gave the most damaging testimony when he stated that the Order had only one objective, that of protecting and avenging its members.

The trials had successfully taken a new turn. Now an entire secret society, the same secret order which had so terrorized the coal regions during the Civil War, was to be tried. To dramatize the connection, General Albright appeared in court wearing his old military uniform. If the jury was unable to grasp the uniform's symbolism, Gowen would not hesitate to draw the direct line. When, during one of the trials the defense tried to portray McParlan as an agent provocateur, Gowen objected, drawing attention to the murders of George K. Smith in 1863, David Muir in 1865, and others during the great crime wave.[21]

The effect was startling. The public had always thought that a secret society was responsible for coal region violence; now Gowen and others confirmed the belief. But still there was no direct evidence linking the secret society so active during the Civil War and the order the coal companies had uncovered. John Kehoe's trial for the murder of F.W. Langdon in 1862 was the missing link. Langdon, it will be remembered, was killed after an encounter with Kehoe. At the time, Kehoe was believed guilty, but there was so little evidence that the case was dropped without coming to trial. Fourteen years later witnesses suddenly appeared. Kehoe and four others were indicted for the 1862 crime. Two men, Neil Dougherty and John Campbell, were found guilty of second degree murder; the other two, Columbus and Michael McGee, were declared innocent. Kehoe alone faced a first degree murder indictment. Despite conflicting testimony on both sides, the jury found him guilty and the judge sentenced him to hang. Kehoe's trial completed the circle—the county delegate of 1875 had committed the first Molly murder in 1862!

The last trial took place in Columbia County. Daniel Kelly, a self-confessed perjurer, promised to turn state's evidence against Patrick Hester, a widely celebrated "Molly" at Locust Gap, for robbing and murdering Alexander Rea in 1868. The state arrested Patrick Hester, Peter McHugh, and Patrick Tully for the crime and convicted them on Kelly's uncorroborated testimony.

The Molly Maguire investigation and trials ended with the eventual execution of 20 men, but the meaning of the episode is still open to interpretation. McParlan undoubtedly uncovered a relatively small group of desperadoes operating in the eastern end of the southern basin. But he also discovered the existence of other terrorist groups. Indeed, the first murder he reported was that of a Molly Maguire by the "Chain Gang"; McParlan feared a gang war would break out between the two organizations. The Pinkerton detective knew and reported the existence of three underworld organizations, but unfortunately he brought only one—the Molly Maguires—to trial.

This selectivity is puzzling. McParlan went to the coal regions believing that the Molly Maguires, alias the Ancient Order of Hibernians, was the only Irish secret society operating there. Perhaps he lost his objectivity and conveniently forgot the Modocs and the "Chain Gang," an oversight also convenient for his employer, Franklin B. Gowen.

Gowen sought to identify the mine workers' first union, the Molly Maguires, as a secret terrorist group. Not known beyond their immediate locale, neither the Modocs nor the Chain Gang could be that. But the Molly Maguires had had wide notoriety since the Civil War. Moreover, the arrest and conviction of the Molly Maguires would vindicate Gowen's failure as district attorney of Schuylkill County.

The trials reflected Gowen's needs. The trial of an entire terrorist group rather than a few offenders gave credibility to his earlier charges of a secret society, and, as already noted, Kehoe's trial provided the necessary connection between the two crime waves. The same logic was the basis of Hester's arrest. Prior to his apprehension and indictment the Molly Maguires were thought to be geographically restricted, but during the trial of the Locust Gap Hibernian the Mollies took on the image of an organization encompassing the entire Schuylkill region. At Hester's trial F.W. Hughes, the Philadelphia and Reading attorney on loan to the state, sought to impress upon the jury that they were trying the same terrorist group that had been tried in Mauch Chunk and Pottsville: "I want you men of Columbia County to help in this movement that has become a necessity for life in the coal regions of Pennsylvania, to help exterminate this hellborn organization, and send it back to the Prince of Darkness whence it came."[22]

Gowen also used the trials as a rostrum for his opinions. His implying of a connection between the W.B.A. and the Molly Maguires allowed Martin L'Velle for the defense to describe the trials as an antiunion attack. During the trial Gowen paused to repair his tattered reputation by remembering his disappointments as district attorney and announcing: "I made up my mind that if human ingenuity, if long suffering and patient care, and toil that stopped at no obstacle, and would confront every danger, could succeed in exposing this secret organization to light of day and bringing to well earned justice the perpetrators of these awful crimes, I would undertake the task."[23] Seen in this light, the Molly Maguire episode becomes a story of Gowen's personal success rather than a tale of justice triumphing over evil.

But the episode had much wider ramifications than one man's success or failure. The hanging of 20 men in the southern anthracite regions proclaimed a new order—the corporation-dominated society. By beating down labor in 1875, the corporation provided what neither labor union nor state seemed capable of providing: protection from and prosecution of criminals and terrorists. F.P. Dewees signaled the corporation's new role:

> To counteract the influence of terrorism the efforts of the civil authorities, backed with the money, the power, and the influence of the Lehigh and Wilkes-barre [sic] Coal Company, were evoked; and as the assassination of Yost had been perpetrated by men from Carbon County in consideration of the murder of Jones, the cost of their prosecution was also assumed by the company.[24]

If the Molly Maguire episode represented corporation dominance to the anthracite regions in general, it represented something more ominous for labor. Gowen successfully tarred labor with the name of terrorism. Many people would henceforth not only equate with terrorism any response of labor to industry problems, but would see labor itself as the source of terrorism—as terrorism itself. Indeed, within a year the Molly Maguires were being used as justification for the shooting down of mine workers in the street.

Wages plunged as the depression deepened during 1877. In July the monthly pay of employees of the Pennsylvania Coal Company averaged $30. John Mucklow, a contract miner in Taylorsville, reported that he received only 63 cents for each car of coal he sent to the top.[25] Dissatisfaction over low wages smoldered until the great railroad strikes fanned it into an open flame.

The railroad strikes of 1877 began early in July on the Baltimore and Ohio Railroad after the company announced a reduction in wages. The strike quickly spread to the other major lines and on July 23 reached the Delaware, Lackawanna, and Western Railroad. From the D.L.&W. the strike spread to the other roads serving the Wyoming and Lehigh regions. Since coal could not be transported, the mines shut down.

Thrown out of work, the mine workers decided to press their claims for higher wages by refusing to return to work when the railroad strike was over. On July 25 the D.L.&W. miners demanded a 25 percent pay increase. The Lackawanna Coal and Iron Company miners joined the strike the next day. The Lehigh men walked out with the railroaders, and the miners in the Shamokin area also struck. As would be expected, the railroad strikes of 1877 created a series of uncoordinated and violent coal strikes.

With violence enveloping the anthracite regions in 1877, memories of the Molly Maguires were revived. Furthermore, the railroad and coal strikes began just as the Pittsburgh riot ended.[26] Shocked by the attack on private property which this riot represented, the middle class citizenry of the anthracite regions determined that their towns would not become other Pittsburghs. Their fear and determination quickly became a volatile mixture requiring only the smallest spark to burst into violence.

The first explosion occurred in Shamokin. During the evening of July 25 vandals broke into and looted the Philadelphia and Reading Railroad station. An armed group of townspeople fired a volley at the looters, killing one person and wounding several

others.[27] After the shooting two vigilante committees patrolled
the streets for two weeks.[28]

There was also a vigilante committee, nominally directed by
the mayor, in Scranton. Feeling that the city's ten-man police
force was inadequate, Mayor Robert H. McKune had asked the
city council to create an emergency force to protect Scranton
during the crisis. The council rejected McKune's request.
McKune then appointed an advisory committee of seven citizens
who agreed to raise a special police force.

Unknown to the mayor, there was already an incipient private police force. McKune received most of his support from
workingmen, "and hence held a questionable position in the
confidence of the great mass of law-abiding citizens." Believing
that "when civil authority is overcome and defied, the honest
citizen is a law unto himself," the skeptical citizens secretly
formed a "Citizens' Corps," which met at the Forest and Stream
Sportman's Club.[29] After the appointment of the advisory committee, the Citizens' Corps placed itself at McKune's disposal.

Although deputized as the mayor's Special Police Force,
there was little doubt as to who had inspired the vigilante
committee. The Special Police Force met and trained in a room
over the Lackawanna Coal and Iron Company's store, the same
company which provided nearly all of the Special Force's
weapons and ammunition. The L.C.&I. went even further by
furnishing 30 of the 46 special policemen. It was inevitable,
then, that W.W. Scranton, general superintendent of the
company, should take command of the special force when the
expected trouble came.

At a mass meeting on August 1 the Scranton strikers decided
to enlist new recruits in their cause. Marching in a body, they
had some success at the silk mill and at the L.C.&I.'s blast
furnaces, and were heading for the Dickson Manufacturing
Company when they encountered the mayor. McKune stepped
into the street to stop the crowd, but was seized and wounded.
Suddenly the Special Police, commanded by W.W. Scranton,
appeared.

Scranton was not averse to violence; he wanted a confrontation with labor. On the eve of the riot, commenting on the
possibility of troops being sent into the city, Scranton had
said: "I trust when the troops come—if they ever get here—that
we may have a conflict, in which the mob shall be completely

worsted. In no other way will the thing end with any security for property in the future."[30] The troops did not arrive in time, and Scranton ordered his Special Police "to shoot low, and to shoot to kill if they shot at all."[31] Scranton's men did just that; they fired into the crowd, killing six and wounding 54.

Immediately after this incident 5,000 members of the Pennsylvania National Guard were sent to Scranton from Harrisburg. The Guard entered the coal regions with a great display of power. A crew with a Gatling gun preceded the trains, while skirmishers surrounded the town of Plymouth, arresting everyone in sight. Despite the miners' request that the troops be withdrawn, the Guard, now partially relieved by the United States Army, occupied the area for the duration of the strike.

The strike continued, spreading despite the presence of troops. In mid-August the Hazleton men walked out, making the strike in the Lehigh region complete. The Schuylkill region, however, remained on the job. There had been some hope that the Schuylkill men would join the effort in early August when the miners around Shenandoah met to discuss the strike. But the Philadelphia and Reading miners refused to sanction any strike call. Meeting again on August 10, the Shenandoah men voted against the strike.

Not discouraged, the northern mine workers continued their strike. By September events apparently had vindicated them. The Hazleton men returned to work with a promise that wages would be restored when coal prices increased. Employees of independent mine operators near Wilkes-Barre won a restoration of their wages. The Lehigh Valley Railroad at first refused to haul coal from the reopened mines, but public protest forced the railroad to move the coal.

With the smaller operators surrendering, employees of the large corporations felt they could safely open negotiations. A committee of miners from the Delaware and Hudson; Delaware, Lackawanna, and Western; and Pennsylvania Coal Companies went to New York to confer with the companies' presidents. The initial efforts of the committee failed—the presidents of the Delaware and Hudson and Pennsylvania Coal refused to see them. The committee was finally received two days later, but during the ensuing conference the corporation heads announced that the depression would not allow them to grant a wage increase.

The committee returned home, where the strikers greeted

their report with mixed emotions. The Delaware, Lackawanna, and Western men voted 1,262 to 144 to continue the strike. The Delaware and Hudson mine workers also refused to work. But the Pennsylvania Coal Company employees could not sustain the strike and returned to work.

The Wyoming-Lackawanna miners supported their strike by a variety of methods. Some sought work in the Schuylkill region. The strikers also canvassed the southernmost region for relief funds. After the Hazleton and Wilkes-Barre miners had returned to work they contributed to the strike fund. But the support was not enough; in October the Pittston relief committee could distribute only 14 ounces of flour, a half-bushel of potatoes, and four pounds of fish per week per family. "Hundreds of families are suffering the pangs of hunger," reported the British Consul.[32] Faced with starvation, the miners capitulated.

The trial of the Scranton Special Police provided an epilogue to the 1877 strikes. A coroner's inquest determined that the deaths of the riot victims were the result of murder, and ordered the arrest of the Citizens' Corps. In the trial the jury returned a verdict of not guilty.[33] Some historians have questioned the verdict, but the Pennsylvania legislature agreed with it:

> Too much praise cannot be awarded the mayor and citizens' special police force of Scranton for the admirable organization they created, and for the prompt and vigorous measures taken when the emergency arrived. Had the action of the City Council been approved and its advice taken, no special force would have been raised, or had there been timidity among them when called out, Scranton would, no doubt, have suffered as badly as did Pittsburgh; for nowhere in the State was there a harder set of men than at Scranton and vicinity, many of the Molly Maguires, driven out of Schuylkill County, having gathered in and about that city, besides the scores of other hard cases who had been there for years.[34]

The verdict of not guilty in the Scranton vigilante trial may be interpreted as the guilty verdict in the Molly Maguire cases was—as a personal success story. W.W. Scranton and Franklin B. Gowen took advantage of violence to achieve their own ends. But this, of course, does not explain the presence of violence in the first place.

The violence is understandable only in terms of an institutional breakdown. The economic collapse of 1873 forced wages down at the same time the weakening of the W.B.A. left the mine workers with no reasonable means of protesting poor working conditions or low pay. Denied these means, the miners turned to direct, violent action. Superficially poles apart, the Molly Maguire episode and the Scranton riot reflected the institutional vacuum.

The mine workers quickly learned that in a violent confrontation management commanded overwhelming power. The Molly Maguire episode resulted in the Coal and Iron Police becoming the most effective law agency in the area. Vigilante action in both the Molly Maguire episode and the strikes of 1877 demonstrated that recourse to terrorism sent local businessmen into the operators' corner. Finally, the use of the National Guard to protect private property showed that the state was aligned with management. Thus outgunned, the mine workers again turned to the idea of a union to resolve their problems.

Reorganization and Collapse

The strikes of 1877 spurred the anthracite mine workers toward reorganization. In early August the Wyoming-Lackawanna strikers called for the reestablishment of an industrywide union, a call that went unheeded; but the activities of the relief committees in the Schuylkill region kept the possibility of interregional cooperation alive.

The Knights of Labor built the cooperative spirit. Organizers for the Knights of Labor had secretly entered the hard coal fields in 1871, but the existence of established unions precluded their success. The collapse of the Workingmen's Benevolent Association and the Miners' National Association, however, gave organizers for the secret union an open field, and on July 3, 1876 the Scranton miners formed Local Assembly 216 which provided some leadership during the 1877 strikes. Following the strikes the new union spread quickly throughout the coal fields; within the year local assemblies flourished in the Schuylkill region.

Opposition from the Roman Catholic Church hindered the growth of the Knights. Parish priests in the coal regions, ignoring Bishop Wood's sanction of the Knights of Labor, denounced the organization. One priest opposed the new union to the extent that he created the Catholic Workingmen's Society as an alternative for his parishioners. The hostility of the local pastors reflected their suspicion of secret societies in general and their awareness of the popular linking of labor and the Molly Maguires.

The secrecy of the union may have renewed fears of a terrorist group, but the local press quickly dispelled these. In

May 1878 the *Weekly Miners' Journal* published the preamble to the Knights of Labor's constitution and in November printed and explained the union's meeting notice. The ability of an enterprising newspaper to penetrate a clandestine society convinced many of the legitimacy of the Knights of Labor.

But Franklin B. Gowen rekindled suspicions in order to prevent a strike. Because of financial difficulties the Philadelphia and Reading stopped paying its mine workers in October 1878. In early January 1879 employees at the Reading's Beechwood, Brookside, and Luke Fiddler collieries struck for back wages. In mid-January rumors that Reading mine workers at Centralia and Girardville would also strike were circulated. Faced with a potentially disastrous strike, Gowen took the fight to the Knights of Labor.

Gowen began his offensive with an open letter to the *Weekly Miners' Journal* in which he shattered the Knights' secrecy by listing the locations, numbers, and officers of the local assemblies. After demonstrating his complete knowledge of the union Gowen tried to array regional loyalties behind himself by contending that the society was "gotten up in other regions with a view of keeping Schuylkill County in idleness." The most important part of the letter suggested a link between the secret union and the terrorist group, the Mollies. The Knights of Labor, Gowen alleged, contained a section called McNulty's gang whose assignment was "to burn breakers and destroy property."[1]

Gowen's letter had the desired effect. The *Weekly Miners' Journal* congratulated the Reading's "perfect police" for exposing a union gang "whose mission partakes so much of the character of the extinct order of Mollie [sic] Maguires."[2] Parish priests were quick to use the letter against the Knights. In Shenandoah Father Henry O'Reilly read the letter and denounced both the union and the McNulty gang. The priest connected the McNulty gang and the Molly Maguires by naming "Muff" Lawler as a member of the new, allegedly terrorist, group.

Now on the defensive the Knights of Labor sought to improve their reputation. R.E. Diffenderfer, president of Local Assembly 887 in Pottsville, and other Knights petitioned the Schuylkill County Court to arrest the McNulty gang. The court in turn gave the petition to the district attorney, who, not knowing quite what to do with it, let the matter rest.

While the dispute over McNulty was running its course, the Knights of Labor were helpful to the mine workers, and got the credit when the Reading finally paid its employees. In the Shamokin area miners at the Mineral Mining Company had struck against a reduction in the piece rate; supported by the other regions, the strikers had waged a successful seven-week battle against the company.

Encouraged by this limited success the Knights renounced their secrecy on July 23, 1879, by giving a public picnic in Shenandoah. A crowd estimated at ten to fifteen thousand attended the outing and listened attentively to noted speakers U.P. Stephens and Terence V. Powderly. To the uninformed layman the well-attended picnic indicated that the Knights had successfully weathered the storms of opposition raised by the Catholic Church and Franklin B. Gowen. But the cloud of dual unionism was already gathering on the horizon.

Skeptical of the inclusiveness of the Knights, many miners wanted a union exclusively for mine workers. During February 1879 the Lehigh region mine workers moved toward craft unionism by forming the Workingman's Protective Association of the Lehigh Region. At its first meeting the association called for a union embracing both the anthracite and bituminous coal miners. To achieve that end, the Protective Association invited all hard coal miners to send three delegates for every ten collieries to Hazleton on March 1 to consider the possibility of organizing an anthracite group.

A sufficient number of delegates appeared in Hazleton to establish an executive committee composed of representatives from each county. The new industrial union accepted the position of its predecessor, that the difficulties of the mine workers lay in the basic weakness of the anthracite coal mining industry, which they still saw as overproduction. The executive committee also agreed with the now defunct W.B.A. that the mine workers could best help themselves if they would "restrict and systematize productivity." As the first step toward control of production the new union officials called a strike for March 15. The executive committee, hoping to establish a statewide union, requested the bituminous miners to send representatives to meet with the anthracite committee in Harrisburg. At the Harrisburg meeting the representatives confirmed the principle of unity among all mine workers and seconded the strike call for the anthracite industry.

But the anthracite mine workers did not go out on strike. Disappointed by the failure to strike, the Lehigh men began to desert the W.P.A. The weakness of the new union was emphasized when a poorly attended delegates meeting on April 19 agreed not to press any demands on the operators.

A successful strike in the Mahanoy City area, however, prompted the W.P.A. to reconsider.[3] Meeting on July 5 the Lehigh men resolved that "when coal comes under $3.00 per ton we cease work", and demanded a 20-percent increase in pay. The industrial union told the operators to meet the new wage demand by July 10 or face a strike.

The operators ignored the ultimatum, but there was no strike. The miners met on July 16 to discuss what course of action to take, but were unable to decide on anything. They called another meeting for three days later. At the July 19 meeting the association canceled its strike call. Fear that the other regions would not join the strike had dictated the cancellation and prompted a Hazleton newspaper, *The Mountain Beacon*, to advise:

> In union there is strength! Were the miners a unit throughout the anthracite region in their deliberation and resolves, they could control wages, keep coal up at a fair price, and, in fact, be complete "masters of the situation." But ill-advised strikes at a few collieries while the other sections continue to ship coal to their fullest capacity, should be avoided. Why don't the miners organize so that when a strike is ordered the order will be promptly obeyed from Carbondale to Pottsville and Shamokin and not a pick lifted?[4]

The only industrial organization that appeared capable of reuniting the mine workers was their first union, the W.B.A. In 1880 sixty veterans of the W.B.A. held a reunion in Thompson's Hall in Pottsville and proudly proclaimed the resurrection of the union. "The time is auspicious," they declared, "for it rising phoenix-like from its own ashes and continuing for years to come to be a credit to its members and a means of keeping the coal trade in a prosperous condition."[5] But the sanguine sixty had misread the times; within two months the reincarnated W.B.A. sank back into its ashes.[6]

While the W.B.A. failed as an industrial union alternative to the Knights of Labor, it did provide the foundation for a new union—the Miners and Laborers' Amalgamated Association. In 1883 the bituminous coal miners in Illinois, Ohio, Pennsylvania, and Maryland formed the Amalgamated Association of Miners of the United States. Hoping to enroll the anthracite mine workers, the association sent an organizer, George Harris, into the hard coal fields.

Harris opened his campaign in Mount Carmel in May 1884. He made his headquarters Woll's Tavern in Pottsville, the old headquarters of the W.B.A. Progress was slow, but by November enough Schuylkill County miners were enrolled to necessitate a formal structure. The new union, however, admitted that the response of the mine workers had failed to meet expectations, and published an appeal for support. The appeal stirred John Parker, a leader and organizer of the old W.B.A., to offer his services to the fledgling union.

Assisted by Parker and other old labor leaders Harris achieved spectacular success during 1885. In May mine workers in Northumberland County perfected an organization. Later that summer the Philadelphia and Reading miners formed a grand district of the Amalgamated. In late November the Schuylkill unit received its charter, and miners in Carbon and Luzerne Counties gradually formed organizations. In late December the Amalgamated reached for the newly arrived immigrants by translating its constitution into Polish.

The new immigrants formed a growing and, for labor, questionable element in the anthracite coal regions. The East Europeans had appeared in the coal fields during the 1860s. During the Civil War the Polish community in Shamokin became large enough to organize the Saint Stanislaus Kostka Beneficial Society. From the southern fields the Slavs moved north; in 1868 Louis Hajdukiewicz, a Pole, arrived in Nanticoke in the Wyoming region after a brief stay in Hazleton. The Italians began to appear during the following decade; by 1878 there was an Italian community in Stockton in the Lehigh region. As can be seen in Table 27, the newer immigrants supplied an ever-increasing proportion of the anthracite laboring force.

Labor men viewed the "Slav invasion" with concern. The new arrivals' lower standard of living posed a serious economic threat.[7] Also, the clannishness of the immigrants and the hostile nativistic reactions disrupted the effort to achieve a truly collective response among the anthracite mine workers. Recognizing the need to enlist the Slavs and Italians, both the Knights of Labor and the Amalgamated tried to accommodate the new

TABLE 27
Immigrant Groups in Anthracite Mines,
by Decades (Percentage)

Decade	Slav and Italian	British and German
1861–1870	1.05	77.30
1871–1880	6.44	57.46
1881–1890	17.65	52.72

Source: Roberts, *Anthracite Industry*, 19.

immigrants. But they were unsuccessful; the Knights remained basically an Irish organization, while the Amalgamated enrolled 30,000 English, Welsh, and German mine workers.

Throughout its existence the Amalgamated maintained a symbolic connection with the Workingmen's Benevolent Association. John Parker played an important role in the organization of both unions. Headquarters of the new organization were in the same building as the old had been, and the M.&L.A.A.'s charter proudly hung next to that of the W.B.A. Each association tended to blame the economic woes of the mine workers on a glutted market. With these links, the Amalgamated probably owed its success to the anthracite mine workers' nostalgia and respect for their first union.

The existence of the Amalgamated, however, could have been a major barrier in the mine workers' attempt to form a union capable of dealing effectively with the mine operators. Attempts at reorganization had resulted in the creation of two unions, each of which could be played against the other by an astute operator. Aware of this danger, the leaders of both organizations sought to coordinate their policies. In November 1885 the executive council of the Amalgamated met with the Knights of Labor and established a joint committee as liaison between the two unions.

Assured of mutual support, both unions attempted to increase wages. On the eve of the joint meeting the Amalgamated demanded that the miners receive nothing less than base wages. The joint committee ratified the demand and requested a consultation with the operators over wages. Most operators ignored the invitation, but the Philadelphia and Reading agreed to pay basis wages during November and December.

Encouraged by its success with the largest company in the

Schuylkill region, the joint committee met in December and specified more detailed demands. It insisted that prices at New York harbor and Philadelphia markets be used in determining coal prices when fixing the basis and that representatives of the mine workers sit with the operators on the wage committee. The two unions also demanded that the wage schedule be not less than the 1875 Lehigh basis and that all inside boys between the ages of 15 and 18 be considered second-class laborers. The committee was partially successful in securing its demands. The Schuylkill Coal Exchange recognized the body and allowed its representatives to sit with the Exchange's wage committee.

The Amalgamated worked for most of the wage demands, but followed the Knights' lead in fighting for the eight-hour work day. In April the joint committee set May 1, 1886 as the deadline for the operators to grant the shorter day. Victory appeared within reach when the Reading agreed to the eight-hour day provided that the other operators also agreed. Unfortunately, the remaining operators were not as generous as the Reading, and the joint committee quietly dropped the issue.

The committee could nevertheless claim some success. Through its efforts the Schuylkill region mine workers gained representation on the wage committee for the first time in 11 years. The most powerful corporation in the southern region had yielded to demands for basis wages and the eight-hour day. But despite this qualified success, inter-union tension soon threatened to destroy the Joint Committee.

The tension between the two unions erupted in 1887 when the Amalgamated issued a demand for a 10-percent increase in wages. The Knights agreed to support the new wage schedule. But when the miners around Scranton, who were mostly Knights, refused to ask their employers for the wage increase, the joint committee withdrew the demand. Quick-tempered members of the industrial union considered the action of the Scranton Knights a breach of faith. Writing to the *Weekly Miners' Journal*, "Miner" described the Knights as "being composed of the giddy youth" and advised that "one organization is all that is necessary in the coal region."[8]

Discord between the Knights and the craft unions also tended to disturb the harmony created by the joint committee. The executive board of the Miners and Mine Laborers' National Federation, to which the M.&L.A.A. maintained some allegiance, called for abolishing the methods of National Trade

Assembly 135, the Knights' mining organization. The Amalgamated refused to join in the Federation's war.

Weakened by grassroots acrimony and national discord, the
joint committee nevertheless attained a substantial victory at
Harrisburg for the mine workers. During 1887 both unions
lobbied for a law requiring the semimonthly payment of wages.
Despite lobbying by the operators in return, the legislation
was passed.

The Amalgamated was encouraged by the success in Harrisburg to reopen the wage question. In August it demanded a 15
percent increase in wages. The joint committee ratified the
action of the Amalgamated by calling for a strike on September
10 against any operator who refused to grant the demand or to
negotiate.

Reaction to the strike call varied from region to region. The
poorly organized Wyoming-Lackawanna region did not obey the
call, and the Schuylkill region largely evaded the strike when
the bankrupt but still powerful Philadelphia and Reading
opened last-minute negotiations. The railroad agreed to an 8
percent increase until January 1, 1888, pending settlement in
other areas. Most Schuylkill independent operators followed
the Philadelphia and Reading's lead.[9]

The Lehigh independents, however, led the large companies
in rejecting labor's ultimatum.[10] Ario Pardee Sr., spokesman
for the Hazleton independent operators, bluntly stated: "Our
position always has been and is now that we are unwilling to
treat with anyone outside our employ, who knows nothing of
our business and who is no way connected with us, and we are
just as firm in that position as we ever have been."[11] Twenty
thousand miners tested the firmness of the operators by walking
out.

Mine operators adopted two strikebreaking strategies—
reopening and starvation. As labor leaders feared, the operators
tried wooing the new immigrants back to work, but to the surprise of everyone, the Slavs and Italians supported the strike.
Many immigrants even left the region rather than take part in
strikebreaking. In management's view, if resident Slavs and
Italians refused to fight management's battle, willing immigrants could be found elsewhere; as early as September 11,
Calvin Pardee brought in a group of Italians to break the strike.

The strikers greeted the "black legs" with violence. At the
Humbolt colliery near Hazleton, Hungarian strikers attacked

Hungarian "scabs" and both sides suffered casualties. Soon there was more extreme violence. In November unknown assailants shot two strikebreakers, John and Henry Miller, as they returned home from work. Many citizens also suspected the strikers of being guilty of arson after three breakers burned to the ground within a week.

The mine operators might have been able to use the acts of violence to rally public support behind them had they not alienated many by their use of strikebreakers. In December there were rumors that the operators were importing Belgian miners, which brought a strong protest:

> The talk of the Lehigh operators importing Belgians to operate their mines is the merest subterfuge. Such action would not only be a violation of law but would be fruitful of consequences which would consign its projectors to ignominy such as would make them wish they themselves had gone to Belgium instead of bringing Belgium to the anthracite coal regions of Pennsylvania. Can it be possible that these operators are becoming demented to talk such stuff?[12]

In Washington, Congressman Charles N. Brumn (Republican-Greenbacker) supported the interests of his labor constituents by submitting a resolution requesting the President to enforce the 1885 immigration act. The Treasury Department instructed its Boston, New York, Philadelphia, and Baltimore customs men to detain any Belgian miners entering those ports. The scare subsided when the Philadelphia customs office detained 12 Belgian miners.

Significantly, at least one large company, the Lehigh-Wilkes-Barre Coal Company, did not join with the independents in their drive to break the strike. W.H. Tillinghast, the company's president, noted earlier actions by independent operators and advised his superintendent in the Lehigh region: "whilst I would be glad to start one or two of our collieries, I would *not risk any contest* with the men." "If we could only resume by the request of our men," Tillinghast later explained, "it would be a great point gained."[13]

By November the independent operators saw the wisdom of Tillinghast's advice and, using the base wage as bait, tried to lure the mine workers from their unions. Higher coal prices resulted in an automatic 4½ percent increase in wages. The operators offered to pay the normal increase but refused to recognize the unions, while the strikers spurned what they felt to be a bribe.[14]

Unable to reopen, management waited until the necessities of the men forced them back. Operators evicted strikers from company housing, but labor staved them off by obtaining a temporary restraining injunction. Temporarily assured of shelter, the miners faced the greater threat of hunger.

The operators used various means in attempting to reduce the miners to starvation. A. Pardee and Company's flour mill shut down and refused to deliver flour to the company's stores. Other company stores simply refused to advance credit to the strikers. Coal also became scarce; by December the mining town of Freeland faced a "coal famine."

Not content with denying their employees access to company stores and coal, the mine operators attempted to prevent the strikers from trading with other merchants. G.B. Markle and Company in Hazleton refused to pay August wages to its striking employees at the end of September. When in October the company finally paid for work done in August, the paymaster deducted four months advance rent, which left the men with little or no cash. Individual operators used their influence to prevent the strikers from getting temporary employment. In October superintendents of G.B. Markle and Company toured a drainage ditch construction site between Eckley and Harleigh and pointed out strikers, who were promptly fired. Ario Pardee put pressure on the Hazleton Steam Heating Company to discharge striking miners. Undeterred, the strikers sang:

> In looking o'er the papers now
>   A funny thing appears,
> Where Eckley Coxe and Pa dee say
>   They'll stand for twenty years,
> If God should call us miners off,
>   We'll have children then alive,
> Who will follow in our footsteps
>   Keep the strike for thirty-five.[15]

There were two reasons for the miners being able to withstand the starvation campaign. Many found work elsewhere. Both the Schuylkill and Lackawanna regions, operating full time, found in the strikers a willing pool of skilled manpower; in the Schuylkill region the Philadelphia and Reading hired 500 Lehigh miners and the Delaware, Lackawanna and Western in the Wyoming region found room for 400. Strikers also sought work in the cities or in the West. Indeed, it was estimated that not less than 5,000 strikers found work in other areas.[16]

Strikers who stayed where they were received outside support. Organized labor raised relief funds. The national executive board of the Knights of Labor issued a "red circular" and distributed it along with a personal appeal by Terence V. Powderly for donations. District and local assemblies responded generously; the Reading railroaders pledged a relief fund of $100,000, and contributed a day's wages toward their goal. The Schuylkill miners agreed to a 5 percent assessment for the benefit of the Lehigh strikers. By issuing orders drawn on local merchants rather than opening their own stores, the strikers astutely distributed the relief funds.

Businessmen supplemented the support of organized labor. Local editors viewed the strike as an issue on which they had to take a stand:

> For years have the intelligent people of this region been looking upon this picture of despair, but they like the toilers have been deaf, dumb and blind until now. The time has come, however, when silence ceases to be a virtue, and we believe that if the strikers will stand united they may be successful.[17]

Finding their voice, local newspapers chastised the operators:

> The tactics of the petty nabobs of Lehigh are more like the antics of the old time Russian despots in dealing with their serfs, than the conduct of American employers towards American workingmen.[18]

> It [the strike] points out very clearly that public opinion is moulded in favor of the miners in this struggle of might against right; the defiant stand taken by operators against what is only fair and just, has awakened the American people to the fact that a few millionaires have combined together to defeat the mining class of people in their endeavors to get a fair compensation for a fair days [sic] labor.[19]

Editors not only defended the miners' cause, they furthered it by pointing out that the philanthropy of the local independent operators benefited other areas and the "petty coal kings" kept company stores which were a "drawback to legitimate business houses."[20]

It was understandable that local businessmen would attack the company stores by supporting labor. Hazleton merchants subscribed to *The Plain Speaker*'s relief fund. Businessmen in the Schuylkill region aided the miners in their fight against "autocrats who do not possess the ordinary instincts of good Christians nor respectful citizens" by organizing themselves as financial auxiliaries to the unions.[21] Pottsville merchants, for example, organized the "Business Men's Relief Organization of Pottsville" to raise funds for the strikers.

Other members of the "middle class" in the anthracite regions also supported the strikers. Reverend T.M. Bateman, pastor of the Hazleton Primitive Methodist Church, gave a series of ten lectures to raise money for a Christmas dinner for the striking miners, and Roman Catholic priests refused to exert their influence against the strike. Even the civil authorities supported the strike by detaining would-be strikebreakers for "nonpayment of taxes."

Merchants took an active role in the strike. Labor believed that the Lehigh Valley Railroad was helping the more resolute independents to maintain the strike by threatening wavering operators with rate increases. Spurred by the threat of being boycotted themselves, local merchants joined labor's boycott against the Lehigh Valley. Attention, however, soon switched to the Reading.

The Reading's decision in September to negotiate created excellent labor relations which the company cultivated by hiring Lehigh strikers and selling excursion tickets to a benefit for the Lehigh miners at the Philadelphia Academy of Music. But as the strike continued, labor began to question the good intentions of the Reading, whose greatly increased production aroused suspicions that it was helping the Lehigh operators meet their contracts. Many miners also feared that the Reading agreed to enter the battle when its temporary agreement with the unions pending settlement in other areas expired.

A strike on the Reading substantiated these suspicions. The strike occurred when the Reading at Port Richmond dismissed Knights of Labor who refused to deliver a carload of flour to the Philadelphia Grain Elevator Company. Determined that "the company will hereafter operate its own road if it takes a regiment of military at every point," the Reading fired and blacklisted the striking Knights; even Operator Kane, who had lost a leg in railroad service, was caught in the sweep.[22] The Reading enjoyed the services of a valuable ally in its fight against the Knights; a spokesman for the Brotherhood of Locomotive Engineers gloated: "The Knights are knocked out, and the Brotherhood had a hand in doing it. We are pledged to stand by the Company and we have a man ready at any moment to take charge of every engine on the entire system."[23]

The Reading's action spread fear and anger among the

Schuylkill miners. In December they requested a continuation of the 8 percent increase due to expire January 1, 1888. Arguing that coal prices would not permit an extension, Austin Corbin, the president of the Reading, refused to negotiate, and his miners walked out on January 3, 1888. Independent operators were willing to grant the continuation to avoid a strike, but ran afoul of the railroad strike when their miners refused to dig coal which would be hauled by the Reading. The Schuylkill strike was a combination of two strikes, both aimed at the Reading.

Proclaiming that the Reading had driven "the individual coal operators out of business," labor began a legal campaign to separate the railroad from its coal mining subsidiary. Labor cited Pennsylvania's 1874 Constitution, which prohibited railroads from owning mining property, and, supported by the Constitutional Defense Association, petitioned state authorities to initiate quo warranto proceedings against the Reading. But the state authorities could do little since the Reading enjoyed ex post facto protection.[24]

Frustrated at the state level, labor turned to Washington, where the unions petitioned the House of Representatives to investigate the Reading. The response to the petition triggered intra-party strife when Samuel J. Randall, Democratic state chairman of Pennsylvania, sought to extend the scope of the investigation to embarrass his chief rival, William L. Scott, who owned coal mines in the Shamokin area, and Eckley B. Coxe, who, rumors held, was being considered as a candidate for state chairman by anti-Randall forces. The political maneuvers resulted in an investigation of the anthracite labor troubles. Under Chairman George D. Tillman, "Pitchfork Ben's" brother, the investigating committee discovered a pool of anthracite operators regulating production and prices, along with a conspiracy to destroy labor unions. The committee suggested legislation divorcing railroads from mining.

But the Congressional investigation was a hollow victory. No legislation was passed, and the miners succumbed to the power of the Reading. Before the strike the Reading had attempted to overawe the mine workers by increasing its Coal and Iron Police force. After the strike began the company tried to break the strike by importing immigrants. It brought in 260 Italians to reopen its Mahanoy City colliery, for example.

If the strikebreaking technique was not a complete success

immediately, management entertained no doubts over the out-come of the strike. Testifying before the Congressional com-mittee, A.S. Whiting, the Reading's general superintendent, explained his confidence:

> Question: "You say these striking men will come back and go to work?"
>
> Whiting: "Yes, sir."
>
> Question: "On your terms?"
>
> Whiting: "At the old rates; yes sir."
>
> Question: "What force do you rely on to bring these men back?"
>
> Whiting: "Well, sir, their necessities."
>
> Question: "Starved out, do you mean?"
>
> Whiting: "I did not say we would keep them out until they starve. I did not propose to put it in that shape."[25]

If the Reading did not overtly propose to starve the men into submission, it nevertheless did all it could to hasten the day when "necessities" would force the men back to work at the old rates. The company evicted strikers. Lacking company stores, the Reading could not deny credit, but it added to the discomfort of the strikers by refusing to sell coal in the region during the strike.

The starvation tactics of the Reading only reinforced the miners' faith in unionism. Fathers denounced sons who broke the strike and children refused to share their schoolbooks with "scabs." But the men could not live by faith alone, and the Schuylkill strikers failed to obtain adequate relief funds.

Unable to view the strikes against the Reading as an attack on the company store, as they viewed the Lehigh strike, local businessmen refused to support the miners.[26] Local editors, having come full circle now, violently disagreed with the metro-politan newspapers which considered the strike as being "pro-voked by rank injustice," and insisted that the Reading was not under any obligation to continue the compromise agreement. Schuylkill newspaper publishers described the Congressional committee as "These Boors," and lectured the committee on the moral difference between a pool formed to regulate an industry suffering from overproduction and one formed for speculative purposes. Merchants, anxious to end the strike, urged Reading's president Corbin to make minor concessions, but labor would not settle for less than a contract extension, so Corbin refused to negotiate. Rebuffed by both capital and labor, local business turned against labor. Storekeepers wrote public letters denouncing the strike and its leaders and added force to their words by denying credit. No Protestant minister stepped forward to aid the strikers, and the Catholic clergy denounced the unions and their strikes.

Loss of public support and a growing disenchantment within the ranks was seriously weakening the Schuylkill strike. As the strike began to collapse, the mine workers became violent. Attacks on black legs became more frequent. Some mine workers threatened the strikebreakers with death; once again Molly Maguire notes circulated. The growing tendency toward violence among the strikers and a full complement of heavily armed private police could only result in a riot.

The riot occurred in Shenandoah in February 1888. The Shenandoah strikers had become restive in late January when the manager of the William Penn colliery posted notices that he would reopen in February. On February 2nd angry strikers threw stones at black legs as they entered the mine, but failed to stop the reopening. Elated by the success of the William Penn, yet cautioned by the rock-throwing, other mine operators started to reopen under Coal and Iron Police protection. At quitting time on February 3, a crowd gathered at the West Shenandoah colliery, attempting to discourage the strikebreakers from returning to work the next day. As they began to throw rocks the Coal and Iron Police moved in and arrested several strikebreakers. During the scuffle one officer was knocked to the ground whereupon he and other policemen fired into the crowd, wounding three.

The angry crowd followed the Coal and Iron Police to Squire Shoemaker's and demanded the release of the arrested stone-thrower (the others had escaped during the excitement). The stoning of his home convinced Shoemaker that discretion was the better part of valor, and he released the prisoner. Meanwhile the city authorities arrested two Coal and Iron policemen and took them before Squire Monaghan. A crowd quickly gathered at Monaghan's and demanded that the policemen be turned over to them, but were dispersed by a sheriff's posse.

On February 4 another crowd of miners assembled at the Keehley Run colliery to hurl both their scorn and something more substantial at the strikebreakers. The Coal and Iron Police escorts contained the crowd until the workers safely escaped. Their job done, the police were retreating to their base at Indian Ridge colliery when a stone struck an officer. The police fired a volley which wounded six. The second shooting ended the riot and by that evening order had been restored.

With the successful reopening of the William Penn colliery the strike effort was seriously weakened; wholesale desertion followed. The frustrated miners tried to stem the adverse tide with violent means, but the presence of heavily armed Coal and Iron Police was proof to the miners that management still commanded overwhelming power.[27]

With its front crumbling, labor sought peace. W.T. Lewis, Master Workman of the Miners' National Trade Assembly, ordered the Knights of Labor back to work on February 17. The Amalgamated, however, held out six days longer and returned with a face-saving reduction in the cost of mining supplies. The victorious Corbin magnanimously donated $20,000 for the relief of the destitute miners. The Lehigh strikers, discouraged by the Schuylkill example and by the systematic discharge by Lackawanna operators of those hired earlier in the strike, had to forget their promise to hold out 35 years; they began to return to work in late February. On March 4 the unions capitulated. The defeated miners, however, did not receive charity from the victorious operators in the Lehigh region: "Dont suppose any of our men made themselves particularly obnoxious during the strike; if they did you can gradually, without causing comment, weed them out after work is resumed."[28]

The failure of the 1887-88 strikes completely demoralized the anthracite mine workers' second attempt to organize. Disillusioned and frustrated, the mine workers began to desert their unions. Although not completely destroyed, neither the Knights of Labor nor the Miners' and Laborers' Amalgamated would regain its former strength.

Chapter

11

The Final Organization

The mine operators defeated but did not destroy the two unions in the 1887-88 strikes; now both the Knights and the Amalgamated vainly endeavored to regain lost ground. Officers of the Miners' National Trade Assembly of the Knights of Labor devoted some time to salvaging their disintegrating organization in the anthracite coal fields. In January 1889 Robert Watchorn, secretary-treasurer of the National Assembly, made a lecture tour of the hard coal fields. John Hart, an organizer, went with Watchorn and concentrated on rebuilding Division 12, which encompassed the Schuylkill region.

Hart had only temporary success with rebuilding. The 29 delegates attending the division's April meeting reported an increase of 1,300 members. Hoping to further swell its membership, the division imported five "General Speakers" to spread the message about unionism during a month-long series of lectures. The revival meeting technique, however, proved ineffective; poor attendance forced the cancellation of the June assembly.

Not dismayed by the poor response, national officers of the M.N.T.A. continued their efforts to reorganize the hard coal fields. To increase the stature of the union among the mine workers, they convened their 1889 national assembly at Wilkes-Barre. But the boast that the M.N.T.A. had 25,000 members failed to impress the anthracite mine workers.[1] The efforts of the national officers of the Knights of Labor benefited somewhat the few remaining local and district unions in the anthra-

131

cite fields, but the Knights failed to provide adequate leadership in the anthracite mine workers' quest for reorganization.

The Amalgamated also failed. The Miners' and Laborers' Amalgamated Association tried to renew interest in unionism among the mine workers by importing top-level speakers. In May 1888 Daniel McLaughlin, a member of the Illinois legislature, president of the Miners' Protective Association of Illinois, and vice president of the American Federation of Labor, accepted an invitation by the Amalgamated to stump the region on behalf of the union. Unfortunately the effect of McLaughlin's tour cannot be measured, but in July the Shamokin miners reorganized their local union. Heartened by this action, the executive council of the Amalgamated called on all mine workers to help themselves by "enrolling under the banner of organization."[2] Apparently few miners wished to help themselves, for the council renewed its appeal the next month.

Developments at the national level, however, were encouraging. In late 1888 the Amalgamated was invited to a merger meeting of National Trade Assembly 135 and the American Miners' Federation (the A.F. of L.'s miners' union). During the meeting William T. Lewis, Master Workman of Trade Assembly 135, and his partisans bolted the Knights of Labor and joined the federation, which promptly reorganized itself as the Miners' National Progressive Union.

The M.N.P.U. strove to draw the anthracite regions into its organization. In February 1889 Thomas W. Davis and J.J. Fritzpatrick, vice president and member of the new union's executive board, respectively, spoke in the Mahanoy City area. After Davis and Fritzpatrick had left, the mine workers held a mass meeting in Ashland to discuss the possibility of affiliating with the new union. Hearing of the proposed meeting, the executive board of the M.N.P.U. sent the anthracite mine workers an open letter reminding them that "God helps those who help themselves."[3] The miners resolved to help themselves by associating with the new union.

Elated by the display of confidence in Ashland, the M.N.P.U. aided the organizational drive of the Amalgamated by sending P.H. Donnely, an organizer, into the hard coal regions. Donnely remained in the field for several months, but was unable to increase the union's membership. The executive council of the Amalgamated held sporadic meetings throughout 1889, but, with the exception of planning and erecting a monument to the late John Siney, it was unable to accomplish anything.

Although helped by national organizations, the Knights of Labor and the Amalgamated failed to recover the ground lost during the 1887-88 strikes. The refusal of the mine workers to reenlist in a collective effort gave the operators the opportunity to scrap the unions' earlier achievements. Wages quickly dropped; in June 1888 Schuylkill region miners received 10 percent less wages than in the same month the previous year. Small independent operators refused to comply with the semi-monthly wage guidelines. Independent mine owners also forced their employees to sign the "dockage confession," by which the miners waived their right to seek redress for illegal dockage. "If 'the dockage confession' should become a recognized institution in this country," warned the *Daily Republican*, "there would no longer be any question of the subjugation and practical enslavement of the miners who risk their lives continually that coal barons may live in luxury on the profits of their toil."[4]

Alarmed, the mine workers turned again to unionism for protection. A group of miners met in Pittston in October 1889 and proposed the formation of a new union to "comprise all miners of the Anthracite regions."[5] They demonstrated some political know-how by suggesting that the organization should nominate legislative candidates. Economically the new union would create a "Labor Exchange," consisting of the union's general superintendent, general secretary, and grand adviser, which would meet and discuss problems with the coal pool. The delegates at the Pittston meeting nominated Franklin B. Gowen for the post of grand adviser and recommended that the grand adviser receive a $10,000 annual salary, a suggestion too ludicrous for serious consideration.

The mine workers, however, did pay some attention to renewed efforts on the part of the Amalgamated to reestablish itself. In November 1889 the Amalgamated's executive council opened its reorganization campaign by boasting of its record: "During the active days of the M.&L.B.A. in this region wages were higher and times generally better than any period in many years, in fact no percentage reductions were made between November, 1885, and July, 1888, or until the men themselves grew indifferent towards organization."[6] After their braggadocio the executive council appealed to the men "to organize for mutual protection." In December the union attempted to stimulate enrollment by abolishing its initiation fee.

The executive council had some success in its drive to enlarge the union; mine workers in Park Place and Saint Clair reorganized their defunct branches. Elated by the renewed activity, the Amalgamated called a mass meeting of mine workers for February 22, 1890 and explained:

> ... the object of said meeting to be, to consider and take such action as is deemed necessary on the advisability of cementing existing organizations and urge all unorganized men into one organization covering the whole anthracite region that will look after the interests of the mine workers of this section and endeavor by practical organized effort to bring about more satisfactory results.[7]

The explanation is important because it demonstrates that the anthracite mine workers had local unions; they lacked only a general association.

Thirty-three delegates attended the February meeting to discuss the founding of an industrywide union. After some deliberation the representatives agreed to meet during the following month, and resolved that there should be "one organization for the whole anthracite region and that the organization should be an open one."[8] Slightly more delegates (41) convened for the second conference and voted in favor of one union, to be called the Workingmen's Benevolent and Protective Association.

During the April meeting the delegates outlined the W.B.P.A.'s objectives. The new union proposed to organize all mine workers and cooperate with other labor unions to secure fair wages. It would enforce existing laws and urge the passage of others for the mine workers' benefit. The new union also demanded a strict enforcement of the anti-contract labor laws. The most interesting aspect of the new organization was its conservative attitude. The W.B.P.A. promised that it would substitute arbitration for strikes and that it would "cultivate a closer relationship between employer and employee." To guarantee the closer relationship the new union pledged itself to "discountenance and ignore any attempts on the parts of its members to infringe upon the rights of his employer."[9]

In June the new movement gained momentum as the Wyoming-Lackawanna men began to organize, and representatives from every anthracite county attended the meeting that month. The meeting considered favorably a demand by the delegate from Saint Clair that an organizer be placed in the field, and appointed John Bell to that position. The W.B.P.A., however, was unable to maintain its impetus; in August the prospect of poor attendance forced the cancellation of the delegates' meeting.

To some extent, the W.B.P.A.'s decline can be attributed to opposition from the operators. The Philadelphia and Reading fired its employees who had attended the March organizational meeting and prevented three others from attending the April conference by insisting that they remain at work. "In some countries, this would be called tyranny," remonstrated the *Daily Republican*, "in free America it is practiced with impunity, and there is no redress for the oppressed."[10]

But tyranny did not completely account for the decline of the union. The W.B.P.A. was amazingly lax; until spurred by the Saint Clair men, it did not put an organizer in the field. Moreover, the conservatism of the union had as little appeal for the rank and file as the Pittston meeting's suggestion that Franklin B. Gowen be appointed grand adviser to labor.

Numerous strikes during this period indicate that although the mine workers shunned the W.B.P.A. they had not discarded the idea of a union, of organized protest. Most strikes were local, and usually ended in defeat. Failure at the local level made the miners keenly aware of the need for wider action. Unable to found a general organization by themselves, they turned to the United Mine Workers of America.

The United Mine Workers of America was the result of a merging of Miners' National Trade Assembly 135 of the Knights of Labor and the American Miners' Federation. In 1885 the Federation replaced the defunct Amalgamated Association of Miners as an industrial and open union alternative to the Knights of Labor. After a bitter fight the two organizations held an unsuccessful merger conference in 1888; as mentioned above, only a portion of the Knights joined the Federation to form the Miners' National Progressive Union. The two unions finally settled their differences in 1890, however, and formed the United Mine Workers.

The Saint Clair men were the first anthracite miners to notice the U.M.W. In their appeal to the Workingmen's Benevolent and Protective Association for an organizer, the Saint Clair local suggested that the W.B.P.A. request the services of either the American Federation of Labor or the United Mine

Workers if an organizer could not be found within the W.B.P.A. The appointment of John Bell precluded the establishing of a liaison with the new U.M.W.

In June 1892 the Shamokin men organized a U.M.W. local union, thus bringing the U.M.W. into the anthracite regions. But the national union experienced some difficulty in spreading beyond its Shamokin base; it took more than a year for word of a new organization to circulate. It was in November 1893 that George Harris, the organizer of the Miners and Laborers' Amalgamated Association, stumped the Schuylkill region on behalf of unionism. A stimulating speaker, Harris usually left an embryonic local union in his wake.

After Harris had laid the groundwork, the United Mine Workers began to blossom. In August 1894 the new union was strong enough to call its first district convention. Not much is known about this meeting, but delegates from the entire Schuylkill region attended the district's second convention in November. By January 1895 the district boasted 63 local unions and sent ten delegates to the U.M.W. national convention.

Despite its quick blossoming the U.M.W. failed to put down deep roots in the anthracite regions. The new organization represented only the Schuylkill region, and past experience had shown that a union that did not include all three regions died quickly. Within the Schuylkill region the U.M.W. failed to enlist the new immigrants who were fast becoming the major element in the anthracite labor force.

The failure of the new union to establish itself firmly among the anthracite mine workers explains the reaction of management. The operators ignored the request of the U.M.W. for representation on the wage committee. During the Centralia strike of 1896 the Lehigh Valley Coal Company refused to let the union intercede because mediation would be viewed as recognition of the union.

The U.M.W. acknowledged its own weakness; with the exception of an occasional bid for employer recognition and a declaration against the basis system of wages, it concentrated its activities on politics. In September 1895 the new union gathered data on the violation of the 1887 semimonthly wage law, which it turned over to the state factory inspector. The U.M.W. also fought a bill allowing tax collectors to attach the wages of miners. The union joined the middle class in the coal regions in launching a legislative campaign against the company store. The anti-company store movement accomplished nothing.

The U.M.W. did succeed in securing one desired law. John Fahy, the U.M.W. organizer, was convinced by nativist propaganda and the new immigrants' hesitancy to join the union that the two factors were a major obstacle to the organization of the anthracite regions. Accordingly he traveled to Harrisburg to lobby for an anti-immigrant law. Aided by two other union leaders Fahy secured the passage of the Campbell Act, which taxed employers three cents per day for each adult immigrant on their payrolls.[11]

The anthracite mine owners shifted the burden to the immigrant by deducting the tax from his wages.[12] By doing so, the operators also shifted the odium of the tax from the union to themselves. During the strike of 1897 the operators would reap the consequences.

The strike of 1897 began as a reaction to one man's personality. Gomer Jones looked upon his appointment to the superintendency of the Honeybrook division of the Lehigh-Wilkes-Barre Coal Company, near Hazleton, as a challenge. Replacing weaker men, Jones restored discipline through sternness and wholesale firing; his men hated him, while the middle class in the area condemned his "arrogance."[13] Oblivious to these feelings, Jones further alienated his employees by inaugurating several economies. Part of his retrenchment program called for a centralized stable at the Company's Audenreid stripping operations.

Noting that the location of the new stable would require two hours of extra work per day, 35 immigrant mule drivers at Stripping Number 5 struck on Saturday, August 14, and set up a picket line. Jones viewed the strike as a disciplinary problem; brandishing an ax handle he threatened the pickets with corporal punishment. Seeing the object of their resentment thus armed, the men attacked Jones. Jones, aided by a friend, managed to escape, but not before he hit a striker with his club. News of the event quickly spread; by that evening 800 mine workers around Audenreid walked off their jobs in protest. On Monday 2,000 joined the mule drivers' strike by refusing to work until the company discharged Jones.

The strike increased without benefit of "any recognized leader." Realizing the need for organization the strikers requested the aid of John Fahy in forming a U.M.W. local. In the interim the miners created a temporary committee and elected Joseph Keshilla, a Hungarian, president and Nille Duse, an Italian, vice president. The election reflected the strike's personnel: immigrants had started and maintained the strike while the "American" miners refused to participate. The fact that the immigrants were no longer docile came as a welcome surprise; local editors gloated over what they considered to be poetic justice: "The strike now in progress on the South Side has furnished an object lesson that it will be well for the operators in this section to make note of. The day of the slave driver is past, and the once ignorant foreigner will no longer tolerate it."[14]

The company tried to end the dangerous lesson quickly. It fired foremen and clerks who sympathized with the strikers. Two squads of Coal and Iron Police patrolled the area with Winchester rifles. Neither tactic impressed the strikers; they stood firm. "Never in all our experience." reported the *Daily Standard*, "have we met a more determined body of strikers than was found in the several patches."[15]

Unable to frighten the miners back to work, the company next tried diplomacy. Its first offer was a promise to negotiate after the men returned to work. But the immigrants refused to consider the proposition. Finally General Superintendent Elmer H. Lowall ended the strike by revoking the stable order and promising to investigate Gomer Jones within ten days.

But industrial peace did not return to the Hazleton area. The alien tax law went into effect on August 21, and on August 26 the immigrants at Coleraine struck for a wage increase that would cover the new tax. The foreigners spread the strike by marching to Milnesville and Beaver Meadows. Meanwhile the original strikers at Audenreid grew impatient as the Lehigh–Wilkes-Barre Coal Company proved lax in opening the Gomer Jones investigation; when the ten-day period expired they joined the strike.

As they had in the first strike, immigrants provided the initiative and leadership. "Holy Mother!" exclaimed an Irishman, "is it mesilf that's quittin fer the shallow faced spalpeens?"[16] Under immigrant leadership the strikers formulated their demands: a 15 percent wage increase; the right to select and pay their own physician; and an end to the company store. To these traditional demands the immigrants added another of their own—the same wages as "Americans." Armed with a pro-

gram the strikers marched from colliery to colliery forcing the
men at each one to quit work. By September 6 the marchers
had closed down most of the mines on the south side of Hazleton.

On September 6 the operators called for police protection.
Three counties—Luzerne, Carbon, and Schuylkill—touched
Hazleton's south side, and the counties' three sheriffs responded. Sheriff Alexander Scott of Schuylkill County took a
posse to McAdoo, but finding the marchers in McAdoo orderly,
he returned to Pottsville after reading a riot proclamation. Upon
his return to the county seat, Scott stated that his trip was a
waste of the taxpayers' money because the strikers were not a
threat to private property. Sheriff James Martin of Luzerne
County did not agree with Scott, nor did he worry about the
taxpayer. Coal and Iron Police formed most of his 150-man
posse while the operators furnished the posse's arms and wages.
On September 10 Sheriff Martin used part of his well-endowed
posse to protect private property in Lattimer.

At first the strike bypassed A. Pardee and Company's mine
patch of Lattimer, which lay on Hazleton's north side. But when
Pardee's Harwood mine employees organized a U.M.W. local
the immigrants at the Lattimer mine requested the aid of the
Harwood men in closing down the Lattimer mine. The south-
side strikers could not resist the temptation to shut down the
entire Hazleton area. After several disappointing sorties they
began their march northward on September 10 without arms
and behind two American flags.

At the Hazleton city limits the marchers met Mayor Altmiller,
who refused to permit the men to parade through the town.
The strikers then took a circular route and confronted Sheriff
Martin in West Hazleton. Martin vainly tried to stop the march.
Angered by their failure, Martin and his deputies took a trolley
to Lattimer, where they established a picket line across the
public highway. When the marchers arrived in Lattimer the
sheriff repeated his demand that the parade cease. Suddenly
Martin either fell or was pushed aside and his posse fired into
the unarmed strikers. The deputies fired with cool and deliber-
ate aim, hitting some of the marchers in the back as they ran
for cover. When the smoke finally cleared, more than 50 strikers, mostly immigrants, lay dead or wounded.

"Strikers shot in cold blood," screamed the *Pottsville Republican*, and most of the middle class in the coal regions agreed.[17]

The Daily Standard editorialized: "It was not a battle, because the strikers were not aggressive, nor were they on the defensive, because they had no weapons of any kind and were simply shot down like so many worthless objects, each of the licensed life takers trying to out-do the other in this butchery."[18] Mayor Altmiller also protested the shooting:

> When the men declared their intention to march through the city on Thursday, I told them I would not permit it. They advanced as you know to the line and I met them. They then took a circuitous route without quarreling with anyone and without disturbance. They were handled on this occasion without difficulty and I believe that they could be handled in the same manner all along..[19]

The citizens of Hazleton joined in the chorus at a mass meeting in which they expressed sympathy for the victims and adopted the following resolution:

> Whereas a sad calamity has befallen this community and an unwarranted and uncalled for attack has been made upon peaceful persons seeking redress Resolved, that we, as a body, condemn and deplore such actions which were perpetrated on the public highway without justification or excuse.[20]

The citizens also called for the arrest of the sheriff and requested the governor to keep troops out of the region. But Governor Daniel H. Hastings, perhaps alarmed by the news that a crowd of immigrant miners had raided homes in McAdoo in search of arms, sent the Third Brigade to the Hazleton region the following morning. Local editors viewed the arrival of the troops as another example of the operators running roughshod over the townspeople's wishes.

The citizens of Hazleton, however, refused to be denied. In cooperation with several immigrant societies, they swore out warrants for the arrest of Sheriff Martin and his deputies. Some deputies fled into the militia's lines and the troops refused to allow the warrants to be served. The National Guard finally relinquished its protection and the court held Martin and 73 deputies for trial. The court set bail at $4,000 per person, which the City Trust, Safe Deposit, and Surety Company of Philadelphia provided. The following day the court increased the bail to $6,000 per person and the same company provided the necessary bond.

The wheels of justice ground slowly, but each turn seemed favorable to the prosecutors. In late September the coroner's inquest found the killings unnecessary. The grand jury returned true bills against the sheriff and his deputies in October. But after a five-week trial the jury returned a verdict of not guilty.

The strike continued while interested citizens sought to bring Sheriff Martin and his deputies to justice. The Lattimer shooting had a profound effect on the mine workers. Before the incident, immigrants maintained the strike while the older ethnic stocks remained aloof, but the shooting brought all ethnic groups into the strike. Recognizing defeat, the operators, except for Eckley B. Coxe and Brothers, agreed to readjust their pay scales. Despite the opposition of some angry women, the men returned to work at higher wages.

The anthracite mine workers gained an organization as well as higher wages in the 1897 strike. By early October John Fahy announced that he had completed the organizing of the Hazleton area. But the desire to enroll in the union was not unique to the Hazleton area; shocked by the shooting, mine workers throughout the anthracite fields sought to express their unity with the Lattimer "martyrs" by joining the United Mine Workers. It would take time to perfect the organization of nearly 150,000 men, but the Lattimer shooting made that organization impossible to stop.

During its organization drive the U.M.W. adjusted to the realities of the anthracite regions. John Fahy accommodated ethnocentrism by organizing each immigrant group into separate locals which used the native language of their members. The district form of government allowed the union to resist the centrifugal forces of regionalism. When finally organized, the United Mine Workers divided the anthracite fields into three districts whose boundaries corresponded to regional lines. The Anthracite Tri-District Convention enabled a unification of policy while the powers retained by the national union guaranteed that a district—region—would not be allowed to go its own way.

Thus the anthracite mine workers, demoralized by their defeat in the 1887-88 strikes, rejected the early reorganizational drives by both the Knights of Labor and the Miners and Laborers' Amalgamated Association. The haste of the mine operators to undo the unions' accomplishments, however, stimulated the mine workers to seek protection through collective action, and the hard coal miners at length turned to the United Mine Workers. The U.M.W. saw "new immigrants" as the greatest obstacle to organization and tried to remove them by lobbying for anti-immigrant legislation, but ironically the "new immigrants" made possible the complete organization of the anthracite coal fields by spontaneously striking against the arbitrary actions of Gomer Jones and by shedding their blood during the Lattimer shooting. The Lattimer shooting gave all mine workers a common identity which they expressed by joining the union.

The collective response had been largely a failure; its major achievement was the basis system of wage determination. Yet the basis system did little to restructure the reward system, since the failure of the unions allowed management to manipulate the system for its own benefit. Even if the unions had survived, however, it is doubtful if the basis system would have benefited labor. By tying wages to coal prices, the basis system made labor a victim of the anthracite industry's basic sickness—overinvestment.

Both management and labor realized separately that they were victims of a sick industry. Both mistakenly concluded that the illness was low prices due to overproduction and both applied the same remedy—price maintenance. Price maintenance, however, abated but did not arrest the industry's true disease. Management's technique of maintaining prices, a pool governed by productive capacity, stimulated further investment. The basis system encouraged the existence of marginal capital by automatically reducing labor costs as prices fell. To a large extent, the anthracite mine workers' low wages were the result of the inability by both management and labor to fathom economic reality.

The mine workers had also tried to improve their reward system through the political process. Through their unions they secured legislation granting them the right to hire a checkweigh man and to receive a semimonthly pay. But both laws became dead letters after the collapse of the unions. As in the case of higher wages, the collective response through legal action produced only temporary results.

Yet the fleeting results testified to the value of collective ability. The anthracite mine workers were quick to correlate higher wages and better legal protection with the lifespan of their unions. This correlation, plus the demonstrated futility of direct and violent reaction, convinced the mine workers of the need to restructure their reward system and improve their working conditions by a unified effort.

The Collective Response:
The Physical Plant

The anthracite industry's physical plant produced two major problems for the mine workers. First, it was necessary to reduce the high accident rate of the mines by upgrading safety standards. Since the high cost of improving the safety of a particular mine would be damaging to the competitive position of the operator, management would never acquiesce to such a proposal unless assured that all operators would simultaneously comply. Faced with the need for inclusive and simultaneous compliance, the mine workers turned to the state, which alone possessed enough coercive power to compel universal acceptance of safety standards.

Second, because of the simple fact that even with the cooperation of the state the mines could never be accident-free, the mine workers needed welfare provisions for the victim and his family. A variety of techniques could be used to solve this problem. The state could be asked to provide a welfare program. The mine workers could help their unfortunate colleagues. And management could help its distressed employees, although operators were not likely to establish welfare programs unless they were forced to.

Each of the several techniques for solving the problems projected by the productive system's physical plant presupposed collective activity. Low wages precluded individual savings and made the group the mainspring of self-help. Most important, although the mine workers possessed numbers, the raw material of political power, this resource became meaningful only when organized and directed.

Mine
Safety

The anthracite mine worker, who worked in some of the most dangerous mines in the world, now actively sought higher safety standards. The insistence of the operators that safety regulations be universally applied compelled the mine workers to use political methods to achieve their goal.

Third-party politics provided a means by which the mine workers could attempt to make the political system responsive to their demands. The Workingmen's Benevolent Association had early tried to use this means. Rooted in the eight-hour movement and associated with the political-minded National Labor Union, the W.B.A. naturally joined the Labor Reform movement, and the first Labor Reform Party convention under the auspices of the union in Schuylkill County began on August 16, 1870 at Saint Clair. Each delegate cast one vote for every 300 men represented, and the convention nominated a ticket which crossed major party lines. The new political party expected its candidates to pay their own campaign expenses, but appointed a five-man campaign committee and asked each union district to have three men distribute ballots on election day.

The Labor Reform Party, however, suddenly withdrew its ticket. Nobody explained this action, but the strongly Republican *Miners' Journal* implied that the W.B.A. had made a deal with the Democrats. John Siney, the president of the W.B.A., added credence to the *Journal*'s charges by writing an open letter to the W.B.A.'s newspaper, the *Anthracite Monitor*, after the election urging the formation of a labor party again now that "the election is over."[1]

The labor union held another political convention during the following year, but not because John Siney urged it. The Democratic Party had outraged the union by failing to renominate James McKeon, the "friend of the workingmen," for the legislature. The Labor Reform Party, borrowing occasionally from the larger political organizations, nominated a full ticket. Its platform called for anti-monopoly measures, repeal of the conspiracy act, economy in government, and the establishment of a Bureau of Labor Statistics. The new party endorsed the protective tariff, once again demonstrating the W.B.A.'s identification of labor's welfare with that of the employer. This time the ticket was not withdrawn and the Labor Reform Party showed surprising strength in its first election by receiving approximately one-fourth of the vote in Schuylkill County. The Labor Reform Party in Carbon County received a smaller percentage, while the Northumberland County W.B.A. did not engage in politics.

Exhilarated by its performance, the Schuylkill County Labor Reform Party convened for a second time on August 13, 1872, with great expectations for the forthcoming campaign. Viewing itself as a separate party, the committee on credentials refused to seat delegates who were Democrats. After John Siney, the permanent chairman, quieted a few representatives who had had too much to drink, the convention began selecting candidates. After some debate the party nominated a full ticket, but few liked the results. Siney grumbled about "murdering the infant," and the Mahanoy City branch refused to support the ticket.

The nomination of Cyrus L. Pershing for president judge had caused the disillusionment.[2] Pershing was a native of Cambria County, Pennsylvania, and had never been in Schuylkill County. Prior to his candidacy, he had for 20 years been an attorney for the Pennsylvania Railroad, and many considered him to be Franklin B. Gowen's personal choice. Ironically Pershing was one of the few labor candidates who won the election.

Few mine workers were interested in their third party after the 1872 fiasco; only through the insistence of the Mahanoy City branch was a county convention called in 1874. The convention did not nominate a full ticket, and most of its candidates also sought election under the banner of the Republican Party.

While the Labor Reform Party in Schuylkill County declined, the Wyoming-Lackawanna miners also ventured into third-party politics. In September 1875 a group called the Independent Labor Movement Committee met in Scranton. Concluding that the major parties had ignored the wishes of labor, the committee called for a convention. To insure that the convention would represent only workingmen, the committee requested that each labor union forward to it a list of its delegates. The convention assembled but was unable to adopt a program. The Independent Labor Movement Committee, however, continued to hold meetings during the campaign.

The declining fortunes of the Labor Reform Party led to a merger of this party with the Greenback Party. Greenbackism strongly appealed to the anthracite regions. Heavy capitalization demands made many independent operators receptive to the idea of an inflated currency. In order to service an expanding market, local businessmen favored cheaper credit which, they felt, an inflation would produce. All classes identified the welfare of the anthracite industry with the iron industry, and many iron producers favored the greenback.[3]

In 1877 the Luzerne County Labor and Greenback Parties officially merged, following the state and national trend. The platform of the Greenback-Labor Reform Party called for the abolition of prison labor, criminal rather than civil action against violators of the 1875 wage law requiring standard scales, and a more equitable system of taxation. The party also supported Hendrick B. Wright's Homestead Bill, which would give the prospective homesteader a federal grant to enable him to go west. Thus armed, the Greenback-Labor Reform Party carried the county. The following year the remnants of the Labor Reform Party in Schuylkill County merged with the Greenbackers and carried Mahanoy City, Ashland, Frackville, Gilberton, Shenandoah, and Cass Township.

Despite its early victories the Greenback-Labor Reform Party soon failed. In 1881 the Schuylkill County organization acknowledged its impotency by fusing with the Republican Party; it remained an adjunct to the minority party thereafter. In Luzerne County the third-party organization sought refuge in the Democratic Party.

The failure of the Greenback-Labor Party produced a lull in the mine workers' interest in third parties until Henry George's single tax crusade inspired a revival of political activity. The major result of the renewed interest was the formation of the Land and Labor Party of Luzerne County. During the 1887 campaign the Land and Labor Party called for the application of a single tax, municipal provision of light, heat, and water, postal savings banks and telegraph service, and federal ownership of railroads.[4] The platform had little appeal and the party rapidly declined. With the exception of some flirtation with the Populists, the Land and Labor Party was the last attempt by the anthracite mine workers to create a third party devoted to their interests.

The third-party movement was clearly a failure. The labor parties never enjoyed the allegiance of a majority of the mine workers. Even if all the mine workers had supported the third parties it was improbable that they could control the state legislature; by bloc voting the mine workers could gain control of four counties, hardly a majority in either legislative house.[5]

The anthracite mine workers acknowledged the futility of third-party movements by lobbying within the established system. The mine workers commanded considerable power within the political structure. No local or regional candidate could afford not to respond to their wishes. At the state level, neither party wished to alienate the largest bloc of voters in one of the most populous districts of the Commonwealth. Finally, by dramatizing the humane aspects of safety legislation, the mine workers could enlist other groups in the fight for safer mines.

The Workingmen's Benevolent Association was the first union to organize and direct the miners' political influence. In 1869 the General Council created a Committee on Political Action to guide its political policy. The Committee proposed and the General Council adopted a directive demanding that "each county take judicious action in relation to this fall's election and all bogus legislation and bogus legislators."[6]

After the election the Schuylkill County executive board sent a committee to Harrisburg to lobby for a mine safety law. The lobbyists secured the passage of an act "for the better regulation and ventilation of mines and for the protection of lives of the miners in the County of Schuylkill." The act required the ventilation of mines by either furnace or suction fan and the placing of automatic closing doors (air blocks) to direct the air current. Doors in main passages had to be attended by a boy whose sole function was to prevent their being left open. The act also demanded the employment of a "mine boss" to examine the mine each morning and prohibit miners from entering dangerous places.

The law also took cognizance of the dangers inherent in the mine's transportation system. The state required mine workers to install a signal system between the surface and the bottom of the mine. The act prohibited mine workers from riding loaded cars to the surface under the penalty of a fine not to exceed $50.

A state inspector of mines enforced the safety law. Applicants for the office had to furnish proof of at least ten years' experience in the mines and pass an examination before a board consisting of five practical miners and one mining engineer. Once appointed, the inspector received an annual salary of $3,000 to enable him to devote his full time to the inspection of mines, attending coroner's inquests of mine accident victims, and ascertaining the cause of every serious accident. To better fulfill his duties, the inspector received the power "to enter and inspect the mines and machinery at all reasonable times by day and night."[7]

The 1869 safety act supported the demands of the mine workers that the state enforce safety standards throughout the anthracite industry. Taking advantage of the public concern generated by the Avondale disaster, the General Council sent a committee made up of one member from each county union to Harrisburg to demand more legislation. The lawmakers acquiesced by passing another mine safety act in 1870.

The 1870 law, which was more detailed than the previous act, applied to every anthracite mine in Pennsylvania. Under its provisions a mine operator had to provide two accurate maps of each mine. The mine inspector received the original copy; if the operator failed to submit a map the inspector had the authority to have the map drawn at the expense of the operator.

The act gave mine operators four months to provide their mines with two or more outlets. To make this possible, the operator was given the authority, under court scrutiny, to enter and provide a second outlet upon adjacent lands. If the mine operator refused to provide two or more outlets within the prescribed time, the courts could, upon application of the mine inspector, issue an injunction stopping operation of the mine.

The legislature increased the number of mine inspectors to

six and lowered the experience requirement to five years in anthracite mines. Mine inspectors received the power of a coroner to hold inquests, compel the attendance of persons to testify, and administer oaths. Two boards, one appointed by the court of common pleas in Luzerne County and the other appointed by the Schuylkill County court, composed of three practical miners and two mining engineers, examined candidates for the office. The act provided for the removal of a mine inspector upon the petition of 15 "reputable coal operators or coal miners or both" and an investigation by the court.

The 1870 act also looked beyond the normal safety requirements. Section six required the mine operator to provide and maintain a building "supplied with soft water and properly lighted and warmed, for the use of the men employed in such mine, to wash and change their clothes when entering the mine and when returning therefrom." Section ten prohibited the employment of boys under 12 years of age inside the mines.

Mine operators were understandably anxious to test the constitutionality of the act. They had their opportunity when Inspector T. M. Williams applied for an injunction restraining an operator from working a mine without two openings. The court issued a preliminary injunction, but the operator responded that the act was unconstitutional, and that therefore the injunction should be dissolved. In presenting its decision, the court argued:

> If through the legislature she [the state] can attach conditions, rules, and regulations, which are to be observed by her citizens in the use of their own peculiar property, what is there about coal mines, or the owners thereof, that should especially exempt them from her supervision and control? If she recognizes, almost as part of her organic law, applicable to the property of her citizens, the rule, long ago grown into a maxim, *sic utere tuo ut alienum non laedas*, why may she not make it equally applicable to the lives of her citizens?

"Of its constitutionality," the court concluded, "we have not the slightest doubt."[8]

Although the courts had no doubts over the constitutionality of the law, they were careful to apply only the letter and not the spirit of the law. In 1872 the Court of Common Pleas in Luzerne County refused to issue an injunction to restrain the operation of a mine with only one opening. The court based its decision on the fact that the mine in question was a tunnel, while the act of 1870 specifically stated that slope or shaft mines should contain the second opening.

The mine inspectors, however, did not complain as much about the court's strict interpretation of the law as the delays experienced in getting the cases heard. T. M. Williams grumbled: "The inspector entered this suit after being advised to do so by the district attorney, intending that it should be tried promptly; but despite all his efforts to that effect, it was postponed from one term to another for a year and a half, and the effect intended to produce was entirely lost through the long and tedious delay."[9] It is equally instructive to note the identity of those refusing to obey the law. In 1879 the inspector in the Schuylkill region reported that the Philadelphia and Reading instructed its foremen to comply with all suggestions from the mine inspectors as well as the law. Other inspectors also praised the large corporations for their cooperation and implied that the independent operators were the most troublesome.

The act itself, however, was the major obstacle to enforcement. The inspection districts described in the act were too large to permit a careful examination of all mines. And the hasty writing of the act left many loopholes and oversights. The only chance lay in a revised law.

The mine workers sought a stronger law, but as the strength of the W.B.A. declined the state became less responsive to its demands. In a six-year period the miners were able to secure only two minor amendments to the 1870 act. In 1873 the legislature passed and the governor agreed to an amendment which allowed the examining boards of prospective mine inspectors to act on a majority decision. Three years later the miners secured a supplement to the act which made refusal to supply the mine inspector with adequate and correct maps a misdemeanor.

The 1877 strikes sparked a reorganization drive among the anthracite mine workers; once again the legislature appeared receptive to their demands. In successive sessions the lawmakers passed two minor supplements to the 1870 act. The first amendment enlarged the northern inspection area to include Wayne and Susquehanna Counties. The second required the operators to provide an empty car or cage whenever a group of ten men wished to leave the mine. But the miners did not achieve legislation requiring the furnishing of props.

Traditionally the miners brought propping from a central

timber pile on the surface to their chamber. The practice, however, was conducive to accidents as few miners "wasted" time by going to the surface whenever they needed a prop. The mine inspectors called attention to this potential source of accidents and suggested several remedies. One inspector felt the company should do the propping; another advised extra compensation for timbering; a third suggested that the operator deliver necessary timber to the breasts. During the 1883 session the legislature accepted the third recommendation and required that props be provided upon the miner's request; violators were made liable for any and all damages resulting from their neglect.

During the same session the lawmakers authorized a commission to revise the anthracite mining code. Significantly, the legislature delegated its authority to experts by defining the membership of the commission as the six state mine inspectors and one miner and one operator from each major anthracite county. In 1885 the commission presented a draft law which the legislature adopted with very few changes.

Organized into 19 topical articles and containing tightly defined terms, the anthracite mining act of 1885 was a model piece of legislation.[10] The new law applied to all mines employing more than ten men and boys; it preserved and enlarged with greater precision the provisions of previous laws.

The 1885 act increased the number of inspectors to seven. The inspectors had to visit and examine every mine in their respective districts at least four times a year. If the inspector discovered a dangerous practice which was not covered by the act, he could nevertheless demand that the practice cease. The operator, however, could submit the inspector's demand to an arbitration board consisting of a member selected by each party and a third chosen by the two board members. Any decision reached by a majority of the board was binding.

The act also attempted to provide proper discipline in the mines.[11] Article XII contained 52 "general rules" which applied to every mine. The "general rules" described the duties of all employees and prescribed basic safety regulations. Article XIII permitted the establishment of "special rules" to meet peculiar conditions at particular mines. "Special rules" went into effect 30 days after the mine inspector's approval, and carried the same authority as an enacted law.

Another important feature of the 1885 act was that it required certification of foremen. The Secretary of Internal Affairs granted a certificate of qualification to a prospective foreman after he had given evidence of at least five years' practical experience and had passed an examination before a board composed of the state mine inspector, a practical miner, and an owner or superintendent. Mines could not operate longer than 30 days without the supervision of a certified foreman.

In 1891 the legislature passed another anthracite mining law which increased the inspection districts to eight and changed several "general rules." The lawmakers abolished the provision for "special rules." Under the new act any citizen and not just the mine inspector could begin prosecution for violation of its provisions. The 1891 act also made mandatory the certification of assistant foremen as well as foremen.

The certification of foremen and assistant foremen had unforeseen results. In 1895 the Pennsylvania Supreme Court held that an operator could not be held liable for his foreman's negligence. Certification, the court argued, made the foreman an agent of the state and not of the operator. With the exception of the mine owner's liability for his foreman's actions, the mining acts of 1885 and 1891 successfully withstood court tests.

Enactment of several mining laws did not appreciably reduce the number of accidents; indeed, the accident rate continued to mount. Obviously with an eye on the increasing number of immigrants entering the industry, the miners argued that the laws would become effective after the elimination of inexperienced miners. They therefore clamored for the certification of miners.

In 1889 the legislature gave in to the miners' argument and passed a law providing that only certified miners should be employed in the anthracite mines. To become certified the candidate had to demonstrate that he had at least two years' experience as a mine laborer and pass an examination. Men engaged as miners at the time of passage of the law could be examined and registered after furnishing evidence of having been so employed. The presiding judge in each county appointed the examining board, which consisted of nine miners with at least five years' experience. The examining board received a 50-cent fee for examination and registration out of which the members received their $3-per-day compensation. The act imposed a fine of not more than $100 on persons employing noncertified miners.

The miners, however, discovered many discrepancies in enforcement of the act. They charged the examining boards with being more interested in collecting their fees than in weeding out incompetent candidates. The law failed to prevent the "new immigrants" from becoming miners. Indeed, the requirement of two years' experience as a mine laborer tended to work against the British and German immigrants. Being unskilled, the "new immigrants" had to begin as laborers, but British and German miners refused to become apprentices again. Disappointed, the miners urged major revision and, in extreme cases, the repeal of the act requiring the certification of miners.

It was not until the United Mine Workers began to organize the anthracite industry that the legislature paid attention to the wishes of the miners. In 1897 the legislature passed an amendment to the 1889 act requiring each candidate to answer at least 12 questions in English. The amendment also provided for the imprisonment of violators of the act, but failed to provide for the payment of the examining boards out of the state treasury rather than from board fees. The certification of miners, however, failed, as did the provision of safety regulations by the state, to reduce materially the number of accidents in the anthracite mines.[12]

Chapter
13

Welfare

Adequate care could be provided for injured mine workers only by a hospital, yet in the anthracite regions there were only two hospitals. Through the generosity of Delaware, Lackawanna and Western officials, Scranton boasted a hospital, and in 1872 the citizens of Wilkes-Barre established the City Hospital.[1] But the remainder of the anthracite regions had no hospitals. In the Lehigh region, for example, injured miners requiring hospitalization had to be taken to Bethlehem.

The regions' middle class could not fill the hospital deficiency. It was not that area businessmen were callous toward the suffering around them; many realized that a hospital would not only alleviate suffering but increase the stature of the community. But many realized, too, that, given the fact of the low wages of the mine workers, an effective hospital would have to be run as an enterprise of charity, which few coal region towns could support. The middle class, therefore, looked to the state for aid. In 1849, for example, the *Miners' Journal* called for the establishment of a "miners' hospital" to be financed by a voluntary tax of one cent per ton of coal which would be paid by the consumer.

The *Journal's* appeal went unnoticed. It was not until the mine workers organized the Workingmen's Benevolent Association that the legislature considered establishing hospitals in the anthracite fields. In 1870 the legislature passed an act incorporating "the Miners' Hospital and Asylum of Schuylkill County." According to the act the hospital would provide free medical care to those injured in mining and transporting coal. A tax of one cent per ton of coal mined or transported in Schuylkill

155

County was authorized to support the free hospital. A board of directors elected by the borough councils in the county was to govern the institution.

But the hospital aroused community jealousies. In 1874 the Shenandoah merchants decided that their city needed a medical institution. After holding a fund-raising ball, the merchants joined with the mine workers in asking the executive board of the W.B.A. to assume direction of the project. The executive board accepted the obligation and appointed a hospital committee which promptly organized the Anthracite Hospital Association. The association went to Harrisburg and got a grant of $15,000 from the legislature. The grant, however, carried a proviso that it had to be matched by the investment of a like sum in grounds and buildings.[2] But when the Shenandoah merchants learned that the W.B.A. wanted to put the hospital outside Shenandoah they refused to turn over the funds raised by the ball. Unable to meet the proviso, the association did not establish another hospital.

As the accident rate in the mines increased, it became obvious that a free hospital open to all anthracite miners was needed. In 1879 John Welsh, former president of the W.B.A., led a successful drive for a hospital for miners, which resulted in legislation creating a commission composed of two members from each anthracite county. The commission was to select a site for and erect the hospital provided that the land be donated and the building costs stay within a $60,000 limit. Once built, the hospital would be turned over to a board of trustees who would give injured mine workers preference "over paying patients." Appropriations from the state treasury would defray operating costs. The commissioners named Fountain Springs near Ashland as the site for the new hospital.

The southern location of the hospital was inconvenient for mine workers in the Lehigh and Wyoming regions; they wanted a more central location. The northern mine workers received valuable support from the state mine inspectors; in 1886 James E. Roderick, inspector for the fourth district, suggested that a hospital be located in Hazleton. The legislature accepted Roderick's proposal in 1887 and authorized the establishment of a second state hospital in the middle coal field. After 1887 the legislature responded to the increasing demands of the mine workers by establishing a system of seven state hospitals in the anthracite regions.[3]

The state hospitals, however, would be of little use if there was not rapid transportation, which the anthracite mine owners were unwilling to provide. Joseph F. Patterson, a W.B.A. veteran, reported the experience of a man badly burned in an explosion. Friends carried the injured man to the surface and asked the foreman to send him home on a company car. The foreman said he could not furnish a car at that moment because the boiler house was blocked up with ashes. He did, however, place an extra man at the boiler house to expedite matters. Meanwhile, they laid the injured man under a tree and poured oil over his burns after which, having no bandages, they covered the wounds with "blasting paper."[4]

The mine operators appreciated the need for emergency transportation, but were unwilling to assume the extra cost unless assured that other operators would also provide ambulances. In 1875 Colonel Henry Pleasants, general superintendent of the Philadelphia and Reading, explained the position of his company to the miners and suggested that they secure legislation requiring such transportation. But 1875 marked the demise of the W.B.A., and the mine workers were unable to get what they wanted in Harrisburg.

In 1879 the anthracite mine workers secured the introduction, but not passage, of a bill requiring the transportation of injured miners. Encouraged by the authorization of a state hospital during the same session, the miners renewed their efforts in 1881 and were successful. Applying to all anthracite mines employing more than 20, the ambulance act of 1881 required operators to provide either an ambulance or two stretchers at every mine unless the owner operated two mines within a mile of each other. Noncompliance would be punishable by a $150 fine or 30 days' imprisonment.

The Pennsylvania legislature also provided for the care of injured miners, but refused to go further and create a welfare state. In 1872 the mine workers petitioned the House of Representatives to establish a relief fund for disabled miners, widows, and orphans by taxing coal. The bill passed in the House, but a Senate committee reported it negatively.

Labor received some outside support in its quest for a tax-supported relief fund. In 1878 *The Mountain Beacon* suggested that a special tax of one dollar be levied on all taxables in the anthracite regions, to go into the county treasuries. The county treasurer would use the money to pay injured miners $10 per week during disability and a $500 death benefit to the family in event of a fatal accident. In 1882 Mine Inspector James E. Roderick called attention to the suffering of the disabled miners and concluded: "humanity demands that something be done to relieve them, and that as speedily as possible."[5] But the demands of humanity were not heard in Harrisburg.

Finally in 1891 the mine workers secured the introduction of a relief bill in the House of Representatives. The bill provided for a semiannual tax of one cent on each ton of anthracite mined, which would be paid into the county treasuries. The county commissioners would use the funds to pay $1 a day to disabled miners. If the accident resulted in a loss of limbs, the victim would receive $60 for the limb lost. In fatal accidents the commissioners would pay a death benefit of $60, and the widow would receive $8 a month and $2 a month for each child under 14 years of age. The bill ran into stiff opposition after it was amended to include all mines in the state and only passed the House after it was agreed that the Senate would exclude the bituminous coal mines from its application. But again a Senate committee reported the bill negatively.

Unable to get a tax-supported relief program, the mine workers attempted to provide their own. The anthracite coal regions abounded with beneficial societies serving particular ethnic groups. The Lithuanian Church in Shenandoah, for example, was the focal point of 14 such societies. The ethnic group society, however, could not completely minister to the mine workers' needs, so they turned to their unions.

The W.B.A. maintained a well-defined relief program. The union provided financial aid to disabled miners and required members to visit their unfortunate brethren. In case of death, the W.B.A. assumed the deceased member's burial expenses.

Later unions also doubled as beneficial societies. The Knights of Labor established a relief fund with the proceeds from the 1879 public picnic. The Miners and Laborers' Amalgamated Association levied an occasional ten cents per capita tax to aid accident victims. The United Mine Workers considered the establishment of a benevolent fund. The short lifespans of the various unions, however, made them a questionable source of protection.

The middle class in the anthracite regions supplied some charity to the unfortunate miners. The ladies of Wilkes-Barre organized the Christian Benevolent Association in 1887 to care for the poor of the city, and the leading citizens of Pottsville supported the Benevolent Association of Pottsville. But usually the charitable organizations were so afraid the undeserving would take advantage of their good intentions that they made it difficult for injured miners to receive aid. The Wilkes-Barre Relief Association, for example, required its applicants to pick culm banks or break stones, tasks few maimed miners could do.

Occasionally the middle class responded directly to the needs of an injured miner. In 1874 the citizens of Mahanoy City sponsored a show consisting of trapeze and singing performances for the benefit of Abel Davis who was maimed in a mine accident. The people in Saint Clair held a benefit ball for Hugh Duffy, "a father of a large family," after he was injured in the mines.

While the general public was sympathetic to individual needs, it reserved its aid for "disaster" victims. Appalled by the Avondale mine disaster, Reverend T. P. Hunt collected $155,825.24 for the relief of the victims' families. In 1886 the Scranton *Truth* raised $2,740 for the support of the families of the five victims of the Fair Lawn disaster. Indeed, almost every major accident prompted the formation of a committee to raise funds for the victims and their families.[6]

A disaster relief committee assured protection to those miners killed or injured en masse, but most mine workers suffered individually. The individual mine accident victim faced an uncertain future. His ethnic group and labor union provided inefficient and sporadic relief. Regulations of organized charities made it difficult, if not impossible, for the injured miner to receive aid, while the general public only occasionally came to his rescue. Yet the increasing number of mine accidents made the provision of individual relief a pressing need in the anthracite coal regions.

Surprisingly the large mine operators eventually supplied the need. At first, however, they gave aid only to the victims of disasters. In 1846 the Delaware and Hudson Company donated $1,500 to the Carbondale disaster victims' families. The Pennsylvania Coal Company contributed $5,000 and the Delaware, Lackawanna and Western gave $20,000 to the Avondale disaster relief fund. Although the large operators donated generously to the relief of disaster victims, they did not move to provide for the welfare of the individual miner until the mine workers organized their first union.

In 1869 the Wilkes-Barre Coal and Iron Company, later the Lehigh–Wilkes-Barre Coal Company, established a relief fund for its employees. Under the plan the company donated a day's product each year and the mine workers contributed one day's wages to the fund. Members received $6 a week during disability caused by mine accidents. Upon accidental death the fund paid $50 toward funeral expenses and a pension of $3 a week to the widow and $1 a week for each child under 12 years for a period of one year. By 1874 the benefit fund had received $65,599.38 and distributed $41,336.47 among its members.

During the 1875 "long strikes," Franklin B. Gowen attempted to woo his employees from their union by announcing the creation of a relief program by the Philadelphia and Reading. Under the program there were three classes of contributors: miners and inside laborers paid 30 cents a month; outside laborers 20 cents; and boys and old men either 5 or 10 cents. The company endowed the fund with $20,000 and met whatever deficiencies existed at the end of the year. For occupational death the fund paid $30 toward funeral expenses and weekly payments of $7 to the families of first- and second-class contributors and either $2.40 or $1.40, depending on the monthly payment, to families of third-class members. Injured first- and second-class members received $5, while third-class membership paid either $2 or $1 per week during the first six months of disability.

The plan went into effect in 1877 and was an immediate success. By 1880 the mine inspector reported that 95 percent of the injured miners in Schuylkill County were members of the fund. But the plan was also expensive; in 1889 the Reading announced that during its first 12 years the relief fund had overdrawn its account by $131,763.50 and that the Reading was reorganizing the plan to place it on a self-supporting basis. The second plan created four classes of contributors and raised the monthly premiums while maintaining the old benefits.

Other large operators followed the lead of these two corporations. In 1878 the Lehigh Valley created a relief fund supported by the donation of one day's wages per year, which the company matched. The fund paid the same benefits as the Lehigh–Wilkes-Barre Coal Company's relief program. The Lehigh Valley's beneficial fund, however, contained several innovations. The program devoted part of its funds to the support of the Wilkes-Barre City Hospital. A committee composed of the foreman and two elected employee representatives managed the program at the colliery level. The Delaware and Hudson Company, the Susquehanna Coal Company, and the Mineral Mining Company, the latter two being subsidiaries of the Pennsylvania Railroad, adopted similar beneficial plans.

In 1883 the Lehigh Coal and Navigation Company inaugurated a different plan. Under its program the company paid a royalty of a half cent per ton of coal mined, while the employees contributed ½ or ¼ per cent of their earnings to the fund. Injured members received one-half of the average wages for their class during the first six months of their injury. Benefits would be paid only if the member furnished a certificate of his disability from a fund-appointed doctor every two weeks. Upon accidental death the plan paid $30 toward the funeral expenses and a weekly pension of 50 percent of the average earnings of the deceased for a period of 18 months to his widow.

The Delaware, Lackawanna, and Western did not offer a welfare plan, but it did provide free hospital care for its employees and their families. The corporation also gave its blessing to the mine workers' several "keg funds." Miners redeemed their empty powder kegs for ten cents; the money was used to establish a relief fund to which the other mine workers contributed. The fund was entirely an employee project and was usually local in scope. In 1891 the various groups formed the Amalgamated Miners' Accidental Funds which provided general supervision and greater financial stability.

With the exception of a few "keg funds," Eckley B. Coxe was the only independent operator to provide a relief system for his employees. Coxe did not create a relief fund to which his employees contributed; instead he personally donated $50 toward funeral expenses upon accidental death and gave the widow $3 a week, provided she remain unmarried, and each child under 12 years $1 a week for a period of one year. Injured men received $5 a week during disability. In addition, the company provided hospital care to its employees at the nominal fee of six cents a day.

In seeking to provide for their welfare the anthracite mine workers turned to the state. Although the legislature provided a system of state-supported hospitals and required the operators to maintain emergency vehicles at each mine, it refused to accept the responsibility for the relief of injured miners. Not the union nor the ethnic group nor the community was able to provide welfare for the mine worker injured or killed in an individual mine accident. The large corporation filled the gap by sponsoring relief funds. But the mine workers noted the correlation between the formation of their unions and the establishment of welfare programs and concluded that the action of the corporations was an attempt to weaken unionism and not a generous and compassionate act.[7] The mine workers, therefore, viewed the company-sponsored relief fund as an indirect result of their collective response to the problems confronted in the physical plant of the anthracite industry.

An Overview

The anthracite industry staggered under the burden of overinvestment. Dependent on the domestic fuel market, the industry overbuilt its plant to meet sporadically heavy demands. Heavy capitalization charges and high fixed operating costs prompted the mine owners to outstrip their market. The entrepreneurial order collapsed under the combined weight of increasing capital demands and falling prices.

Motivated by fear of losing their coal tonnage, the carrying companies took advantage of their strategic position and greater capital resources to supplant the individual mine owner. Controlling the mines, the carrying companies restored prices by regulating production through a pool. The coal pool, however, accentuated the real problem of the industry by assigning quotas according to productive capacity. Each company strived for a larger share of the total allotment by increasing its plant.

Both social pressure and outmoded economic conceptions contributed to management's failure to grasp the real problem of the hard coal industry. To retain their position and social esteem managers had to demonstrate competence and prove that they were successful. Yet the public measured success in terms of growth. Management therefore had to strive continuously for a larger share of the total allotment and (even if the coal pool had not existed) increase productive capacity.

Following a socially dictated requirement for growth, management was intellectually incapable of perceiving that expansion for expansion's sake could lead to overinvestment. Management operated on the premise that the economy was a self-regulating mechanism governed by the laws of supply and demand.[1] Given this premise, overinvestment became impossible.

163

The inability of management to define the basic problem of overinvestment created many difficulties for the mine workers. Wages had to be depressed for the operator to earn a return on the high capital charges with a decreasing percentage of capacity. The system of three-fourth, one-half, or one-fourth time and, whenever necessary, the total suspension of work by the coal pool, decreased already low wages. Some independent operators recovered the wages they paid out by charging for a complete system of paternalism. Either unable or unwilling to assume extra expense, management ignored safety precautions; the anthracite mines were thus among the most dangerous mines in the world.

The mine workers could not hope to solve their occupational problems until they overcame their social environment. They lived in a society atomized by geo-economic and ethnic forces. Divided geographically into four basins and regrouped by transportation lines into three economic regions, each district resented the prosperity of the others. Successive waves of immigrant groups produced pressures which caused the disintegration of the social structure within each region. Yet the collective productive system of mining anthracite negated any attempt to solve the problems of the industry on an individual, regional, or ethnic basis, and necessitated a collective response from the mine workers as an occupational class. The need to respond as a group of workers rather than as members of an ethnic or regional group created a crisis of identification for the miners.

The first two attempts to reach a collective solution to the occupational problems failed because the miners did not successfully meet the identification crisis. Regional and ethnic forces, not the power of Franklin B. Gowen, smashed the Workingmen's Benevolent Association. Both the Knights of Labor and the Miners' and Laborers' Amalgamated Association succumbed during the 1887-88 strikes because of regionalism.

The two organizations achieved some noteworthy improvements in the miners' prospects, however. While unionized, the mine workers enjoyed relatively higher wages. Aware of the correlation between their organizational drives and legislative action, the mine workers credited their unions with the passage of advantageous laws. Even company-sponsored welfare plans could be considered a reaction by management to unionism.

The success of unified response and the demonstrated futility of direct and violent action compelled the mine workers to endeavor continually to reconcile their various identifications.

When bloodshed in Lattimer abruptly dissolved the identification crisis, the miners proclaimed their new identity by enrolling in the United Mine Workers of America.

The anthracite mine workers realized that they worked in an ailing industry. Incorrectly diagnosing the sickness as overproduction and falling prices, the workers at first sought to strengthen prices by regulating production with strikes, although their inability to identify themselves primarily as members of an occupational class prevented their success. Even if successful in uniting as a working class, however, their policy would not have cured the real sickness of the anthracite industry, overinvestment. Indeed, the policy of the mine workers may have added to the burden; by tying wages to coal prices through the basis system, labor encouraged the existence of marginal capital by automatically reducing labor costs as prices fell. Yet it must be remembered that labor leaders developed their program from the same economic premise from which management operated. In a very real sense the anthracite mine workers sought their economic salvation in a strong capitalistic system.

But the union became more than an economic institution in the anthracite coal regions. By accommodating the disruptive forces in the area the U.M.W. instilled a spirit of unity among the mine workers. On the eve of the 1902 strike Con Carbon, a coal region minstrel, caught the spirit in a ballad:

Now you know Mike Sokolosky—
Dat man my brudder.
Last night him come to my shanty,
Un me tellin': "V'at you cummin' fer?"
Him tellin' 'bout tomorra dark night,
Every miner all, beeg un schmall
Goin' fer on shtrike.
Un him say t' me: "joe, me tellin' you
Dunt be 'fraid or shcared fer nottink, nevair,
      nevair do."
"Dunt be shcabby fella," him tellin' me again.
I'm say, "No sir! Mike, me out o' sight—
Me Johnny Mitchell man."

Chorus

Me no 'fraid fer nottink,
Me dey nevair shcare,
Sure me shtrike tomorra night,
Dat's de biziness, I dunt care.

Righta here me tellin' you—
Me no shcabby fella,
Good union citizen—
Johnny Mitchell man.

Now me belong t' union, me good citizen.
Fer seven year me livin' here
In dis beeg America.
Me vorkin' in de Prospect,
Vorkin' Dorrance shaft, Conyngham, Nottingham—
Every place like dat.
Vorkin' in de gangway, vorkin' in de breast,
Labor every day, me nevair gettin' rest.
Me got plenty money, nine hoondred, maybe ten,
So shtrike kin come, like son-of-a-gun—
Me Johnny Mitchell Man.[2]

Union membership transformed Joe Sokolosky from a Pole who happened to be a miner in the Wyoming region into a mine worker who happened to be Polish and working in the northern basin. Seen in this light the labor union was an instrument of social integration and the creator of a laboring class identity among the anthracite mine workers.

But the integrative power of the union was not limited to the working class. The middle class in the anthracite regions experienced the same problem of identification as the mine workers. Restricted in outlook to their own business and community, the middle class developed a parochialism which in its most sophisticated stage rarely extended beyond the county line. Only an outside force could break down the parochialism of the middle class and bring it within a larger community.

Industry could have provided the necessary cohesive force. The mines were the largest employers in the area. Coal companies collected taxes, maintained roads, and provided police protection. Churches and charities looked to management for aid.

The takeover by the large companies placed the industry in an even better position to become the integrative force in the anthracite regions. The operations of the corporations were usually regional and therefore provided a larger view for the middle class whose fortunes rose or fell with the operators. Furthermore, the coal pool transcended regionalism.

But the middle class refused to identify with the coal industry. Public-spirited businessmen resented the exploitation by mine operators, both large and small, of the wealth of the area for the benefit of other regions. And the merchants feared the great economic, social, and political power of the industry. Their fear becomes more understandable when it is remembered that bureaucrats, who managed but did not own property, wielded the power of the industry, and that some bureaucrats such as Gomer Jones were considered arrogant in their exercise of power. Suspicious of those in mining industry management, the middle class was more willing to support organized labor.

Several factors encouraged friendly relations between business and labor. Many merchants were former miners and others had family connections with mine workers. On several key issues such as the company store and hospitals, the interests of the middle class paralleled those of labor. "The interest of the merchants in the mining towns of the State," the *Daily Republican* announced, "are identical with those of the mine workers."[3]

The *Daily Republican* overstated the case; businessmen did not join the U.M.W. nor did they support all of its policies. Rather they saw in the union a symbol of a larger community bound together by the problems of work. By identifying with that community the middle class naturally adopted some of labor's values and norms and thus gave the anthracite regions a distinctive character. The social structure of the anthracite regions was unique because it received its direction and inspiration from its laboring class rather than its upper class; it was, in short, a society standing on its head.[4]

The effect of corporate enterprise remains to be measured. Contrary to popular opinion, the corporation was not a soulless exploiter of labor. It is true that the large companies kept wages low, but it must be remembered that the internal logic of the anthracite industry permitted few alternatives. Whenever possible the corporation, unlike the independent operator, provided for the welfare of its employees. The large operators voluntarily discontinued the company store and the company doctor, but the independent mine owner did not. Even Eckley B. Coxe, the most enlightened individual operator, kept a company store. The corporations exerted their influence against legislation proposed by the mine workers, but when the legislation became law they complied. On the other hand, state mine inspectors experienced great difficulty with the independent owners. Finally, most corporations and very few small operators sponsored welfare plans for their employees. Given such evidence, it seems reasonable to conclude that the large corporations with their wider profit margins could afford to be more sympathetic to the needs of the mine workers than the individual entrepreneurs could.

Yet the corporations bitterly opposed labor unions. The large corporations fought every organizational drive among the anthracite mine workers and, superficially, smashed their unions. Such opposition appears inexplicable; both management and labor explained their problems in terms of the market and both agreed that they could achieve their different goals by restricting production. It is possible to explain capital's opposition to its own policy in terms of greed or a desire to preserve managerial prerogatives. While both arguments carry considerable weight, they overlook the vital ingredient of the hostile attitude of management.

Ideology was the crucial ingredient. Gowen's insistence that the Molly Maguires were agents for the W.B.A. in the face of overwhelming facts to the contrary; the popular acceptance of his implications; the *Weekly Miners' Journal's* reassessment of its opinion of the Knights of Labor after the charges relating to the "McNulty gang"; and the violence that attended strikes showed that industrial strife in the anthracite regions reflected an ideological clash. Managers, like most Americans, worshipped individualism. Their hero was the "self-made man" who got ahead by individual initiative; they believed in the Horatio Alger myth.

The collective production system, however, submerged the individual. "The anthracite miner is a peculiar creature," observed George Korson. "As an individual he is unknown. Only collectively does he make his presence felt."[5] Acting collectively, through his union, the anthracite mine worker denied the established American faith. Subscribers to a creed that emphasized the individual could not understand that the mine worker could achieve nothing except as a member of a group. In many respects the posse in Lattimer was shooting at aliens. But the ethnic background of the victims did not make aliens; their presence as a group, in a parade, made them foreigners threatening the established ideology. Native mine workers understood the issue and rallied around their fellow aliens in the union. Ironically, in fighting labor unions big business fought for the values of a society which it had done much to destroy, while the anthracite mine workers spoke, collectively, for industrial man by placing the group above the individual.

Notes

INTRODUCTION

1. J. Cutler Andrews, "The Gilded Age in Pennsylvania," *Pennsylvania History*, XXXIV (January 1967), 23-24. Gail M. Gibson, "The Harrisburg Conference: Research Needs and Opportunities in Pennsylvania History," *Pennsylvania History*, XXXIII (July 1966), 336. Philip S. Klein, "Our Pennsylvania Heritage: Yesterday and Tomorrow," *Pennsylvania History*, XXV (January 1958), 7-8.

2. Several explorations have been made into the area: Marvin W. Schlegel, *Ruler of the Reading: The Life of Franklin B. Gowen, 1836-1889*, Harrisburg: Archives Publishing Company of Pennsylvania, 1947; Victor R. Greene, "The Attitude of Slavic Communities to the Unionization of the Anthracite Industry Before 1903" unpublished Ph.D. dissertation, University of Pennsylvania, 1963; and Rowland Berthoff, "The Social Order of the Anthracite Region, 1825-1902," *The Pennsylvania Magazine of History and Biography*, LXXXIX (July 1965), 261-291.

3. See Table 2.

4. "Children of the Coal Shadow," *McClure's*, XX (1902/03), 435.

CHAPTER 1

1. Peter Roberts, *The Anthracite Coal Industry* (New York: Macmillan, 1901), 3-4.

2. The term refers to the geological formation containing the coal beds.

3. Some writers refer to the period as the Carboniferous Age.

4. There are two other basins, the Loyalsock and Mehoopany, 25 miles northwest of Lackawanna, but they were opened late and their output is included in the northern basin's statistics. John K. Mumford, *Anthracite* (New York: Industries Publishing Co., 1925), 63.

5. On December 18, 1885 the buried valley broke into a mine at Nanticoke and flooded 10,000 yards of working, killing 26 men. The Delaware and Hudson Company, *The Story of Anthracite* (New York: The Delaware and Hudson Company, 1932), 11.

169

6. Frederick M. Binder, "Pennsylvania Coal: An Historical Study of Its Utilization to 1860," unpublished Ph.D. dissertation, University of Pennsylvania, 1955, 2. Alfred Mathews and Austin N. Hungerford, *History of the Counties of Lehigh and Carbon in the Commonwealth of Pennsylvania* (Philadelphia: Everts and Richards, 1884), 754 and 769.

CHAPTER 2

1. Howard N. Eavenson, *First Century and A Quarter of the American Coal Industry* (Pittsburgh: The Author, 1942), 139.

2. The Delaware and Hudson Co., *The Story of Anthracite*, 24-25. Letter from Jesse Fell, December 1, 1826 in *Hazard's Register of Pennsylvania*, III (May 9, 1829), 302-303. Fell is unsure of the date, but he places it at about 1770.

3. Commonwealth of Pennsylvania, Senate, Select Committee upon the Subject of the Coal Trade, "Report of the Committee of the Senate Upon the Subject of the Coal Trade," *Journal of the Senate of the Commonwealth of Pennsylvania*, 1833-34, vol. 2, 472; hereafter cited as the Packer Report.

4. See the *Scranton Republican*, December 21, 1879, 4.

5. Mathews and Hungerford, *History of Lehigh and Carbon Counties*, 658.

6. J. Bennet Nolan, *The Schuylkill* (New Brunswick: Rutgers University Press, 1951), 29.

7. Samuel R. Smith, *The Black Trail of Anthracite* (Kingston, Pa.: The Author, 1907), 74; Daddow and Bannan, *Coal*, 113, 120. Both Allen and Ginter stumbled on outcrops of the southern basin. John Charles discovered the eastern middle basin while digging for a ground hog in 1826, and Isaac Tomlinson found coal near Shamokin in 1790. Smith, *Black Trail*, 79; Delaware and Hudson Co., *Story of Anthracite*, 32-33.

8. Homer Greene, *Coal and the Coal Mines* (New York: Houghton, Mifflin and Co., 1889), 58.

9. *Ibid.*, 91; William H. Williams, "Anthracite Development and Railway Progress," *American-Irish Historical Society's Journal*, XXII (1923), 91; *Hazard's Register of Pennsylvania*, December 10, 1831, 384.

10. Walter R. Johnson, *Notes on the Use of Anthracite in the Manufacture of Iron With Some Remarks on Its Evaporating Power* (Boston: Charles C. Little and James Brown, 1841), 12. Mumford, *Anthracite*, 69.

11. Charles A. Ashburner, *Brief Description of the Anthracite Coal Fields of Pennsylvania* (Author's edition, 1884), 4.

12. Johnson, *Notes*, 9-10 (italics in original).

13. *Hazard's Register of Pennsylvania*, IX (March 9, 1833), 160.

14. *Ibid.*, VIII (September 18, 1831), 192.

15. The minimum distances of the anthracite fields from the cities are: Philadelphia, 90 miles; New York, 140 miles; Buffalo, 265 miles; and Pittsburgh, 250 miles.

16. Eli Bowen, "Coal and the Coal Fields of Pennsylvania," *Harper's*, XV (August 1857), 451-454.

17. Contract between J.O. Cist and Aaron Dean, January 18, 1815. Mss. Coal File 1, Wyoming Geological and Historical Society, Wilkes-Barre.

18. Mumford, *Anthracite*, 43.

19. Hyman Kuritz, "The Pennsylvania State Government and Labor Controls from 1865 to 1922," unpublished Ph.D. dissertation, Columbia University, 1954, 4.

20. United States, Anthracite Coal Strike [1902] Commission, *Report to the President on the Anthracite Coal Strike of May-October, 1902* (Washington: Government Printing Office, 1903), 17.

21. Lehigh Coal and Navigation Company, *Annual Report, 1857*, 19. Joseph H. Harris to G.A. Nicholls, May 1, 1876, Philadelphia and Reading Company Papers, The Historical Society of Pennsylvania.

22. United States, House of Representatives, Subcommittee of the Committee on Interstate and Foreign Commerce, *Report and Testimony in Regards to the Alleged Combination of the Philadelphia and Reading Railroad Company and Other Railroad and Canal Companies and Producers of Coal* (hereafter cited as Coombs Committee), 52nd Cong., 2nd Sess., 1892, Report 2278, 21.

23. Coombs Committee, 139.

24. Commonwealth of Pennsylvania, Legislature, *Testimony Before the Committee to Investigate The Philadelphia and Reading Railroad Company and the Reading Coal and Iron Company* (hereafter referred to as *Reading Investigation*), Legislative Documents, 1876, vol. III, 1045.

25. The carrying companies not only occupied the industry's bottleneck, as Matthew Josephson used term, but also controlled the physical bottleneck. The passes or gaps breaking the mountains surrounding the coal basins were so narrow that usually only one, or at the most, two railroads could be constructed through them. Jules Irwin Bogen, *The Anthracite Railroads: A Study in American Railroad Enterprise* (New York: The Ronald Press Co., 1927), 5-6.

26. The independent nonoperating landowners—those deriving their income from royalties—were weakened during the Civil War. Royalties were payable in currency, and the low value of greenbacks depressed their revenue. G.O. Virtue, "The Anthracite Mine Laborers," U.S. Department of Labor, *Bulletin 13* (1897), 731.

27. *Annual Report, 1867*, 13-14; see also letter from J. Brisbin, president, to Senator (Pa.) George Landon, April 8, 1867, Delaware, Lackawanna and Western Papers, Coal Department, Lackawanna Historical Society.

28. Contracts between the company and individual operators in the Delaware, Lackawanna, and Western Papers. See also Eliot Jones, *The Anthracite Coal Combination in the United States with Some Account of the Early Development of the Anthracite Industry*, "Harvard Historical Studies." Vol. XI (Cambridge, Mass.: Harvard University Press, 1914), 52.

CHAPTER 3

1. Packer Report, 449.

2. *Hazard's Register of Pennsylvania*, I (May 17, 1828), 310.

3. Lehigh Coal and Navigation Company, *Annual Report, 1863*, 28.

4. *The Plain Speaker* (Hazleton), January 28, 1888, 3.

5. W.H. Tillinghast to Reuben Downing, October 14, 1887, Lehigh–Wilkes-Barre Coal Company Papers. Italics in original.

6. William Roberts to W.R. Storrs, March 13, 1876; Delaware, Lackawanna, and Western Papers. See also J.W. Williams to W.R. Storrs, October 26, 1883, Delaware, Lackawanna, and Western Papers.

7. W.S. Jones to D.F. Bound, November 8, 1871, Delaware, Lackawanna, and Western Papers.

8. Thomas Murphy, *Jubilee History Commemorative of the Fiftieth Anniversary of the Creation of Lackawanna County, Pennsylvania*, 2 vols. (Topeka: Historical Publishing Co., 1928), II, 508.

9. J. Brisbin to Samuel Sloan, July 22, 1868, Delaware, Lackawanna, and Western Papers.

10. Eckley B. Coxe was state chairman of the Democratic Party; the Pennsylvania Democratic Party supported Asa Packer, president of the Lehigh Valley Railroad, for governor.

11. W.H. Tillinghast to William F. Vilas, December 2, 1885, Lehigh–Wilkes-Barre Coal Company Papers. Also see J. Brisbin to P.W. Osterhart, December 26, 1868, Delaware, Lackawanna, and Western Papers; and W. Ward to G.E. Wooten, September 20, 1878, Philadelphia and Reading Company Papers.

12. The Northern Central controlled the Mineral Mining Company which operated mines around Shamokin. See H.B. Wright to George Wright, May 19, 1879; A. Pardee and Co. to Hendrick B. Wright, April 7, 1877, Hendrick B. Wright Papers, Wyoming Geological and Historical Society. *Weekly Miners' Journal*, September 16, 1881, 6.

13. W.C. Johnson to Dailey and Robert, March 7, 1896, and W.C. Johnson to Elmer H. Lowall, March 31, 1896, Lehigh–Wilkes-Barre Coal Company Papers.

14. W.R. Storrs to George E. Smith, January 30, 1899, Delaware, Lackawanna, and Western Papers.

15. W.C. Johnson to E.W. Marple, October 11, 1898, Lehigh–Wilkes-Barre Coal Company Papers.

16. April 29, 1890, 2.

17. United States House of Representatives' Select Committee on Existing Labor Troubles in the Anthracite Regions of Pennsylvania, *Labor Troubles in the Anthracite Regions of Pennsylvania* (hereafter cited as *Labor Troubles*), 50th Congress, 2nd session, Report 414, 435.

18. Historians of an earlier generation thought the Mollies guilty. See James Ford Rhodes, "The Molly Maguires in the Anthracite Region," *American Historical Review*, XV (April 1910), 547-561. Later writers such as Anthony J. Bimba thought them guilty only of being union leaders. See *The Molly Maguires* (New York: International Publishers, 1932). The most recent scholar, Wayne G. Broehl, maintains that the Mollies were guilty of crimes, and interprets the episode as a story of personal success and failure in his book *The Molly Maguires* (Cambridge, Mass.: Harvard University Press, 1964).

19. The "new middle class" is usually defined as the white collar worker, whereas the classical bourgeoisie refers to businessmen and property owners.

20. *Daily Republican*, March 29, 1890, 2; March 25, 1891, 2.

21. *The Plain Speaker* (Hazleton), December 3, 1887, 2.

22. Hans Kurath found a major language boundary running between the two regions. *A Word Geography of the Eastern United States* (Ann Arbor: University of Michigan Press, 1949), 11-12.

23. Donald L. Kinzer lists the two organizations as being nativistic and anti-Catholic. *An Episode of Anti-Catholicism: The American Protective Association* (Seattle: University of Washington Press, 1964), 34.

24. *The Scranton Republican*, March 11, 1886, 3.

25. Charles R. Spahr, "Coal Miners of Pennsylvania," *Outlook*, LXI (August 5, 1889), 809.

26. *The Scranton Republican*, December 26, 1884, 3.

27. Quoted by Paul Fox, *The Polish National Catholic Church* (Scranton: School of Christian Living, n.d.), 29.

28. Fox, *Polish Church*, 489.

29. Murphy, *Jubilee History*, 238.

PART II

1. Stanley H. Udy, Jr., *Organization of Work: A Comparative Analysis of Production Among Nonindustrial Peoples* (New Haven: H.R.A.F. Press, 1959), 3.

CHAPTER 4

1. Commonwealth of Pennsylvania, Second Geological Survey of Pennsylvania, *Report on the Mining Methods and Appliances Used in the Anthracite Fields*, by H.M. Chance (hereafter cited as Chance, *Mining Methods*) (Harrisburg: Board of Commissioners for the Second Geological Survey, 1883), 105-106.

2. Chance, *Mining Methods*, 130-132. Franklin Platt, in Commonwealth of Pennsylvania, Second Geological Survey of Pennsylvania, *A Special Report to the Legislature Upon the Causes, Kinds, and Amount of Waste in Mining Anthracite by John Price Wetherhill* (hereafter cited as Platt, *Waste*) (Harrisburg: Board of Commissioners for the Second Geological Survey, 1881), 17A.

3. Commonwealth of Pennsylvania, Mine Inspectors, *Reports of the Inspectors of Mines, 1871-1897, Reports, 1886* (hereafter cited as Pennsylvania Mine Inspectors), *Reports* [date], 2.

4. George E. Stevenson, *Reflections of An Anthracite Engineer* (New York: The Author, 1931), 167.

5. George Korson, *Minstrels of the Mine Patch; Songs and Stories of the Anthracite Industry* (Philadelphia: University of Pennsylvania Press, 1938), 276.

6. Pennsylvania Mine Inspectors, *Reports, 1875*, 70.

7. Quoted by Carter L. Goodrich, *The Miner's Freedom: A Study of the Working Life in a Changing Industry* (Boston: Marshall Jones Co., 1925), 56.

8. Quoted in Pennsylvania Mine Inspectors, *Reports, 1880*, 74.

9. Reports of the Mine Inspectors in Pennsylvania, *Legislative Documents, 1875*, 932.

10. Pennsylvania Mine Inspectors, *Reports, 1889*, 1.

11. Pennsylvania Mine Inspectors, *Report, 1878*, 127.

CHAPTER 5

1. Quoted by J.G. Brooks, "Impression of the Anthracite Coal Troubles," *Yale Review*, VI (November 1897), 307.

2. See Appendix III.

3. *Labor Troubles*, 542.

4. *Ibid.*, 479. Also see *Daily Republican*, September 14, 1887, 3.

5. George M. Gowan to Samuel Sloan, March 15, 1879, Delaware, Lackawanna, and Western Papers.

6. *Daily Republican*, November 15, 1890, 1.

CHAPTER 6

1. "The Anthracite Mine Laborers," 730.

2. *Communities*, 17-18.

3. Anon., *History of Schuylkill County, Pennsylvania With Illustrations and Biographical Sketches of Some of Its Prominent Men and Pioneers* (New York: W.W. Mansell & Co., 1881). Herbert C. Bell, *History of Northumberland County, Pennsylvania* (Chicago: Brown, Runk and Co., 1891). H.C. Bradshaw, ed., *History of Luzerne County, Pennsylvania, With Biographical Selections* (Chicago: S.B. Nelson & Co., Publishers, 1893).

4. *Pennsylvania Laws*, 1891, Law 177, Article VIII.

CHAPTER 7

1. J.G. Brooks, "Impression of the Anthracite Coal Troubles," *Yale Review*, VI (November 1897), 308-309.

2. *Daily Record of the Times*, August 16, 1875, 1.

3. *Public Ledger* (Philadelphia), July 15, 1842, 1. George Korson, *Black Rock: Mining Folklore of the Pennsylvania Dutch* (Baltimore: Johns Hopkins University Press, 1960), 136. Nolan, *The Schuylkill*, 23.

4. Roberts, *Anthracite Industry*, 173.

5. See Appendix IV.

6. There is no mention of an organizational meeting, but the Northumberland County W.B.A. always celebrated its anniversary on this date.

7. Photocopy of the charter in the writer's possession.

8. *Record of the Times*, November 25, 1868, 3.

9. *Record of the Times*, March 24, 1869, 2.

10. Commonwealth of Pennsylvania, Senate, Committee on the Judiciary General, *Report of the Committee on the Judiciary General, of the Senate of Pennsylvania, in Relation to the Coal Difficulties with Accompanying Testimony* (hereafter cited as *Judiciary Committee Report*), Legislative Documents, 1871, 1677-1678, 1709. Charter of the Workingmen's Beneficial and Benevolent Association.

11. Charter of the The Workingmen's Beneficial and Benevolent Association.

12. Quoted by Virtue, "Mine Laborers," 734. See *Miners' Journal*, December 12, 1868, 3.

13. December 1, 1868, 3.

14. *Record of the Times*, June 9, 1869, 2.

15. *Shamokin Herald*, June 17, 1869, 3.

16. *Shamokin Herald*, March 3, 1870, 3. See also *Public Ledger*, February 7, 1870, 4.

17. March 3, 1870, 3.

18. *Shamokin Herald*, March 17, 1870, 3.

19. March 12, 1870, 3.

20. April 30, 1870, 2.

21. *Miners' Journal*, July 2, 1870, 3.

22. Joseph F. Patterson, "Reminiscences of John Maguire After Fifty Years Of Mining," *Publications of the Historical Society of Schuylkill County*, IV (1913/ 1914), 321. "Dead work" included all work that did not produce coal, such as timbering and pumping.

23. *Shamokin Herald*, July 7, 1870, 3. *Shenandoah Herald*, July 9, 1870, 8. A "drawback" was an amount of money returned to the operator after the Reading had collected its bill. The amount fluctuated with the price of coal.

24. *Shamokin Herald*, July 7, 1870, 3.

25. *Daily Miners' Journal*, July 26, 1870, 3.

CHAPTER 8

1. R.E. Rirthorn to W.R. Storrs, June 17, 1870; P.E. Gallagher to W.R. Storrs, September 20, 1870; Delaware, Lackawanna, and Western Papers.

2. *Daily Miners' Journal*, January 12, 1871, 2.

3. January 10, 1871, 1.

4. January 5, 1871, 2.

5. *Judiciary Committee Report*, 1679.

6. Letter from Benjamin James, February 8, 1871, quoted in Alan Conway, *The Welsh in America: Letters from the Immigrants* (Minneapolis: University of Minnesota Press, 1961), 89.

7. January 12, 1871, 4.

8. The Northumberland County W.B.A. agreed to accept the $3 basis with a sliding scale of 33 percent, which would go below the base wages. But some districts refused to accept the contract. *Shamokin Herald*, February 16, 1871, 3.

9. *Judiciary Committee Report*, 1533-1535. The carriers' position is ably discussed by J.B. Hodgkin in his "Latest Phase of the Coal Troubles," *Nation*, XII (April 13, 1871), 254-255.

10. *Daily Miners' Journal*, March 2, 1871, 2.

11. *Ibid.*, May 17, 1871, 2.

12. *Shamokin Herald*, May 11, 1871, 3. Letter from T. Thomas, December 6, 1873 quoted in Conway, *Welsh in America*, 193-194.

13. *Daily Miners' Journal*, May 12, 1871, 2.

14. Gowen had some success. In April he and some union leaders met with Governor Geary, but were unable to come to an understanding. *State Journal* quoted by *Daily Miners' Journal*, April 7, 1871, 2.

15. *Shamokin Herald*, April 20, 1871, 3.

16. The Treverton district of the Northumberland County W.B.A. rejected this decision. *Shamokin Herald*, May 11, 1871, 2.

17. Commonwealth of Pennsylvania, Secretary of Internal Affairs, *Annual Report, 1872-73*, Part III, *Industrial Statistics*, 331. The operators wanted a $2.50 basis with wages at $9, $10, and $12 a week, while the union demanded a $3 basis and wages at $11, $12, and $14 a week. Joseph F. Patterson, "Old W.B.A. Days," *Publications of the Historical Society of Schuylkill County*, II (1909), 364.

18. The middle class, however, would change its opinion of the large corporation; by 1888 it preferred the corporation over the small entrepreneur.

19. *Shamokin Herald*, April 23, 1872, 3.

20. The company's new rules required that the miners leave the mines on foot if they quit work before quitting time. Since contract miners stopped work as soon as they had blown enough coal free to "make their wages," they considered the rule a threat to their status. *Shamokin Herald*, May 29, 1873, 3; *Shenandoah Herald*, May 29, 1873, 2.

21. Benjamin Franklin to Franklin B. Gowen, March 27, 1874, Molly Maguire Folder, The Historical Society of Pennsylvania.

22. Dual unionism occurs when two unions attempt to organize the same craft or industry.

23. Christopher Evans, *History of the United Mine Workers of America from*

the Year 1860 to 1890 (Indianapolis: United Mine Workers of America, 1914), 62-70.

24. *Public Ledger*, November 29, 1874, 4.

25. The coal pool controlled the New York market. The line trade consisted of markets along the railroad's line to Philadelphia. Schlegel, *Ruler of the Reading*, 63.

26. Mules were not brought out of the mines unless a long shutdown was expected or planned. Bringing the mules out of the mines at this time was the best evidence that the companies were not about to yield to the men.

27. Joint Investigation Committee, 1079.

28. Korson, *Minstrels of the Mine Patch*, 225.

29. *Shamokin Herald*, July 8, 1875, 3.

CHAPTER 9

1. Gustar V. Rimlinger, "Labor Protest in British, American, and German Coal Mines Prior to 1914," unpublished Ph.D. dissertation, University of California, 1951, 57.

2. Alexander K. McClure, *Old Time Notes of Pennsylvania*, 2 vols. (Philadelphia: John C. Winston Company, 1905), 548-549. Draft resistance in the coal regions was so great that the army created the Lehigh military district to maintain order and enforce the draft law. William August Itter, "Conscription in Pennsylvania During the Civil War," unpublished Ph.D. Dissertation, University of Southern California, 1941, 140-143.

3. In Carbon County Civil War violence was attributed to a secret society called "The Buckshots"; F. D. Dewees, *The Molly Maguires: The Origin, Growth and Character of the Organization* (Philadelphia: J.P. Lippincott and Company, 1877), 47.

4. To some, the Molly Maguires' great political influence explained why few criminals had been brought to justice. In order to escape the supposedly Irish-dominated political structure, operators and other citizens agitated successfully for a special court and police force.

5. *Report, 1869*, 863.

6. *Judiciary Committee Report*, 1607.

7. *Shenandoah Herald*, January 24, 1874, 2.

8. F.D. Dewees, *The Molly Maguires*, 25.

9. Wayne G. Broehl, Jr., *The Molly Maguires* (Cambridge, Mass.: Harvard University Press, 1965), 106.

10. *Judiciary Committee Report*, 1527. Italics in the original.

11. *Ibid.*, 1531. Italics in the original.

12. Quoted by Broehl, *Molly Maguires*, 148.

13. Benjamin Franklin to Franklin B. Gowen, March 25, 1874, Molly Maguire Folder, The Historical Society of Pennsylvania, Philadelphia.

14. *Ibid.*

15. McParlan knew Dougherty was not guilty, yet did nothing to help him. See Broehl, *Molly Maguires*, 196-197.

16. *Ibid.,* 199.

17. They were mistaken; Thomas was only wounded.

18. The case was rife with inconsistencies. Yost and McCarran identified the attackers as the two strangers in Carroll's tavern. McParlan's report, however, had the villains lying in ambush while Yost was in the tavern.

19. Quoted by Broehl, *Molly Maguires*, 234.

20. Dewees, *Molly Maguires*, 246-247.

21. Franklin B. Gowen, *Argument of Franklin B. Gowen, Esq., of Counsel For the Commonwealth In The Case of the Commonwealth vs. Thomas Munley, Indicted In the Court of Oyer and Terminer of Schuylkill County Pennsylvania, For the Murder of Thomas Sanger, A Mining Boss, At Raven Run, On September 1, 1875* (Pottsville: Chronicle Book and Job Rooms, 1876), 17-18.

22. F.W. Hughes, *Commonwealth versus Patrick Hester, Patrick Tully, and Peter McHugh Tried and Convicted of the Murder of Alexander W. Rea. Argument of Honorable F.W. Hughes, For Commonwealth at Bloomsburg, Pa., February 23 & 24, 1877* (Philadelphia: G.V. Town and Son, 1877), 31.

23. Gowen, *Argument*, 16.

24. Dewees, *Molly Maguires*, 230.

25. Commonwealth of Pennsylvania, Legislature, Riot Committee, *Riot Committee Investigation* (hereafter cited as *Riot Committee*), Pennsylvania Legislative Documents, 1878, Vol. 5, Document No. 29, 3.

26. The strike in Pittsburgh against the Pennsylvania Railroad resulted in a riot causing an estimated damage of $5 million to $10 million. Foster Rhea Dulles, *Labor in America: A History*, 3rd ed. (New York: Thomas Y. Crowell, 1966), 120.

27. *Weekly Miners' Journal,* July 27, 1877, 4. Commonwealth of Pennsylvania, Adjutant General, *Report of the Adjutant General of Pennsylvania, 1877*, 91. Great Britain, Foreign Office, *Commercial Reports. Reports Respecting the Late Industrial Conflicts in the United States* (hereafter cited as *British Consular Reports*), Sessional Papers, 1877, Vol. LXXXIV, 650.

28. The Commonwealth armed the committees. *Report of the Adjutant General*, 90.

29. Samuel C. Logan, *A City's Danger and Defense, Or Issues and Results of the Strikes of 1877* (Scranton: The Author, 1887), 55.

30. Quoted by Logan, *City's Danger*, 79.

31. *Ibid.*, 86.

32. *British Consular Reports*, 670.

33. *Record of the Times*, August 9, 1877, 1, November 28, 1877, 4.

34. *Riot Committee*, 30.

CHAPTER 10

1. *Weekly Miners' Journal*, February 17, 1879, 4, February 21, 1879, 6.

2. February 21, 1879, 5.

3. The Mahanoy City miners won a five-cent increase in the wagon rate. *Weekly Miners' Journal*, July 11, 1879, 8.

4. July 24, 1879, 3.

5. *Weekly Miners' Journal*, March 5, 1880, 8; March 12, 1880, 7.

6. During its brief life the reconstituted union was sufficiently strong for John Farrell, a representative of the striking bituminous miners at Clearfield, to seek its aid in raising relief funds. *Weekly Miners' Journal*, April 8, 1880, 7.

7. Nichele Molinaro, for example, testified that he lived on 20 cents a day. United States, House of Representatives, 50th Cong., 1st Sess., 1888, Select Committee to Inquire into the Alleged Violation of the Contract Labor Law, *Testimony Taken By the Select Committee of the House of Representatives to Inquire into the Alleged Violation of the Laws Prohibiting the Importation of Contract Laborers, Paupers, Convicts, and Other Classes.* House Misc. Document 572.

8. May 27, 1887, 3.

9. There was a small strike in the Shamokin area in which the Mineral Mining Company refused to recognize the union. *New York Daily Tribune*, November 5, 1887, 3.

10. Evidence of independent leadership was evident in the actions of the Lehigh Valley Coal Company. It subscribed to the Reading compromise in the Schuylkill region but refused to grant the increase in the Lehigh region. *Daily Republican*, September 14, 1887, 1. *Wilkes-Barre Telephone*, September 24, 1887, 3.

11. *Daily Republican*, September 16, 1887, 1.

12. *Daily Republican*, December 2, 1887, 2.

13. W.H. Tillinghast to J.I. Hollenbeck, October 15 and 25, 1887; italics in original.

14. *The Record of the Times*, November 11, 1887, 1. *New York Daily Tribune*, November 11, 1887, 3. In Shamokin the Mineral Mining Company offered its men a 10 percent increase with the same result. *New York Daily Tribune*, November 5, 1887, 3. *Public Ledger and Daily Transcript*, November 5, 1887, 1. *The Plain Speaker*, November 10, 1887, 9.

15. *The Plain Speaker*, December 17, 1887, 3. "Pa dee" is a play on Ario Pardee's name.

16. *New York Daily Tribune*, October 4, 1887, 2; *Wilkes-Barre Telephone*, February 18, 1888, 3; *New York Daily Tribune*, September 17, 1887, 2; *The Plain Speaker*, March 8, 1888, 1; *Evening Chronicle*, October 26, 1887, 4.

17. *The Plain Speaker*, September 14, 1887, 4.

18. *The Truth* (Scranton), quoted by *The Plain Speaker*, October 5, 1887, 2.

19. *Daily Republican*, December 6, 1887, 1.

20. *The Plain Speaker*, September 26, 1887, 2; December 3, 1887, 2.

21. *Daily Republican*, November 1, 1887, 2. *Shenandoah Herald*, November 5, 1882, 1.

22. *Daily Republican*, December 27, 1887, 1; December 24, 1887, 1.

23. *Ibid.*, December 28, 1887, 1. Many Knights avenged themselves by working for the Chicago, Burlington, and Quincy Railroad when the B.L.E. struck the line in 1888. *The Tribune*, February 29, 1888, 2. It is also interesting to note the Reading's "gratitude" to the B.L.E.; in February 1889 the Reading gave its employees the alternative of resigning from the Brotherhood or from their jobs. *Daily Republican*, February 18, 1889, 4.

24. The Reading began mining in 1871.

25. *Labor Troubles*, 174.

26. The individual operators, however, did maintain company stores; it appeared to many that labor was trying to destroy the Reading and replace it with independent operators and hence restore the company store in the Schuylkill region.

27. On February 3 the Reading sent a carload of carbines to its Coal and Iron Police at Shenandoah. *Daily Republican*, February 4, 1888, 1.

28. H.R. Maxwell to J.I. Hollenbeck, March 9, 1888, Lehigh–Wilkes-Barre Coal Company Papers.

CHAPTER 11

1. *Daily Republican*, September 19, 1889, 1. In 1889 the anthracite industry employed 119,646 men and boys.

2. *Weekly Miners' Journal*, July 27, 1888, 3.

3. *Daily Republican*, March 6, 1889, 1.

4. *Weekly Miners' Journal*, October 17, 1889, 4. Dockage was the amount deducted from the contract unit for dirt and slate.

5. *Daily Republican*, October 17, 1889, 4.

6. *Ibid.*, November 14, 1889, 1. The council overstated its case; Schuylkill region mine workers received below basis wages until November 1887.

7. *Daily Republican*, February 10, 1890, 4.

8. *Ibid.*, February 22, 1890, 4.

9. *Daily Republican*, April 23, 1890, 1. *Weekly Miners' Journal*, April 25, 1890, 3.

10. April 24, 1890, 2.

11. See Victor R. Greene, "A Study in Slavs, Strikes, and Unions: The Anthracite Strike of 1897," *Pennsylvania History*, XXXI (April, 1964), 202. The courts later declared the act unconstitutional.

12. It should be noted that the Philadelphia and Reading refused to comply with the law.

13. *The Daily Standard* (Hazleton), August 16, 1897, 1. Other superintendents also found fault with Jones' enforcing of "old time rules." W.R. Storrs to Samuel Sloan, August 28, 1897, Delaware, Lackawanna, and Western Papers.

14. *The Daily Standard*, August 20, 1897, 6.

15. August 18, 1897, 1.

16. *The Hazleton Weekly Sentinel*, September 2, 1897, 6.

17. September 11, 1897, 1. Historians Victor Greene and Edward Pinkowski feel that the middle class condoned the shooting. Victor R. Greene, "A Study," 207. Edward Pinkowski, *The Lattimer Massacre* (Philadelphia: Sunshine Press, 1950), *passim*.

18. September 11, 1897, 1.

19. Quoted in *The Hazleton Weekly Sentinel*, September 16, 1897, 2.

20. *Ibid.*, 5.

CHAPTER 12

1. Quoted by the *Shenandoah Herald*, October 29, 1870, 4.

2. The president judge presided over the Court of Common Pleas; one of his functions was to assign judges to various cases.

3. The identification process can easily be seen in the appeal by a group of unemployed miners for state relief. Their relief plan called for increasing the demand for anthracite by the state's stockpiling iron. *Weekly Miners' Journal*, April 26, 1878, 6. See Irwin Unger, *The Greenback Era: A Social and Political History of American Finance, 1865-1879* (Princeton: Princeton University Press, 1964), 55-59.

4. Copy of the platform in the writer's possession.

5. Two of the six anthracite counties, Dauphin and Columbia, contained large nonmining populations.

6. *Morning Republican* (Scranton), quoted in *Shamokin Herald*, July 29, 1869, 3.

7. *Pennsylvania Laws, 1869*, Law No. 845, pp. 852-856.

8. *Commonwealth v. Bonnell*, 8 Phila. 534.

9. Mine Inspectors' *Reports, 1886*, in Pennsylvania, Secretary of Internal Affairs, *Annual Report, 1887*, Part III, *Industrial Statistics*, 77a.

10. For example, the act defined "owners" or "operators" as "any person or body corporate, who is the immediate proprietor, or lessee, or occupier of any coal mine or colliery, or any part thereof."

11. Mine inspectors often complained that the mines' lack of discipline caused many accidents.

12. See Table 10.

CHAPTER 13

1. The Scranton hospital later became the Moses Taylor Hospital. W.H. Storrs to Mrs. Agnes Gladding, December 29, 1898, Delaware, Lackawanna and Western Papers. Pennsylvania, Mine Inspectors' *Reports, 1879*, 88-89.

2. It is interesting to note that the original bill read: "An act for the erection and maintenance of three hospitals in the anthracite coal fields." *Journal of the House*, 1874, 448.

3. The other hospitals were located in Scranton, Coaldale, Shenandoah, Nanticoke, and Shamokin. *Hazleton Standard-Speaker*, September 1, 1966, 6.

4. Joseph F. Patterson "After the W.B.A.," *Publications of the Historical Society of Schuylkill County*, IV (1913/1914), 181.

5. Mine Inspectors' *Reports, 1882*, 261.

6. Two other committees were the York Farm Disaster Fund and the Twin Shaft Disaster Committee.

7. Historians have agreed with the mine workers' contention. Schlegel, *Ruler of the Reading*, 143. Ray Ginger, "Company-Sponsored Welfare Plans in the Anthracite Industry Before 1900," *Bulletin of the Business Historical Society*, XXVII, 118-119.

CHAPTER 14

1. The coal pool was, after all, a corrective response to the workings of that law.

2. Korson, *Minstrels*, 234.

3. January 26, 1889, 2.

4. Rowland Berthoff concluded that the anthracite regions' social structure was "headless" when he overlooked the role played by labor. "Social Order," 276.

5. *Minstrels*, 204.

Appendix I

Production and Employment in the Anthracite Industry

Year	Number of employees	Tons of production
1870	35,600	12,653,575
1871	37,488	13,868,087
1872	44,745	13,899,976
1873	48,199	18,751,358
1874	53,402	17,794,857
1875	69,966	20,895,220
1876	70,474	19,611,071
1877	66,842	22,077,869
1878	63,964	18,661,577
1879	68,847	27,711,250
1880	73,373	24,843,476
1881	76,031	30,210,018
1882	83,242	30,867,301
1883	91,411	33,200,608
1884	101,078	33,561,390
1885	100,534	33,520,941
1886	103,034	34,064,543
1887	106,574	37,137,251
1888	117,290	41,638,426
1889	119,007	30,015,835
1890	109,166	40,080,355
1891	123,345	44,320,967
1892	129,797	45,738,373
1893	138,002	47,179,563
1894	139,655	45,506,179
1895	143,610	51,207,000
1896	149,670	48,074,330
1897	149,557	46,947,354

Data from Peter Roberts, *Anthracite Coal Industry*, 107.

Appendix II

Rules Adopted by the Coal Operators and Mine
Superintendents of the Eastern District of
the Wyoming and Lackawanna Coal Fields,
at the Mine Inspector's Office,
Scranton, Pennsylvania,
December 24, 1881

All persons employed in or about this colliery are hereby notified that the following rules and regulations have been adopted for the purpose of preventing injury to persons or property from negligence or carelessness of the employes.

The attention of each class of workmen is hereby called to the duties assigned them; they are also requested to do all in their power to avoid all unnecessary risk in following their daily avocations.

MINE BOSS

It shall be the duty of the mine boss to direct and generally supervise the whole working of the mine. He shall instruct the workmen in their several duties and vocations.

It shall be his special duty to keep the work in proper shape as it advances. He shall keep a careful watch over the ventilating apparatus, airways, traveling-ways, pumps and sumps, and shall see that the miners timber their places safe from the danger of loose coal, slate, or rock falling upon them. If he shall find a place in a dangerous condition, it shall be his duty to give orders to have it secured by taking down or propping up the loose material, with the least possible delay; or, if necessary, he shall stop the mining of coal at once, until it is secured. He shall also see that the signaling arrangements from bottom to top and top to bottom of the shaft or slope are kept in good condition. And he or his assistants shall examine carefully the workings generating explosive gas every morning before the miners enter the mine; and shall ascertain that the mine is free from danger before the workers are allowed to enter. He or his assistants shall go over the mine every evening and see that the doors along the air-passages are properly closed. It shall also be his duty to measure the ventilation at least once

From Pennsylvania Mine Inspectors, *Report, 1881,* 227-233.

a week at the inlet and outlet; also, at or near the face of all gangways, and the measurements to be reported to the inspector once per month.

FIRE BOSS

It shall be the duty of the fire boss to examine carefully every morning every place in the mine where explosive gas is evolved, and see that it is in a fit state for men to work therein before they are allowed to enter the mine. If any of the working places are in an unsafe condition, he shall notify the parties who work therein by danger-signal or otherwise, and they shall be governed by his advice in the absence of the mine boss.

If explosive gas is found in any of the working places, he shall not allow the men to enter said place or places until he is present to expel or see that it is expelled safely. When a signal board is furnished, he shall mark opposite the number, name, or letter (by which the party is known who works in said place) a mark thus X, indicating danger. It will then be the duty of all persons working in said place to immediately ascertain the cause of danger, and no one will be allowed to enter such place until authorized by the mine boss or fire boss.

He shall also mark the date of the month with chalk upon some conspicuous place at the face of each place examined, every morning, and shall be located at some convenient place designated by the mine boss, where he may be seen after his examining tour by every person working in the mine, and there find out the condition of their working place. Any miner or laborer going into his working place where explosive gas is evolved without ascertaining in person the condition of the same, shall be stopped at once, and the same reported to the mine boss. It shall be his special duty to see that all stoppings, doors, brattices and airways are kept in proper condition, and he shall report any defect which he may find in them to the mine boss. He shall also see that all the safety lamps used in the mine are kept in good order; also, keep a careful watch over the ventilation.

DRIVER BOSS

The driver boss shall see that the drivers are at the stables in proper time in the morning, and ready to begin work at the appointed time. He must see that the mules are regularly fed and watered, and properly attended to, and must see that the mules are not driven up steep grades without frequently resting them. He shall see that the mules are not unnecessarily whipped or abused.

If the safety of persons or animals require a safety-block or latch to be thrown across the track, near the face of the working places, he shall see that one or the other be put on at once. He shall not allow door boys to leave their doors except by permission of himself or mine boss.

DUTY of MINER

It shall be the duty of every miner employed in the mine to examine the roof or other overhanging material in his working place as soon as he shall enter the same in the morning, and if found unsafe he shall immediately take down or prop up the loose material, and see that it is in a safe condition for himself and laborers to work therein. No miner shall leave his place in an unsafe condition when his laborers are allowed to work after he has gone home. If the mine boss shall order bad roof to be taken down, or shall order props to be set under the same, it shall be the duty of the miner to attend to the same without unnecessary delay. It shall also be the duty of the miner to take proper care of his powder from the time it leaves the powder house until it reaches his working place in the mine, at which place it must be properly taken care of, and kept in a box, with cover to place over it, when the miner is not present. This box must be kept well back from the roads. When the miner is making a cartridge he shall keep his lamp at least four feet away from the nearest part of the box. Said lamp shall be placed upon that side of the box which the current of air would carry a spark from the lamp away from the box. He shall not be allowed to make a cartridge with a lamp upon his head, or his pipe in his mouth, nor shall he set his lamp upon his box. When charging a hole, if the cartridge sticks, he must take it out of the hole carefully, and either make the cartridge smaller or enlarge the hole, so that he may be able to push it easily into it. No ramming of cartridge with a drill will be allowed.

When driving an entrance between two chambers it shall be the duty of the miner, before firing a shot, to give timely notice to the men in the chamber towards which he is driving, so that they may find a place of safety. They shall also guard the passages on either side of their place, at every shot, so that no person may come unaware upon it when about to fire. They also shall be careful not to go back too soon to a shot which seemed to have missed fire.

When a shot has been fired, they shall take great care to examine the roof and coal, and see that they are in a safe condition before they go to work under them.

They shall also see that their car is a safe distance before firing a shot. Before loading their car, they, or their laborers, shall see that no tools, powder, or other material is left in the car. They also shall see that the car is properly blocked and spragged before starting to load it, and after every shot they must see that the roof is left clear before the mule shall be allowed to draw the car to the end of the road near the face.

Where explosive gas is evolved they must learn the condition of their working place before entering the same. Where gas is strong and issuing out in great volumes, they shall see that no loose coal or culm is left at the face over night, and that no gas is left burning when they leave their place after the day's work is done. Where blowers of gas are found issuing out of the bottom, no culm or gob shall be left in close proximity to it. They shall also guard against all kinds of accidents, which are liable to occur in a mine, and, as far as practicable, they shall keep· their props and gob at least two feet from the road.

LABORER or HELPER

It shall be the duty of every mine helper or laborer to take proper care in running his car from the face to the gangway. He shall see that it is properly spragged, so that no runaway may occur, whereby persons or property may be injured; and he shall not run his car down to the gangway until called upon. When letting his car down to the gangway, he must not go before it to hold it back, but shall sprag the wheels sufficiently, and, if necessary, push it when it does not run with the proper number of sprags. It shall also be his duty to fill his road properly for the mule to travel in, and, as far as practicable, he shall keep the sides of his road sufficiently clear of culm or other material, so that a person or mule may pass a car with ease. Where head or stopping blocks are provided for cars to rest against, he shall see that they are properly placed upon the road, as he is going up, so that they may be in proper position when the car comes down. He shall also look into his car before loading it, and see that no tools, sprags, or other material excepting coal is left in it. He shall see that the car is properly secured before commencing to load it, by putting a sufficient number of sprags in the wheels, and, if necessary, he shall place a prop securely against the lower end of the car. He shall devote his time principally to cleaning, preparing, and loading his coal, but, when necessary, he shall help his miner to set props and do any other work which requires his aid.

HEADMAN and FOOTMAN

It shall be the duty of the headman and footman, at every shaft where men have to ascend or descend to be at their proper places when the mine shall be regularly at work, or at such times as the mine boss may designate, and they shall see that not more than ten men are allowed to ascend or descend at the same time on any carriage. If more than ten men shall get on at one time, it shall be their duty to call upon some of them to come off. If the person or persons so called shall refuse to do so, they shall report them to the mine boss, whose duty it shall be to punish them as they deserve. They shall not allow any person to step on the carriage after the signal has been given to the engineer to hoist or lower the carriage, not leave the carriage until it has rested upon the bottom or top.

It shall also be the duty of the headman or footman to pay strict attention to the signaling apparatus, and see that they are kept in good condition, so that they may, at all times, communicate with the engineer, and they must see that all of the signals are properly understood between them.

DRIVER

It shall be the duty of a driver to take proper care of his horse or mule, and see that it is properly fed and watered. He must not whip or abuse it unnecessarily, or allow any other person to do so. He shall drive it carefully, and when ascending steep grade allow it to rest frequently. When he leaves his mule or horse at any time, he must be careful to leave it in a place of safety, where it will be secure from runaway cars or other danger. When his mule or horse is drawing cars into place he must be careful not to drive any further than the track is laid, nor into a pile of coal at or near the face, or to leave the car at a place where he has no room to pass it. If the road is in a bad condition for want of filling, he shall report the same to the mine boss. When drawing cars upon a graded road, he shall be careful to sprag or block the cars sufficiently to prevent them from running upon himself or mule. If head or stopping blocks are used at certain points upon the gangway or main road, he shall see that they are properly placed upon the road when going up with the empty cars, so that they may be in a proper position to stop the cars before they go on to the steeper grade.

If any person abuses his mule or horse he must report the same to the mine boss, nor will they be allowed to delegate any other person to take out or return their mules to the barn, nor drive their mules to or from the barn faster than a walk.

COMPANY HANDS

All company hands must be at their proper places in the morning to begin work at the proper time, and must not leave until the breaker stops, or if working full day they are expected to work the ten hours, and they shall see that all instructions given them by the mine boss or foreman are strictly carried out.

DOOR BOY

It shall be the duty of a door boy to be at his post at all times when the mine is regularly at work.

He must not leave his door at the command of any person except the mine boss or other person to whom he may delegate such authority.

OUTSIDE FOREMAN

It shall be the duty of outside foreman to direct and generally supervise the outside business over which he is placed. He shall see that all machinery connected with the breaking and preparing of coal be properly fenced off as required by law, and he or his assistants shall see that all persons are free from the machinery before the signal is given for the engineer to start, and see that the boys are kept in their proper places, and not allowed to play about the machinery or cars.

HOISTING ENGINEER

It shall be the duty of an engineer to keep a careful watch over the machinery, pumps, steam boilers, etc. He shall see that the boilers are properly supplied with water, and that the steam pressure shall not exceed the limit to which the superintendent of machinery or other officer shall consider them perfectly safe to carry. When a fan is used for ventilation he shall keep it running at such speed as the mine boss or superintendent may direct. He shall not slacken its speed unless directed to do so by said officers. If any repairs are to be made to the fan or other parts of its machinery whereby it is required to be stopped, it shall be his duty to give the mine boss timely notice of the same, so that he may have everything left in proper order. He shall also work his engine slowly and with great care when persons are ascending or descending the shaft. He shall also see that the safety carriage is in good order before letting men down in the morning, and must examine the safety-catches, ropes, and cover, and other parts of the machinery daily, and shall run the safety carriage up and down before allowing men to descend in the shaft in the morning. He shall not allow persons to loaf in the engineroom, nor shall he engage in conversation when in the act of lowering or hoisting men or coal. He shall also keep a strict watch over the fireman, and see that he attends to his duties faithfully.

BREAKER ENGINEER

The breaker engineer shall pay strict attention to the signals from the breaker. He shall not start or move his engine until he is satisfied, either by metal tube or other signal, that all persons are free from the machinery. He shall see that no one is allowed to go around any of the machinery for the purpose of oiling or otherwise, except such persons as are authorized by the foreman.

SLATE BOSSES

The slate bosses shall keep the boys in their respective places, and not allow them to go around the machinery or cars. They shall use the greatest caution on all occasions when boys or men are cleaning out rollers or screens, and see that every person is clear of the machinery before giving the signal to the breaker engineer to start his engine.

PENALTIES

For the violation of the above rules and regulations, it shall be the duty of the mine boss or foreman to suspend, discharge, or otherwise punish any person who shall carelessly or willfully neglect to attend to the duties assigned to them.

When damage to property is carelessly or willfully done, the party so offending shall be subject to pay for the full amount of damage, and may be suspended or discharged for the same offense.

GENERAL RULE

All persons are hereby forbidden to enter any of the old workings without the consent of the mine boss or fire boss, or ride upon the cars on any slope or plane, or send out tools upon a car of coal unless they follow them out and take them off the car before ascending the shaft or slope. Any person who opens a door must see that it is properly closed before leaving it. No person shall be allowed to travel upon a slope or plane while the same is in motion. Persons ascending or descending a shaft will not be allowed to enter upon or leave the carriage while in motion, nor shall they be allowed to step on after the signal has been given to hoist or lower the carriage.

Any person knowing of the unsafe condition of any place or of damage done to the doors, brattices, or stoppings or obstructions in the air-passages, shall notify the mine boss or fire boss as soon as possible after said damage has been done.

Any person found guilty of carelessly or wickedly injuring animals or other property shall be held liable for the full amount of damage done to the same.

All persons must familiarize themselves with the above rules and any person violating any of said rules will be dealt with as the superintendent may direct.

I approve the above regulations.

[signed]

Patrick Blewitt,

Inspector of Mines, &c.

Appendix III

Contract Between a Miner and a Store

Messrs. H.H. Ashley & Co.,   No. _____

Gentlemen:

    I wish to purchase goods from your store
from time to time, on credit. I am at
present in the employ of the lessee and
contractor, under the receivers of the
Lehigh-Wilkes-Barre Coal Co., and agree
that you may collect the price of all goods
which you shall furnish me or my family, or
which you have already furnished, from the
same company, their receivers, lessee, or
contractor, or any other party employing
me, out of the amounts they now owe me, or
may hereafter be indebted to me, and that
your receipt to my employers shall be a
full discharge of such indebtedness for
the amounts collected.

Witness_____

_____188-____

We accept the proposition of_____
as above made, and agree to give him credit
on the terms and conditions therein proposed,
to such amounts, and for so long as we may
deem expedient.

Witness_____

_____188-____

From Pennsylvania, Secretary of Internal Affairs, *Annual Report, 1878-79,*
Part III, *Industrial Statistics,* 380.

Appendix IV

Rules to Govern the Mining of Coal in Pittston and
Vicinity as Adopted by the Operators and Miners
This 12th Day of August, 1863

1. Operators are to control their own works in all respects.

2. Operators are to hire any man or boy they deem proper.

3. Miners and others are not to interfere with any company men or boys.

4. It is agreed that when any man is away from his work two days, either from idleness, drinking, or any other cause, except sickness of himself or family, such man shall be discharged.

5. Operators and Miners agree to give each other two weeks notice before making any stop of work (except in case of accident or circumstances beyond their control) for change of price or any other change from the old manner of working.

6. A Committee composed of three coal operators and three miners shall settle and dispose of all difficulties and grievances that may arise between the Miners and Operators, or between those employed by the Operators and Miners, so the work may not be interrupted.

7. Pay day to be the 20th of each month, except when it comes on Sunday.

8. The price of Mining to be six cents per ton more than the price paid when the works stopped and to continue the same, until the 1st of December next.

From Manuscript Coal File 3, Wyoming Geological and Historical Society.

Bibliography

Source Materials

MANUSCRIPTS

Bologna, John. Account Book with G.B. Markle and Co., 1893. Wyoming Geological and Historical Society, Wilkes-Barre.

Cist, J.O. Contract with Aaron Dean, January 18, 1815. Mss. Coal File 1, Wyoming Geological and Historical Society, Wilkes-Barre.

Delaware, Lackawanna, and Western Railroad, Coal Department. Papers. Lackawanna Historical Society, Scranton.

Hand, J.P. Store Book in Account with W.M. Miller & Co., 1894-95. Wyoming Geological and Historical Society.

Land and Labor Party of Luzerne County, Pa. Declaration of Principles. Photocopy in author's possession.

Lehigh–Wilkes-Barre Coal Company Papers. Wyoming Geological and Historical Society.

Miners' Benevolent Association of Archbald. Minute Book, March 28, 1863 to May 8, 1871. Collection of Mr. Joseph Kostick.

Molly Maguire Folder. The Autograph Collection of the Historical Society of Pennsylvania, Philadelphia.

Philadelphia and Reading Company Papers. The Historical Society of Pennsylvania.

Wilkes-Barre. Captains of Police Reports. Wyoming Geological and Historical Society.

Wilkes-Barre. Docket Book. Wyoming Geological and Historical Society.

Workingmen's Beneficial and Benevolent Association of Carbon County. Constitution and By-laws. Photocopy in author's possession.

Wright, Hendrick B. Papers. Wyoming Geological and Historical Society.

GOVERNMENT PUBLICATIONS

Commonwealth of Pennsylvania. Adjutant General. *Report of the Adjutant General of Pennsylvania, 1877.*

———. Coal Waste Commission. *Report of the Commission Appointed to Investigate the Waste of Coal Mining With the View to Utilizing of the Waste.* Philadelphia: Allen, Lane and Scott, 1893.

———. *Laws of Pennsylvania.*

———. Legislature. *Report of the Legislature of Pennsylvania Containing a Description of the Swarta Mining District.* Harrisburg: Boas and Caplan, 1839.

———. Legislature. Joint Committee to Investigate the Philadelphia and Reading Railroad Company and the Philadelphia and Reading Coal and Iron Company. *Testimony Before the Committee to Investigate The Philadelphia and Reading Railroad Company and the Philadelphia and Reading Coal and Iron Company.* Legislative Documents, 1876; Vol. III, 495-1137.

———. Legislature. Riot Committee. *Riot Committee Investigation.* Pennsylvania Legislative Documents, 1878. Vol. 5, Document No. 29.

———. Mine Inspectors. *Reports of the Inspectors of Mines, 1871-1897.*

———. Second Geological Survey of Pennsylvania. *A Special Report to the Legislature Upon the Causes, Kinds, and Amount of Waste in Mining Anthracite With a Chapter on the Methods of Mining by John Price Wetherhill.* By Franklin Platt. Harrisburg: Board of Commissioners for the Second Geological Survey, 1881.

———. Second Geological Survey of Pennsylvania. *Report on the Mining Methods and Appliances Used in the Anthracite Fields.* By H.M. Chance. Harrisburg: Board of Commissioners for the Second Geological Survey, 1883.

———. Secretary of Internal Affairs. *Annual Reports*, Part III, *Industrial Statistics*, 1872-1897.

———. Senate, Select Committee upon the Subject of the Coal Trade. "Report of the Committee of the Senate Upon the Subject of the Coal Trade." *Journal of the Senate of the Commonwealth of Pennsylvania*, 1833-34; vol. 2, 449-572.

———. Senate, Committee on the Judiciary General. *Report of the Committee on the Judiciary General, of the Senate of Pennsylvania, in Relation to the Anthracite Coal Difficulties with Accompanying Testimony*. Legislative Documents, 1871, 1515-1737.

———. Senate, *Journal of the Senate of the Commonwealth of Pennsylvania*.

Great Britain. Foreign Office. *Commercial Reports. Reports Respecting the Late Industrial Conflicts in the United States*. Sessional Papers, 1877, Vol. LXXXIV.

New York. Senate. Special Committee on the Coal Combination. *Report of the Senate Special Committee on the Coal Combination to Inquire Whether a Combination of Corporations or Individuals Has Been Formed With A View of Advancing or Controlling the Price of Coal*. Senate Documents, Vol. IV, Doc. 21, 116th Session, 1893.

United States. Anthracite Coal Strike Commission. *Report to the President on the Anthracite Coal Strike of May-October, 1902*. Washington: Government Printing Office, 1903.

———. Bureau of Statistics. *Labor in Europe and America*. Washington: Government Printing Office, 1875.

———. Commissioner of Labor. *Eleventh Special Report of the Commissioner of Labor; Regulation and Restriction of Output*. Washington: Government Printing Office, 1904.

———. Commissioner of Labor. *Third Annual Report of the Commissioner of Labor; 1887: Strikes and Lockouts*. Washington: Government Printing Office, 1888.

———. Department of Interior. United States Geological Survey. *Mineral Industries of the United States, 1883-1884*. House Misc. Document 36, 49th Congress, 1st Session, 1885.

———. Department of Interior. United States Geological Survey. *Mineral Resources of the United States.* House Misc. Document 42, 50th Congress, 1st Session, 1887.

———. Department of Interior. United States Geological Survey. *Mineral Industries of the United States,* 1891. House Misc. Document, 83, 52nd Congress, 2nd Session, 1892.

———. Department of State. Consular Service. *United States Consular Reports: Labor in Europe.* House Executive Document 54, 48th Congress, 2nd Session, 1885.

———. Industrial Commission. *Report of the Industrial Commission,* Vol. XII, *The Relations and Conditions of Capital and Labor Employed in the Mining Industry.* Washington: Government Printing Office, 1901.

———. Immigration Commission. *Report of the Immigration Commission.* Senate Document 633, 44 vols., 61st Congress, 2nd Session, 1911.

———. House of Representatives. Select Committee on Existing Labor Troubles in Pennsylvania. *Labor Troubles in the Anthracite Regions of Pennsylvania, 1887-1888.* Report 4147, 50th Congress, 2nd Session, 1889.

———. House of Representatives. Select Committee to Inquire into the Alleged Violation of the Laws Prohibiting the Importation of Contract Laborers, Paupers, Convicts, and other Classes. *Testimony Taken By the Select Committee of the House of Representatives to Inquire into the Alleged Violation of the Laws Prohibiting the Importation of Contract Laborers, Paupers, Convicts, and Other Classes.* House Misc. Document 572, 50th Congress, 1st Session, 1888.

———. House of Representatives. Select Committee Relative to the Causes of the General Depression in Labor and Business. *Investigation by a Select Committee Relative to the Causes of the General Depression in Labor and Business, and as to Chinese Immigration.* House Misc. Document 5, 46th Congress, 2nd Session, 1879.

———. House of Representatives. Subcommittee of the Committee on Interstate and Foreign Commerce. *Report and Testimony in Regards to the Alleged Combination of the Philadelphia and Reading Railroad Company and Other Railroad and Canal Companies and Producers of Coal.* Report 2278, 52nd Congress, 2nd Session, 1892.

COLLECTIONS OF DOCUMENTS

Commons, John R. et al. *Documentary History of American Industrial Society.* 10 vols.; Cleveland, Ohio: The A.H. Clark Co., 1910.

Conway, Alan. *The Welsh in America: Letters from the Immigrants.* Minneapolis: University of Minnesota Press, 1961.

NEWSPAPERS

The Daily News (Hazleton).
Daily Republican (Pottsville).
The Daily Standard (Hazleton).
Evening Bulletin (Hazleton).
Evening Chronicle (Pottsville).
Hazard's Register of Pennsylvania.
Hazleton Weekly Sentinel.
Miners' Journal (Pottsville).
Mining Herald and Colliery Engineer (Shenandoah).
The Mountain Beacon (Hazleton).
New York Daily Tribune.
The Plain Speaker (Hazleton).
Public Ledger (Philadelphia).
Record of the Times (Wilkes-Barre).
Scranton Republican.
Seward's Coal Trade, 1877-78.
Shamokin Herald.
Shamokin News-Dispatch.
Shenandoah Herald.
The Tamaqua Courier.
The Tribune (Chicago).
Wilkes-Barre Telephone.

CONTEMPORARY BOOKS AND ARTICLES

Albright, Charles and F.W. Hughes. *The Great Molly Maguire Trials in Carbon and Schuylkill Counties, Pennsylvania. Brief Reference to Such Trials and Arguments of General Charles Albright and Hon. F.W. Hughes, In the Case of the Commonwealth vrs. James Carroll, James Roarity, Hugh McGehan, and James Boyle, Indicted for the Murder of Benjamin F. Yost, Chief of Police of and at Tamaqua, July 6, 1876, In the Court of Oyer and Terminer of Schuylkill County.* Stenographically reported by R.A. West. Pottsville: Chronicle Book and Job Rooms, 1876.

Alden, H.M. "Coal Fields of Pennsylvania." *Harper's,* XXVIII (September 1863), 455-467.

Allison, Robert. "Early History of Coal Mining and Mining Machinery in Schuylkill County." *Publications of the Schuylkill County Historical Society,* IV (1912), 134-155.

Ashburner, Charles A. *Brief Description of the Anthracite Coal Fields of Pennsylvania.* Author's Edition, 1884.

Blanchard, D.E. *A Concise History of the Anthracite Coal Industry of Pennsylvania.* Wilkes-Barre: W.H. Seacord, 1884.

Bowen, Eli. "Coal and the Coal Fields of Pennsylvania." *Harper's,* XV (August 1857), 451-469.

――――. *The Coal Regions of Pennsylvania, Being a General, Geological, Historical and Statistical Review of the Anthracite Coal Districts.* Pottsville: E.N. Carvalho, 1848.

――――. *The Pictorial Sketch-Book of Pennsylvania or Its Scenery, Internal Improvements, Resources, and Agriculture, Popularly Described.* Philadelphia: Willis P. Hazard, 1852.

Brooks, J.G. "Impressions of the Anthracite Coal Troubles." *Yale Review,* VI (November 1897), 306-311.

Chambers, George. *Historical Sketch of Pottsville, Schuylkill County, Pennsylvania.* Pottsville: Standard Publishing Company, 1877.

Chase, H.W. *An Account of the Unparalleled Disaster at the Avondale Colliery, Luzerne County, Pennsylvania, September 6th 1869 By Which One Hundred and Ten Lives Were Lost.* Scranton: J.B. Furman, Publisher, 1869.

Cist, Jacob. "An Account of the Mines in the Region About Wilkes-Barre, Pennsylvania." *Proceedings of the Wyoming Geological and Historical Society,* X (1909), 98-114.

Coxe, Eckley B. "History of Mining Legislation in Pennsylvania." *Journal of Social Science* (1871-1874), 12-32.

"Coal Policy in Pennsylvania." *Hunt's Merchants' Magazine,* XII (1845), 242.

Comparative Views of Most Anthracite Collieries in Pennsylvania. Printed by W.F. Geddes, 1835.

Culin, Steward. *A Trooper's Narrative of Service in the Anthracite Strike of 1902.* Philadelphia: G.W. Jacobs & Co., 1903.

Cushing, L. "The Coal Trade in Pennsylvania." *North American Review,* XVII (January 1836), 241-256.

Dacus, J.A. *Annals of the Great Strikes in the United States.* Chicago: L.T. Palmer & Co., 1877.

Daddow, Samuel H. *Report of the Landed Estate and Mines and Mineral Resources of the Locust Gap Improvement Company.* To Which is Appended the Charter and By Laws of the Company. Philadelphia: Stein and Jones, Printers, 1866.

Daddow, Samuel H. and Benjamin Bannan. *Coal, Iron and Oil; Or the Practical American Miner.* Pottsville: Benjamin Bannan, 1866.

Danville and Pottsville Railroad Company. *Laws and By-Laws of the Danville and Pottsville Railroad Company.* Philadelphia: K.R. Bailey, 1851.

Davis, John et al. *Report of a Committee of Investigation Into the Affairs of the Philadelphia and Reading Railroad Company.* Boston: Eastburn's Press, 1846.

Derby, George. *An Inquiry into the Influence of Anthracite Fires Upon Health; With Remarks Upon Artificial Moisture, and the Best Modes of Warming Houses.* 2nd ed., enlarged. Boston: A. Williams and Co., 1868.

Dewees, F.P. *The Molly Maguires: The Origin, Growth, and Character of the Organization.* Philadelphia: J.B. Lippincott and Company, 1877.

"End of the Anthracite Strike." *Engineering and Mining Journal,* XIX (June 1875), 461.

Evans, Christopher. *History of the United Mine Workers of America from the Year 1860 to 1890.* Indianapolis: United Mine Workers of America, 1914.

"The First Coal Region of Pennsylvania." *Hunt's Merchants' Magazine,* XII (1845), 426-434.

French, Samuel C. *Reminiscences of Plymouth, Luzerne County, Pennsylvania.* New York: Locus Press, 1914.

George, Henry. "Labor in Pennsylvania." *North American Review,* CXLII (1886), 165-182, 268-277, 360-370, CXLIV (1887), 86-95.

Gibbons, P.E. "The Miners of Scranton Pennsylvania." *Harper's New Monthly Magazine,* LV (November 1877), 916-927.

Giering, Eugen. "Wilkes-Barre, Pennsylvania." *Nation,* XVI (1902), 223-225.

Gilberton Coal Company. *Description of the Mines with the Report of P.W. Sheafer of Pennsylvania, Engineer of Mines.* Boston: Wright and Potter, 1864.

Godkin, E.L. "'Cornering' The Public." *Nation,* XII (March 2, 1871), 136-137.

———. "Labor and Politics." *Nation,* XIV (June 13, 1872), 386-387.

———. "Some Questions for the Labor Commission." *Nation,* XIV (January 4, 1872), 5-7.

Gowen, Franklin B. *Argument of Franklin B. Gowen, Esq., of Counsel For the Commonwealth In The Case of the Commonwealth vs. Thomas Munley, Indicted In the Court of Oyer and Terminer of Schuylkill County Pennsylvania, For the Murder of Thomas Sanger, A Mining Boss, At Raven Run, On September 1, 1875.* Stenographically Reported by R.A. West. Pottsville: Chronicle Book and Job Rooms, 1876.

Greene, Homer. *Coal and the Coal Mines.* New York: Houghton, Mifflin and Co., 1889.

Hodgkin, J.B. "Latest Phase of the Coal Troubles." *Nation,* XII (April 13, 1871), 254-256.

———. "True History of the Coal Strike." *Nation,* XII (March 16, 1871), 153-154.

Hudson, James F. "The Anthracite Coal Pool." *North American Review,* CXLIX (January 1887), 43-54.

Hughes, F.W. *Commonwealth versus Patrick Hester, Patrick Tully, and Peter McHugh Tried and Convicted of the Murder of Alexander W. Rea. Argument of Honorable F.W. Hughes, For Commonwealth, at Bloomsburg, Pa., February 23 & 24, 1877*. Stenographically reported by R.A. West. Philadelphia: G.V. Town and Son, 1877.

James, Thomas C. "A Brief Account of the Discovery of Anthracite Coal on the Lehigh." *Memoirs of the Historical Society of Pennsylvania*, I (1826), 321-331.

Johnson, Walter R. *Notes on the Use of Anthracite in the Manufacture of Iron With Some Remarks on Its Evaporating Power*. Boston: Charles C. Little and James Brown, 1841.

Jones, John G. "Impression of the Anthracite Coal Troubles." *Yale Review*, VI (November 1897), 306-311.

Kropff, F.C. *Report Upon the Coal Lands and Coal Work In Beaver Township, Columbia County, Pennsylvania*. Boston: J.E. Farwell & Co., 1865.

Kulp, George B. *Coal, Its Antiquity, Its Discovery and Early Development in the Wyoming Valley*. Wilkes-Barre: n.p. 1890.

Lehigh Coal and Navigation Company. *Annual Reports*, 1863-1897.

Lesley, J.P. *Manual of Coal and Its Topography*. Philadelphia: J.B. Lippincott and Co., 1856.

Logan, Samuel C. *A City's Danger and Defense, Or Issues and Results of the Strikes of 1877*. Scranton: The Author, 1887.

Martin, Edward W. *The History of the Great Riots Being a Full and Authentic Account of the Strikes and Riots on the Various Railroads of the United States and in the Mining Regions and a Full History of the Molly Maguires*. Philadelphia: The National Publishing Co., 1877.

Mathews, Alfred and Austin N. Hungerford. *History of the Counties of Lehigh and Carbon, in the Commonwealth of Pennsylvania*. Philadelphia: Everts and Richards, 1884.

McClure, Alexander K. *Old Time Notes of Pennsylvania*. 2 vols. Philadelphia: John C. Winston, 1905.

McFarlane, James. *The Coal Regions of America*. New York: D. Appleton & Co., 1873.

McNeil, George E., ed. *The Labor Problem Today*. New York: The M.W. Hazen Co., 1887.

Miesse, Charles. *Points on Coal and the Coal Business*. Myerstown, Pa.: Feese and Uhrich, 1887.

Nichols, Francis H. "Children of the Coal Shadow." *McClure's*, XX (1902/03), 435-444.

North American. *Pennsylvania Coal and Its Carriers*. Philadelphia: Crissy & Markley, 1852.

Patterson, Joseph F. "After the W.B.A." *Publications of the Historical Society of Schuylkill County,* IV (1913/14), 168–184.

———. "Old W.B.A. Days." *Publications of the Historical Society of Schuylkill County*, II (1909).

———. "Reminiscences of John Maguire After Fifty Years of Mining." *Publications of the Historical Society of Schuylkill County*, IV (1913/14), 305–326.

"Pennsylvania in Its Industrial Aspect." *Republic*, II (1874), 261-268.

Pinkerton, Allan. *The Molly Maguires and the Detectives*. New York: G.W. Dillingham Co., Publishers, 1877.

Plumb, Henry B. *History of Hanover Township Including Sugar Notch, Ashley, and Nanticoke Boroughs and also a History of Wyoming Valley in Luzerne County, Pennsylvania*. Wilkes-Barre: Robert Baur, 1885.

Rhodes, James Ford. "The Molly Maguires in the Anthracite Region." *American Historical Review*, XV (April 1910).

Rhone, Rossamond D. "Anthracite Coal Mines and Mining." *Review of Reviews*, XVI (1902), 110-122.

Road, Henry. "Mine Laborers in Pennsylvania." *Forum*, XIV (September 1892), 110-122.

Roberts, Peter. *Anthracite Coal Communities*. New York: Macmillan, 1904.

———. *The Anthracite Coal Industry*. New York: Macmillan, 1901.

Rogers, Henry D. "Coal and Coal Mining." *Harper's*, XXIX (July 1868), 163-168.

Roy, Andrew. *The Coal Mines*. Cleveland: Robinson, Savage & Co., 1876.

————. *A History of the Coal Miners of the United States, From the Development of the Mines to the Close of the Anthracite Strike of 1902.* 3rd ed. Columbus, Ohio: J.L. Trauger Printing Company, 1903.

Spahr, Charles R. *America's Working People*. New York: Longmans, Green & Co., 1900.

————. "Coal Miners of Pennsylvania." *Outlook*, LXI (August 5, 1899), 805-812.

Stevenson, George E. *Reflections of An Anthracite Engineer*. New York: The Author, 1931.

Taylor, George. *Effect of Incorporated Coal Companies Upon the Anthracite Coal Trade of Pennsylvania*. Pottsville: Benjamin Bannan, 1833.

Taylor, Richard. *Two Reports on the Coal Lands, Mines and Improvements of the Dauphin and Susquehanna Coal Company and of the Geological Examinations, Present Condition and Prospects of the Stony Creek Coal Estate in the Townships of Jackson, Rush, and Middle Paxtany in the County of Dauphin and East Hanover Townships in the County of Lebanon. With Appendixes*. Philadelphia: E.G. Dorsey, Printer, 1840.

Throop, Benjamin H. *A Half-Century in Scranton*. Scranton: The Author, 1895.

The Twin Shaft Relief Association. *The Twin Shaft Disaster, of June 28th, 1896 and Work of Relief for the Suffers With Charter, By-Laws and Plan of Distribution of the Fund to the Beneficiaries*. Pittston: The Twin Shaft Relief Association, 1897.

Virtue, G.O. "The Anthracite Combinations." *Quarterly Journal of Economics*, X (April 1896), 296-323.

————. "The Anthracite Mine Laborers." U.S. Department of Labor. *Bulletin 13* (1897), 728-774.

———. "Two Features of the Anthracite Industry." Unpublished Ph.D. dissertation, Harvard University, 1897.

Warne, Frank J. "The Effect of Unionism Upon the Mine Worker." *Annals of the American Academy of Political and Social Science*, XXI (January 1903), 20-35.

———. *The Slav Invasion and the Mine Workers; A Study in Immigration*. Philadelphia: J.B. Lippincott and Company, 1904.

Warringer, J. *My Years in Anthracite*. Lansford, Pa.: The Author, 1951.

White, Josiah. *Josiah White's History Given By Himself*. Philadelphia: G.H. Buchanan Company, 1909.

Wright, Carrol D. "An Historical Sketch of the Knights of Labor." *Quarterly Journal of Economics*, I (January 1887), 137-138.

Secondary Sources

BOOKS AND PAMPHLETS

Allen, James B. *The Company Town in the American West*. Norman: University of Oklahoma Press, 1966.

Andrews, Theodore. *The Polish National Catholic Church in America and Poland*. London: S.P.C.K., 1953.

Arnot, R. Page. *A History of the Scotish Miners From the Earliest Times*. London: George Allen and Unwin, Ltd., 1955.

Ash, S.H. "The Buried Valley of the Susquehanna River in the Anthracite Region of Pennsylvania." United States Bureau of Mines, *Bulletin 494*.

Ashley, William James. *The Adjustment of Wages: A Study in the Coal and Iron Industries of Great Britain and America*. London: Longmans, Green and Co., 1903.

Austin, Aleine. *The Labor Story: A Popular History of American Labor, 1786-1949*. New York: Coward-McCann, Inc., 1949.

Bell, Herbert C. *History of Northumberland County, Pennsylvania*. Chicago: Brown, Runk and Co., 1891.

Berthoff, Rowland T. *British Immigrants in Industrial America*. Cambridge: Harvard University Press, 1953.

Billinger, Robert D. *Pennsylvania's Coal Industry, 1762-1954*. Gettysburg: Pennsylvania Historical Association, 1954.

Bimba, Anthony J. *The Molly Maguires*. New York: International Publishers, 1932.

Bogen, Jules Irwin. *The Anthracite Railroads: A Study in American Railroad Enterprise*. New York: The Ronald Press Co., 1927.

Blanchard, Paul. *The Irish and Catholic Power: An American Interpretation*. Boston: The Beacon Press, 1953.

Bradsby, Henry C. ed. *History of Luzerne County, Pennsylvania*. Chicago: S.B. Nelson, 1893.

Brenckman, Frederick. *History of Carbon County*. Harrisburg: James J. Nungessorm, 1913.

Brennan, James M. *From Mine Pit to Pulpit*. Boston: The Christopher Publishing House, 1954.

Brewster, William. *History of the Certified Township of Kingston Pennsylvania, 1769-1929: Together with a Short Account of the Fourteenth Commonwealth*. Wilkes-Barre: Smith-Bennet Corp., 1930.

Broehl, Wayne G. *The Molly Maguires*. Cambridge: Harvard University Press, 1964.

Browne, Henry J. *The Catholic Church and the Knights of Labor*. Washington: Catholic University of America, 1949.

Bulman, H.F. *Working of Coal and Other Stratified Minerals*. London: Benn, 1927.

Carbon County Historical Society. *Centennial Anniversary of the First Shipment of Anthracite Coal From the Lehigh Region at Lausanne, Pennsylvania, August 4, 1814*. Mauch Chunk: Carbon County Historical Society, 1914.

Clark, Thomas H. and Colin W. Stearn. *The Geological Evolution of North America: A Regional Approach to Historical Geology*. New York: Ronald Press Co., 1960.

Coleman, J. Walter. *The Molly Maguire Riots: Industrial Conflict in Pennsylvania's Coal Regions.* Richmond: Garrett and Massie, 1936.

Corlsen, Carl. *Buried Black Treasure.* Dansville, N.Y.: F.A. Owen Publishing Co., 1954.

Cornell, Robert J. *The Anthracite Coal Strike of 1902.* Washington: Catholic University of America Press, 1957.

Dulles, Foster Rhea. *Labor in America: A History.* 3rd ed. New York: Thomas Y. Crowell, 1966.

Dunbar, Carl O. *Historical Geology.* New York: John Wiley and Sons, 1949.

Eavenson, Howard N. *First Century and a Quarter of American Coal Industry.* Pittsburgh: The Author, 1942.

Erickson, Charlotte. *American Industry and the European Immigrant, 1860-1885.* Cambridge: Harvard University Press, 1957.

Fox, Paul. *The Poles in America.* New York: George H. Doran Co., 1922.

––––––. *The Polish National Catholic Church.* Scranton: School of Christian Living, n.d.

Gluck, Elsie. *John Mitchell: Labor's Bargain with the Gilded Age.* New York: The John Day Co., 1929.

Goodrich, Carter L. *The Miner's Freedom: A Study of the Working Life in a Changing Industry.* Boston: Marshall Jones Co., 1925.

Gray, Howard A. *The Coal Industry: A Study in Social Control.* Washington: American Council on Public Affairs, 1940.

Hertzler, J.O. *American Social Institutions: A Sociological Analysis.* Boston: Allyn and Bacon, 1961.

History of Schuylkill County, Pennsylvania With Illustrations and Biographical Sketches of Some of Its Prominent Men and Pioneers. New York: W.W. Munsell, 1881.

Hitchcock, Frederick L. *History of Scranton and Its People.* 3 vols. New York: Lewis Historical Publishing Co., 1914.

Hourwich, Issac A. *Immigration and Labor: The Economic Aspects of European Immigration to the United States.* New York: G.P. Putnam's Sons, 1912.

Hudson Coal Company. *The Story of Anthracite.* New York: The Hudson Coal Co., 1932.

Hussey, Russel. *Historical Geology.* New York: McGraw-Hill Book Company, 1944.

Jones, Chester L. *The Economic History of Anthracite Tide-Water Canals.* Philadelphia: Publishers for the University, 1908.

Jones, Eliot. *The Anthracite Coal Combination in the United States with Some Account of the Early Development of the Anthracite Industry.* "Harvard Economic Studies." Vol. XI Cambridge: Harvard University Press, 1914.

Kasey, Robert and William Douglas. *The Lackawanna Story: The First Hundred Years of the D.L. & W.* New York: McGraw-Hill Book Company, 1951.

Kinzer, Donald L. *An Episode of Anti-Catholicism: The American Protective Association.* Seattle: University of Washington Press, 1964.

Korson, George. *Black Rock: Mining Folklore of the Pennsylvania Dutch.* Baltimore: Johns Hopkins University Press, 1960.

————. *Minstrels of the Mine Patch; Songs and Stories of the Anthracite Industry.* Philadelphia: University of Pennsylvania Press, 1938.

Kurath, Hans. *A Word Geography of the Eastern United States.* Ann Arbor: University of Michigan Press, 1949.

Leighton, George R. *Five Cities; The Story of Their Youth and Old Age.* New York: Harper and Brothers, 1939.

Levasseur, E. *The American Workman.* Translated by Thomas G. Adams. Baltimore: The Johns Hopkins Press, 1900.

Lucy, Ernest. *The Molly Maguires of Pennsylvania or Ireland in America; A True Narrative.* London: George Bell and Sons, n.d.

Moore, Elwood S. *Coal: Its Properties, Analysis, Classifications, Geology, Extraction, Uses, and Distribution.* 2nd ed. New York: John Wiley and Sons, 1940.

Mumford, John K. *Anthracite*. New York: Industries Publishing Company, 1925.

Murphy, Thomas. *Jubilee History of Lackawanna County, Pennsylvania*. 2 vols. Topeka: Historical Publishing Co., 1928.

Nearing, Scott. *Anthracite; An Instance of Natural Monopoly*. Philadelphia: John C. Winston, 1915.

Nicolls, Williams S. *The Story of American Coal*. 2nd ed.; Philadelphia: J.B. Lippincott and Company, 1904.

Nolan, J. Bennet. *The Schuylkill*. New Brunswick: Rutgers University Press, 1951.

Perry, Josephine. *The Coal Industry*. New York: Longmans, Green and Co., 1944.

Pinkowski, Edward. *John Siney, The Miner's Martyr*. Philadelphia: Sunshine Press, 1963.

————. *The Lattimer Massacre*. Philadelphia: Sunshine Press, 1950.

Rayback, Joseph G. *A History of American Labor*. New York: The Macmillan Company, 1964.

Richard, Thomas A. *A History of American Mining*. New York: McGraw-Hill Book Company, 1932.

Rowan, Thomas W. *The Pinkertons: A Detective Dynasty*. Boston: Little, Brown, and Co., 1931.

Schlegel, Marvin W. *Ruler of the Reading: The Life of Franklin B. Gowen, 1836-1889*. Harrisburg: Archives Publishing Company of Pennsylvania, 1947.

Schurick, Adam T. *The Coal Industry*. Boston: Little, Brown, and Co., 1924.

Shalloo, J.P. *Private Police*. Philadelphia: American Academy of Political and Social Science, 1933.

Smith, Samuel R. *The Black Trail of Anthracite*. Kingston, Pa.: The Author, 1907.

The Story of the Old Company. Lansford, Pa.: Lehigh Coal and Navigation Co., 1941.

Suffern, Arthur E. *Conciliation and Arbitration in the Coal Industries of America.* Boston: Houghton Mifflin Co., 1915.

Summers, A.L. *Anthracite and the Anthracite Industry.* 2nd ed. London: Isaac Pitman and Sons, 1922.

Thernstrom, Stephan. *Poverty and Progress: Social Mobility in a Nineteenth Century City.* Cambridge: Harvard University Press, 1964.

Trachtenberg, Alexander. *The History of Legislation for the Protection of Coal Miners in Pennsylvania, 1824-1915.* New York: International Publishers, 1942.

Udy, Stanley H., Jr. *Organization of Work: A Comparative Analysis of Production Among Nonindustrial Peoples.* New Haven: H.R.A.F. Press, 1959.

Unger, Irwin. *The Greenback Era: A Social and Political History of American Finance, 1865-1879.* Princeton: Princeton University Press, 1964.

Walsh, William J. *The United Mine Workers of America As An Economic and Social Force in the Anthracite Territory.* Washington: National Capital Press, 1931.

Ware, Norman J. *The Labor Movement in the United States, 1860-1895; A Study in Democracy.* New York: D. Appleton & Co., 1929.

Wieck, Edward A. *The American Miners' Association.* New York: Russell Sage Foundation, 1940.

Wittke, Carl. *The Irish in America.* Baton Rouge: Louisiana State University Press, 1956.

Yearley, Clifton K., Jr. *Britons in American Labor: A History of the Influence of United Kingdom Immigrants on American Labor.* "The Johns Hopkins University Studies in Historical and Political Sciences," Series 75, No. 1. Baltimore: Johns Hopkins Press, 1957.

————. *Enterprise and Anthracite: Economics and Democracy in Schuylkill County, 1820-1875.* "The Johns Hopkins University   Studies in

Historical and Political Science," Series 79, No. 1. Baltimore: Johns Hopkins Press, 1961.

ARTICLES

Abbot, Edith. "Wages of Unskilled Labor in the United States, 1850-1900." *The Journal of Political Economy*, XIII (June 1905), 321-367.

Accurisa, Sister M. "Poles in Shenandoah, Pennsylvania." *Polish American Studies*, XI (1949), 9-13.

——. "Polish Miners in Luzerne County, Pennsylvania." *Polish American Studies*, VIII (1946), 5-12.

Andrews, J. Cutler. "The Gilded Age in Pennsylvania." *Pennsylvania History*, XXXIV (January 1967), 1-24.

Anspach, Marshall R. "The Molly Maguires in the Anthracite Coal Regions of Pennsylvania, 1850-1890; Being An Inquiry into Their Origin, Growth, and Character and a Study of Absentee Ownership of the Coal Fields." *Now and Then*, XI (October 1954), 25-34.

Arensberg, Conrad M. "Industry and Community." *The American Journal of Sociology*, XLVIII (July 1942), 1-12.

Berthoff, Rowland. "The Social Order of the Anthracite Region, 1825-1902." *The Pennsylvania Magazine of History and Biography* LXXXIX (July 1965), 261-291.

Billinger, Robert B. "History and Development of the Anthracite Industry." Pennsylvania Department of Internal Affairs. *Monthly Bulletin*, XIX (February 1951), 3-9 (March 1951), 13-24.

Bogart, Stephen, "The Much Taxed Jersey Central." *Trains*, XIII (February 1948), 6-13.

Browne, Henry J. "Terence V. Powderly and Church-Labor Difficulties in the Early 1880's." *The Catholic Historical Review*, XXXII (1946), 1-27.

Ehrlich, Leon. "Labor Arbitration in Pennsylvania." *Temple Law Quarterly,* XXIV (June 1953).

Gibson, Gail M. "The Harrisburg Conference: Research Needs and Opportunities in Pennsylvania History." *Pennsylvania History* XXXIII (July 1966), 332-348.

Ginger, Ray, "Company-Sponsored Welfare Plans in the Anthracite Industry Before 1900." *Business History Review*, XXVIII (June 1953), 112-120.

———. "Managerial Employees in Anthracite, 1902; A Study in Occupational Mobility." *Journal of Economic History*, XIV (Spring 1954), 146-157.

Greene, Victor R. "A Study in Slavs, Strikes and Unions: The Anthracite Strike of 1897." *Pennsylvania History*, XXI (April 1964), 199-215.

Hand, Alfred. "Titles to Coal Lands in Pennsylvania and Incidental Monopolies Connected Therewith." *Yale Law Review*, XVI (1907), 167-175.

Hard, Willard. "Route of the Black Diamond." *National Railway Historical Society Bulletin*, XVII (1952), 4-7.

Hayden, Horace E. "Judge Jesse Fell's Experimental Grate." *Proceedings of the Wyoming Geological and Historical Society*, IX (1909), 53-63.

Itter, William A. "Early Labor Troubles in the Schuylkill Anthracite District." *Pennsylvania History*, I (1934), 28-37.

Kennedy, Thomas. "Wages, Hours and Working Conditions in the Anthracite Industry." *Annals of the American Academy of Political and Social Science*, CXI (January 1924), 43-52.

Klein, Philip S. "Our Pennsylvania Heritage, Yesterday and Tomorrow." *Pennsylvania History*, XXV (January 1958), 1-8.

Kline, J. Simpson. "Railroads of Northumberland County." Northumberland County Historical Society. *Papers*, XXXVII (1933), 160-186.

Korson, George. "Early History of the Anthracite Industry in Pennsylvania." *Pennsylvania History*, XXVIII (January 1951), 35-46.

Kuritz, Hyman. "The Labor Injunction in Pennsylvania, 1891-1931." *Pennsylvania History*, XXIX (July 1962), 306-321.

Leighton, George R. "Shenandoah, Pennsylvania; The Story of An Anthracite Town." *Harper's*, CLXXIV (1937), 131-147.

Lovejoy, Owen R. "Coal Mines in Pennsylvania and Child Labor." *Annals of the American Academy of Political and Social Science*, XXXVIII (1911), 133-148.

Miller, Eugene W. "The Southern Anthracite Region: A Problem Area, 1820-1952." *Economic Geography*, XXXI (October 1955), 331-350.

"The Molly Maguires: Their American Record." *National Review*, No. 358 (December 1913), 637-648.

Moody, John. "The Reading Railroad System." *Moody's Magazine*, V (January 1908), 95-102.

Plummer, W.W. "Franklin Benjamin Gowen." *Dictionary of American Biography*, VII, 460-461.

Rashleigh, Alice. "The Story of Carbondale and 'The Black Stone,'" Pennsylvania Department of Internal Affairs. *Monthly Bulletin*, XIX (November 1951), 11-18.

Reynolds, Robert. "The Coal Kings Come to Judgement." *American Heritage* (April 1960), 55-61; 94-100.

Rezneck, Samuel. "Distress, Relief and Discontent in the United States During the Depression of 1873-1878." *Journal of Political Economy*, LVIII (December 1950), 494-512.

Schlegel, Marvin W. "America's First Cartel." *Pennsylvania History*, XIII (January 1946), 1-16.

———. "The Workingmen's Benevolent Association: First Union of Anthracite Miners." *Pennsylvania History*, X (July 1943), 243-267.

Stevens, Sylvester K. "The Reading System; One of the Nation's Most Important 'Bride' Roads Has Been Making History for Over a Century." *Commonwealth*, II (March 1948), 213-216.

Thompson, Edgar. "Mines and Plantations and the Movements of Peoples." *American Journal of Sociology*, XXXVII (January 1932), 603-611.

Warner, W. Lloyd and J.O. Low. "The Factory in the Community," in *Industry and Society*, ed. William Whyte. New York: McGraw-Hill Book Company, 1946.

White, D. and R. Thiessen. "The Origin of Coal." U.S. Bureau of Mines, *Bulletin 38* (1913), 67-84.

Wiest, W. Irwin. "The Centennial of the Cameron Colliery." Northumberland County Historical Society. *Papers*, IV (1937), 149-167.

Williams, William H. "Anthracite Development and Railway Progress."
American-Irish Historical Society's Journal, XXII (1923), 86-96.

UNPUBLISHED DISSERTATIONS AND THESES

Auble, Arthur G. "The Depressions of 1873 and 1882 in the United
States." Harvard University, 1949.

Binder, Frederick M. "Pennsylvania Coal: An Historical Study of Its
Utilization to 1860." University of Pennsylvania, 1955.

Bradley, Erwin S. "Post-Bellum Politics in Pennsylvania, 1866-1872."
Pennsylvania State College, 1952.

Clifford, Albert J. "The Reorganization of the Philadelphia and Reading Coal and Iron Company." The Wharton School, University of
Pennsylvania, 1952.

Felt, Thomas Edward. "Early Unionism in the Anthracite Industry."
Unpub. M.A. thesis, Columbia University, 1954.

Fenton, Edwin. "Immigrants and Unions; A Case Study: Italians and
American Labor, 1870-1920." Harvard University, 1957.

Flynn, Eleanor J. "Public Care of Dependent Children in Pennsylvania." University of Pennsylvania, 1963.

Greene, Victor R. "The Attitude of Slavic Communities to the Unionization of the Anthracite Industry Before 1903." University of Pennsylvania, 1963.

————. "The Molly Maguire Conspiracy in the Pennsylvania Anthracite
Region, 1862-1879." Unpub. M.A. thesis, University of Rochester,
1960.

Hughes, Margaret M. "The United Mine Workers of America as a
Social Control." University of Pittsburgh, 1937.

Itter, William August. "Conscription in Pennsylvania During the Civil
War." University of Southern California, 1941.

Kildeen, Charles E. "John Siney: The Pioneer of American Industrial
Unionism and Industrial Government." University of Wisconsin, 1942.

Kurtiz, Hyman. "The Pennsylvania State Government and Labor Controls from 1865 to 1922." Columbia University, 1954.

Lewis, Raymond John. "The Social and Economic Background of the Anthracite Strike of 1902." Unpub. M.A. thesis, Pennsylvania State College, 1938.

Ricker, Ralph R. "The Greenback-Labor Movement in Pennsylvania." Pennsylvania State College, 1955.

Rimlinger, Gustav V. "Labor Protest in British, American, and German Coal Mines Prior to 1951." University of California, 1951.

Shegda, Michael. "History of the Lehigh Coal and Navigation Company 1840." Temple University, 1952.

Turnback, Sister William Marie. "The Attitudes of Terence V. Powderly Toward Minority Groups, 1879-1895." Unpub. M.A. thesis, Catholic University of America, 1950.

Young, Henry B. "The Anthracite Coal Industry." Unpub. M.A. thesis, Pennsylvania State College, 1924.

Zeilger, Martin. "Social Legislation for the Protection of the Coal Miners in Pennsylvania." Unpub. M.A. thesis, Pennsylvania State College, 1947.

Index